STAND UP AND FIGHT

A...n English's books include *Munster: Our Road to Glory* and
G...d *Slam: How Ireland Achieved Rugby Greatness*. He was
al... the ghostwriter of Brian O'Driscoll's autobiography, *The
Te...*, and Paul O'Connell's memoir, *The Battle*. He spent twelve
ye...s at the *Sunday Times* and close to a decade as editor of
th... *Limerick Leader*.

Stand Up and Fight

Sits comfortably among the best books ever written on Irish sport. Not unlike the classic *Seabiscuit* in style, it takes the countless threads from the day Munster beat the All Blacks and weaves them together word perfectly.

Malachy Clerkin, *Sunday Tribune*

One of the best five books ever published on rugby. Only 80 minutes of a dull Munster day in 1978, when the local heroes beat New Zealand. But what a literary feast that win gave rise to. This classic re-wrote the manual for rugby books by mocking the drive towards unsatisfying surface rubbish. It is of supreme depth and colour and after reading it you will finally grasp Munster, and working-man rugby passion.

Stephen Jones, *Sunday Times*

This book allowed me to live the match as it happened. There is all the vulnerability, the doubts, the drive that made that day epic. These feelings still resonate in the Munster of today.

Keith Wood

The most engaging book on rugby that I've read in many a year – well-researched, splendidly put together with a deft control of narrative. The craft of the novelist with the graft of the hack – it's a winning formula.

Mick Cleary, *Daily Telegraph*

A modern classic … The momentum of the book never slackens. I'm not Irish and I don't know a great deal about rugby, but I found this book absolutely riveting and frequently moving. Twelve thousand people attended the match; 100,000 claimed to have been there. Readers of this book will feel that they were … The kind of read that you devour in socking great chunks.

Andrew Baker, *Daily Telegraph*

New Zealand came, saw and were conquered. English's approach has depth, strength, pace, power and end product.

***Irish Independent* 50 Best Sports Books**

We were there too: Thomond, Halloween 1978, Munster and the All Blacks. Or at least it feels that way after reading Alan English magnificently convey the lead-up, atmosphere and drama of that game so many wish and claim they were at. But as much as that win was something of a once-off, there was nothing overnight about it.

English brings us through the genesis of a Munster rivalry and fascination with the All Blacks, how rugby captured the heart and imagination of the city and people of Limerick, and the education of a coach in Tom Kiernan, all of which culminate in a day of days. Thankfully it is now suitably chronicled in the rugby book of rugby books.

Kieran Shannon, *Irish Examiner* Ireland's 40 Greatest Sports Books

The dedication of the amateur players of the time is wonderfully captured in Alan English's exceptional book.

Matt Cooper, *Irish Examiner*

A compelling dissection of Munster's celebrated 1978 win over the All Blacks.

Observer **Books of the Year**

For those of us centrally involved it drags us back in time as if the intervening 27 years haven't happened at all. English has left no stone unturned. Brilliant in its portrayal, *Stand Up and Fight* is the definitive account. It captures the essence of what makes Munster rugby and its provincial team so unique. I highly recommend it and its appeal will extend way beyond the rugby aficionados.

Tony Ward, *Irish Independent*

The success of the book is the richness of its characters and the tales they have to tell. It is from another life, another era, and the deeper we get into the blandness of the professional era the more we will appreciate how it used to be. This book slaps a preservation order on that time. Read it.

Brendan Fanning, *Sunday Independent*

It is not so much the game itself but the stories around it that compel. English celebrates the day without sentimentalising it.

Observer Sport Monthly

A terrific combination of intelligent reportage and open-eyed mythmaking.

Robbie Hudson, *Sunday Times*

The story of the day may be dog-eared but there is nothing jaded about the way English fleshes it out through the reminiscences of many of the principals. An apposite celebration of a great and historic occasion, this is an excellent book, rugby or otherwise.

John O'Sullivan, *Irish Times*

English weaves a rich tapestry … The background is deftly stitched in as the book builds up to the day, then the author applies his precision needlepoint to bring together all the leading protagonists. If this book sells as it should, English can add another few hundred thousand claimants to the 'I was there' brigade, so skilfully and diligently has this Munsterman recorded the details of that historic day.

David Llewellyn, *Independent*

Wonderfully researched and evocative … This book is as much a celebration of the All Blacks' legend and a discourse on Limerick's socio-economic and rugby background as anything else.

Gerry Thornley, *Irish Times*

What sets *Stand Up and Fight* apart from the vast, vast majority of books written about Irish sporting achievement is that it goes far beyond recounting what happens between the white lines during a match. The reader is given an extraordinary feel of what it must have been like to have been present on the day. But be warned: once you pick up *Stand Up and Fight* you won't be able to put it down.

Colm Kinsella, *Limerick Leader*

A fantastic story ... those fifteen Munster men, along with coach Tom Kiernan, opened the door of self-belief for a nation and Alan English has captured its full meaning and significance in this book.

John Collins, *Irish World*

As much a social history as a book about one game, this is sports writing at its finest. More than 100,000 people claimed to have been at 12,000 capacity Thomond Park when Tom Kiernan's Munster laid low Mourie's 1978 All Blacks: they'll all read this to get the *real* inside story.

Scotland on Sunday

Alan English conducted more than 150 interviews during his research and the result is a marvellously evocative page-turner.

Alan Pearey, *Rugby World* **Book of the Month**

268 pages on ancient Limerick's most unforgettably florid 80 minutes ever. Irresistible.

Frank Keating, *Guardian*

Enthralling ... on the way to relating the story of a single match, English segues into moving social and personal histories, uncovers astounding detail and then, finally, offers the chance to relive the action itself through the eyes of the key participants ... It is a chance to savour the most unique occasion in the history of Irish sport, and because so much has changed, one that will never come again.

Dave Hannigan, *Evening Echo*

Outstandingly researched and written. English weaves into the book the history of Irish and Munster rugby.

Joseph Romanos, *Listener* **(New Zealand)**

A seminal account.

Chris Barclay, *New Zealand Herald*

Alan English has done a top job outlining the build-up and post-match events as well as the match in such a way that the book will not only appeal to rugby fans but anyone with a soft spot for the Irish.

Shane Hurndell, *Hawke's Bay Today*

It's the sort of book that makes you wish you were there … Should be on the bookshelf of any Munster fan and deserves a greater audience.

Rugby Times

Excellent … captures the intensity of battle; Gerry McLoughlin in particular provides a unique insight into life at the sharp end of top-flight rugby.

Peter Sharkey, *Belfast Telegraph*

A tale that has been recounted on many occasions in the past, yet English still manages to make it seem fresh. Arguably the sports book of the year.

James Laffey, *Western People*

This was a sporting shock writ incredibly large and Alan English has done a brilliant job of recording that unbelievable tale in fascinating detail. This is a book that any rugby fan should 'jackal' into their grasp by any means necessary, but its appeal should cross all sporting divides.

Kenny Archer, *Irish News*

Alan English has assembled his material in such a way as to make the build-up read more like a thriller than history. Expertly marshalling his witnesses – players, officials, supporters – he also manages to convey Munster's unique, bred-in-the-bone working-class passion for rugby at a time when it was said you had to be a doctor, Protestant or Dubliner to stand much chance of playing for Ireland. Perhaps English's finest hour, or 80 minutes, is his account of the match itself. The tale of that day and its heroes has often been told, even dramatised, but nobody has told it better, and probably never will.

Simon Redfern, *Independent on Sunday*

STAND UP AND FIGHT

When Munster Beat the All Blacks

Alan English

Yellow Jersey Press
LONDON

1 3 5 7 9 10 8 6 4 2

Yellow Jersey Press, an imprint of Vintage
20 Vauxhall Bridge Road
London SW1V 2SA

Yellow Jersey Press is part of the Penguin Random House
group of companies whose addresses can be found at
global.penguinrandomhouse.com.

Penguin
Random House
UK

First published by Yellow Jersey Press in 2005
Updated edition published in 2007
This edition published in 2018

penguin.co.uk/vintage

A CIP catalogue record for this book is available from the British Library

ISBN 9781787290365

Printed and bound in Great Britain by Clays Ltd, Elcograf S.p.A.

Penguin Random House is committed to a sustainable future for our
business, our readers and our planet. This book is made from Forest
Stewardship Council® certified paper.

For Anne, Aisling, Holly and Jack.
And in memory of my father, Tom English, 1932–2018

Contents

The Cast   xvii

   Prologue: Locky's Story   1
 1 The Silent Lambs   5
 2 Limerick Rugby Miracle   16
 3 All Blacks and Angel Rapers   29
 4 He Was in the World Before   40
 5 Locky the Warrior   59
 6 The Politician   74
 7 London Mauling   83
 8 Worst Dump in the World   99
 9 Brendan Foley's Story   104
10 Enter the Friendly All Blacks   109
11 Stu Wilson's Story   121
12 Horses for Courses   126
13 Seamus Dennison's Story   136
14 Tickets and Tape   140
15 Be a Thinker   148
16 Tony Ward's Story   163
17 The Killaloe Kids   167
18 The First Half   173

19 The Second Half   204
20 The Immortals   227

    Epilogue: Three Stories   240
    Afterword: Forty Years Later   247
    Appendix I   284
    Appendix II   299
    Appendix III   301
    Bibliography   307
    Acknowledgements   309
    Index   313

The Cast

The coaches
JACK GLEESON, New Zealand, a publican
TOM KIERNAN, Munster, an accountant

The Munster players
LARRY MOLONEY, full-back, a bank official
MOSS FINN, wing, a student
JIMMY BOWEN, wing, a finance officer
SEAMUS DENNISON, centre, a teacher
GREG BARRETT, centre, a bank official
TONY WARD, out-half, a teacher
DONAL CANNIFFE, scrum-half, an insurance official
GERRY McLOUGHLIN, prop, a teacher
LES WHITE, prop, a purchasing manager
PAT WHELAN, hooker, a builder
BRENDAN FOLEY, lock, a sales rep
MOSS KEANE, lock, an agriculture official
COLM TUCKER, flanker, a sales rep
CHRISTY CANTILLON, flanker, a student
DONAL SPRING, Number 8, a student

The All Blacks
BRIAN McKECHNIE, full-back, an accountant
STU WILSON, wing, a sales clerk
BRYAN WILLIAMS, wing, a lawyer
LYN JAFFRAY, centre, a meat buyer
BRUCE ROBERTSON, centre, a sales rep
BILL OSBORNE, centre, a stock agent
EDDIE DUNN, out-half, a teacher
MARK DONALDSON, scrum-half, a bank clerk
BRAD JOHNSTONE, prop, a builder
GARY KNIGHT, prop, a salesman
JOHN BLACK, hooker, a trainee manager
FRANK OLIVER, lock, a forestry contractor
ANDY HADEN, lock, a property officer
GRAHAM MOURIE, flanker, a farmer
WAYNE GRAHAM, flanker, a stock agent
ASH McGREGOR, Number 8, a farmer

The officials
CORRIS THOMAS, referee, an accountant
JOHNNY COLE, touch judge, a revenue collector
MARTIN WALSH, touch judge, a factory worker

Also
GEORGE DIXON, 1905 All Blacks manager,
    an accountant
RUSS THOMAS, 1978 All Blacks manager, a grocer
EARLE KIRTON, 1963 All Blacks, a dentist
KEITH MURDOCH, 1972 All Blacks, a lorry driver
STEPHEN HEALY, a plasterer
SEAN HEALY, a plasterer
SUSAN HEALY, a schoolgirl
TERRY McLEAN, a journalist

BILL O'BRIEN, a draper
JOE KENNEDY, a stores worker
JIM TURNBULL, a charity executive
HUGH CONDON, a student
PAUL COCHRANE, an All Blacks supporter
DINAH MAXWELL-MULLER, a secretary
JOE McCARTHY, a cameraman
DAN CANNIFFE, an office manager
KIERAN CANNIFFE, an insurance broker
BILL WALSH, a fish merchant

Rugby was life in Limerick. The heroes of Limerick rugby are my heroes. Gladiators, square-jawed warriors who represent us on the battlefield.

Richard Harris

Rugby football was the best of all our pleasures: it was religion and desire and fulfilment all in one. This phenomenon is greatly deprecated by a lot of thinkers who feel that an exaggerated attention to games gives the young a wrong sense of values. This may well be true, and if it is true, the majority of New Zealanders have a wrong sense of values for the whole of their lives.

John Mulgan, *Report On Experience*

Any game of rugby is confrontational. It's all about not taking steps backwards, not being seen to be intimidated.

Martin Johnson

Prologue

Locky's Story

My name is Gerry McLoughlin. I used to be a rugby player. Some called me 'Locky', others 'Ginger'. No one called me a coward. You could say I had my moments. A long time ago I played for Munster against the All Blacks. One hundred thousand people say they were at Thomond Park that day. Ninety thousand of them are liars. They've been at it for more than twenty-five years. Imagine lying to your grandchildren about a rugby match. I know why they do it, though. What happened that day can never happen again.

I have the match ball in my attic. I swear to God it's the actual ball – I defy anyone to go under the lie detector against me. At thirteen minutes past three Tony Ward kicked it over the wall and into my cousin Marge Kenihan's yard. Her brother Jude was standing on a ladder, watching the match for free, and I gave him £100 for the ball. Some day I'll auction it for charity. Or if I go broke I might sell it for myself. There are other people claiming they have the ball and the whole bloody lot of them can go and scratch.

I was a prop forward. Loosehead or tighthead, I could play both sides of the scrum. And the front row is where it all happens. Where I'm from, the boys in the front row get respect. Our people like the hard men. Not too many backs ever became legends in Limerick. Tom Clifford, Gordon Wood, Keith Wood, Peter

Clohessy – what do they all have in common? They all played in the front row.

Back then, the scrum was the key to winning any match. It was the only chance you had to wear down the opposition pack. It was the be-all and end-all. Without a good scrum, it didn't matter a damn what else you did on the field.

Whoever said scrummaging is an eight-man effort is a liar. For a start, the hooker doesn't worry about the props. You should never be hoping for too much from your back row either. You wouldn't want to rely on them. In the Munster team that day I wouldn't say Donal Spring ever broke his back with a push, you had Colm Tucker wanting to carry the ball and Christy Cantillon flying off looking for fucking tries. The last thing on their mind was scrummaging. All they wanted to do was get out. So in the Munster pack, in actual fact, you're not going to get much help from your back row and the hooker's doing his own thing. You only have one or two friends in there.

If you want to beat the All Blacks, the first thing you've got to do is stand up to them, show them you're not afraid. Some people see fifteen men in black jerseys and they're beaten before the match even starts. In the front row, it's all about intimidation. If you allow them to intimidate you, the match is over – I don't care how good your backs are. Some people said they'd kill us in the rucks, that they'd kick the shit out of us when we went down on the ball. But we were used to getting kicked and raked. The rugby we played was fierce. It was nothing new to us to have to take a shoeing.

At Thomond Park, I was always aware that people who knew about propping were watching me. They'd say, 'You were in trouble there. This was wrong, that was wrong.' Nobody told you if you'd played well. So the last thing you wanted to do was go backwards. You just couldn't let it happen, not in front of your own people. We knew where they lived, where they drank, what they did for a living, where they liked to stand in the ground.

I was up against Gary Knight that day. Two stone heavier than me and three inches taller, but I didn't fear him. I never feared any prop in my life. He came on the field with a bandage wrapped around his face, but I never gave that a second thought. I found out later that he had herpes. I found out because they told me I had it myself. In all this time I've never been able to shake it off. Some souvenir.

I'd never have played for Ireland if it hadn't been for the All Blacks match. You didn't get capped out of Limerick. Bias, bias, there was unbelievable bias against us. We knew it. It was a fact of life. We'd been told it as kids. I went to see Munster play the All Blacks in 1963. My father took me, I was twelve. They didn't win, but they gave as good as they got. The Munster hero that day was the tighthead prop.

'Who's the fella covered in blood, Dad?'

'That's Mick O'Callaghan. He's related to you.'

'But I never saw him before.'

'He's a cousin of your mother's.'

'Does he play for Ireland?'

'No. One miserable cap, he got. You see, he plays for Munster and if you come from Munster you have to be twice as good as the fella that plays for Leinster or Ulster.'

'What about if you come from Limerick?'

'If you come from Limerick, you have to be three times as good as the fella from Dublin. At least.'

'What about if you play for Shannon?'

'If you play for Shannon, it doesn't matter how good you are.'

I was a Shannon man. My father was a bus driver, seven days a week, all hours. Same as all the lads in Shannon, we were a working-class family. Our kind of people didn't get on in Irish rugby. One year Shannon were sent up to Dublin to take on the full Irish team in a practice match. First scrum, the push came on and

Mick Fitzpatrick, the Irish prop, went up in the air. He had Moss Keane behind him. Noel Ryan put him up in the air, legs split. They only brought us up once. They knew if they'd brought us up again we'd have scrummaged the Irish team off the park. We'd done two hundred scrums a night for the previous seven or eight years. That's a lot of scrummaging. We knew how to get to a team, how to break them. It wasn't just a yard of a push, it was two or three yards. After half an hour of that, they'd be exhausted, dead on their feet. We knew the only way of getting on the Irish team was playing in a match where you could put yourself in the limelight.

Three of us got picked for Munster against the All Blacks that day. Ireland were playing them the following Saturday and the selectors didn't bother waiting for our match. They picked the Irish team three days previous. RTE didn't bother sending any cameras down to film it – they thought it was a waste of time. Nobody gave us a prayer. Some people were afraid for us. They didn't think we belonged on the same pitch.

The only man who believed we could win was Tom Kiernan, our coach. They called him the Grey Fox. He could make you believe no team was unbeatable. Not even the All Blacks.

He told us we had to stand up to them. He said, 'They won't go round you, they'll try and go through you.'

No one was going to go through me.

Chapter One

The Silent Lambs

Limerick, 31 October 1978

It was lunchtime but the hotel restaurant was empty, except for a man in a light grey suit who stood with more than twenty chairs in front of him, waiting for his audience to show up. Tom Kiernan, coach of the Munster rugby team, was thirty-nine years old but hair that had long turned grey made him appear five or six years older. In less than two hours his players were going to face the best team in the world. For six weeks he had lived the match, day and night, over and over. Now he had twenty-five minutes to tell his team how to beat the New Zealand All Blacks – perhaps less, because they were running late and traffic was building outside, where twelve thousand people were making their way to a small ground one mile away on the northern edge of town. Not one of them gave his players a chance.

At another hotel, a short walk away, the All Blacks were preparing to board a coach parked outside on O'Connell Street, the main thoroughfare. Each man wore a black blazer with light grey slacks, a white shirt and a black tie embossed with the team's emblem, a silver fern. The All Blacks always looked smart: it was expected of them. Lyn Jaffray, selected in the centre against Munster, even insisted to his team-mates

5

that the silver ferns on their cufflinks pointed the same way.

In seventy-three years of trying, no Irish team had ever beaten the All Blacks. Some said none ever would, that the gap would only get wider. More than any other rugby nation, New Zealand knew how to win. Time and again, down the years, they had rescued themselves when defeat seemed certain, driven on by uncommon desire and sometimes by the fear of failure. For no matter how brilliantly a team representing New Zealand might play, the bottom line was that they win.

Every touring side lived in the long shadow cast by the All Blacks of 1905, who came to Britain and Ireland and shook the game there so severely it was as though they had reinvented rugby itself. In beating their colonial masters so devastatingly at their own game, they did more for their country's self-regard than any group of men before or since. The 1978 touring side, the eighth to leave New Zealand, were fast acquiring the air of invincibility many regarded as the All Blacks' birthright. On all known form, Munster were facing annihilation. Four games into an eighteen-match tour the New Zealanders had the look of a side that would remain unbeaten. 'The Eighth All Blacks are cutting through British rugby like an armoured division piercing thin lines of infantry,' Clem Thomas had written in the *Observer* three days previously. In the *Cork Examiner* that morning Dermot Russell had sifted the evidence and found only a glimmer of hope.

The known facts are that Munster have been bad this year and that the All Blacks have mopped up all opposition so far. The imponderable now is the preparation which coach Tom Kiernan has given his charges through sessions at Fermoy and, since Sunday, at Limerick. Has he been able to motivate this ordinary team to the stage where it could be potentially great? Only time will tell.

The chatter of rugby supporters echoed from the lobby, but Kiernan did not hear it. His players began moving towards the restaurant. They had no blazers or ties or cufflinks with the three crowns of Munster: they wore whatever they wished. No coach was parked outside to take them to the ground: there was no money for that; they would have to travel in their own Escorts and Cortinas.

It was a time before replica jerseys, a time when Munster played only a handful of games every year, mostly against the three other Irish provinces – Leinster, Ulster and Connacht – in front of modest, sometimes paltry crowds. The days when Munster supporters would queue all night in heavy rain for tickets were more than twenty years away. Of the six counties that make up the province of Munster, rugby was widely played in only the biggest two – Cork and Limerick. There, the province played second fiddle to dominant clubs like Cork Constitution, Garryowen and Shannon, who contested with a ferocious intensity the Munster Senior Challenge Cup.

Every once in a while, however, Australia, South Africa or New Zealand would turn up and a Munster team drawn from these clubs would give them a game. On these rare days, generally years apart, the Munster team and the red jerseys they pulled on came to mean something. The feelings they stirred among their supporters back then were no different from those that would be felt by a future generation, for against the touring teams they played with a fierce passion. But this time, few were expecting much of a match. In their most recent outing of any significance, against Middlesex five

7

weeks before, Munster had been humiliated. They had not won outright the championship contested by the Irish provinces for ten years. If the match had been a prizefight, they would have had the credentials of a bum.

Donal Canniffe, the captain and scrum-half, was first to walk through the restaurant door. Nobody had greater pride in the jersey, but he was a Munster man by cruel accident. The course of his life had changed early one morning in 1951, in Dromod, County Leitrim, where his father was stationed as the local sergeant. Cycling home on her new bicycle, Donal's mother Maisie was thrown over the handlebars and killed. Her youngest son, Donal, was ten days short of his second birthday. Dan Canniffe moved his seven children south, and Donal was reared in Cork city by his father's sister, a woman who had once smuggled revolvers past the Black and Tans at South Gate Bridge by concealing them in her underwear.

Kiernan believed he had the right captain. Canniffe stood a fraction over six feet tall; he was like a ninth forward, able to take punishment. He mightn't have been the slickest or the quickest or have the most natural ability, but he was durable and he could lead men.

The others followed Canniffe in twos and threes. Larry Moloney, the full-back, was with his great friend Seamus Dennison, the outside centre. Moloney was a man bred close to the soil, a butcher's boy from Bruree in County Limerick, De Valera country. Kiernan reckoned he had a cigarette coming out of his mouth every time you looked at him. He was so laid-back, the coach would say, it was a job just trying to keep him awake. At his club, Garryowen, they called him The Prince, and maybe there was something regal about the way he cruised into the line. There was only eleven and a half stone of him, but he could hit.

As a kid in winter he had pulped turnips by hand every night, enough to feed thirty or forty cattle two buckets each, which was a lot of pulping. In the summertime he saved hay, scoured ditches and cleaned drains. A life on the land was never an option for him, though. 'There's four more after you, so you keep going. Go out into the world and make your own way through it,' Paddy Moloney had said when he reached school-leaving age. He found a job in a bank, behind the counter. As work went, it was easier than saving hay. Just not as satisfying.

Dennison, a schoolteacher, was even smaller, but if anything he hit harder. He was a shopkeeper's son from Abbeyfeale, on the Limerick–Kerry border. Like his friend he had been sent to boarding school in Limerick city, where they played rugby. He had three international caps, the last of them won three years back. Plenty of people said he should have been given ten times that many, that his lack of size had cost him. Balding and bearded, he didn't look much like a rugby player, which was why men who didn't know him were often knocked backwards by the juddering force of his commitment.

Alongside him in the centre was Greg Barrett, a bank official from Cork, six feet two and lightly built, not much of a ball handler but never slow to tackle, which was just as well.

The props, Gerry 'Locky' McLoughlin and Les White, had played together only rarely. White was an Englishman. Nobody was quite sure how old he was, but it was plain that he had plenty of miles on the clock. Kiernan had recruited him from London Irish and among the lads the joke was that White's qualification was down to his mother being seduced by a sailor in Cobh.

The garrulous, ginger-haired Locky was another teacher,

but far from the usual wielder of chalk. He would arrive on Monday mornings sporting cuts and scratches from Shannon matches, sometimes a beaten-up nose, or a swollen ear or a black eye and, every so often, all of these at once. Here was vivid proof of his hard-man status, a weekly reminder that of the local warriors who went about their business in the front row, none was more committed than he. He was desperate to beat the All Blacks and he didn't care who knew it. He felt his chances of ever playing for his country were hanging on this one match.

Colm Tucker, a wing forward, played in the same Shannon pack as Locky. He was a travelling sales rep, the kind of job a rugby man got when his face was his calling card. Tucker was probably the best ball-carrier in Ireland, but the national selectors had ignored him too. Alongside him in the back row Tucker had the mobile Christy Cantillon and a gangling Number 8 from Trinity College in Dublin who could run fast and hard, Donal Spring.

The hooker was Pat Whelan, ruthless and rampaging and capped eleven times. The second-row forwards were also internationals: Moss Keane, from Currow in County Kerry, a great bear of a man, and Brendan Foley, from the heart of working-class Limerick city. On the wings were a pair of twenty-one-year-olds from Cork, Moss Finn and Jimmy Bowen. Kiernan did not expect either to see a lot of ball against the All Blacks. The game plan he had devised would see to that, all going well. More than anything, this strategy depended on Munster's out-half having one of the games of his life.

Tony Ward was weeks away from being named European Player of the Year. He was like nothing Munster rugby had ever seen: bewitching and glamorous and utterly instinctive, with a jink that left people tackling thin air. When it looked like he had no options open to him, nowhere to run, he would suddenly make something happen.

There was a vulnerability about Ward, a contradiction that few rugby people understood in this, his first year on the major stage. So devastatingly confident with the ball in hand, he was less self-assured off the pitch. Earlier in the year, on the eve of his third international match, against Wales in Dublin, he had been alone in a lift at the Shelbourne hotel when the doors opened and six or seven Welsh players walked in. He didn't know what to do or where to look, and he didn't imagine that any of them would recognise him, so he just stared at his shoes and waited for his floor. When the doors opened again he began to walk out and then a voice said, 'See you tomorrow, Tone', and he looked back, incredulous that Gareth Edwards knew his name.

How many of these men might be good enough to make the All Blacks' best team? Most rugby writers would have made a firm case for Ward, pondered the claims of Keane and Whelan and drawn a line through the rest. But for Kiernan, they were all he had and they would do. They would have to do.

The ferocity of Kiernan's tongue had once been such that timid young team-mates expecting a lashing would feign injury and wait for the storm to pass, rather than face him at his most fulminating. But during his university years he began to mellow. He became a wiser and more skilful leader. There was something mesmeric about him; an urgency in the eyes, a talent for persuasion.

As a player he had been a general who led from the back and shot from the lip, barking out commands to his backs, focusing on every facet of the game, not just his own part in it. More than any other Munster rugby man, alive or dead, he had been there and done it. Captain of his country, captain of the Lions, ever present in the Ireland team for fourteen years, he had the respect of every man in the room. He rose from his chair and spun it around. He lifted his right foot and rested it on the seat, then moved forward, crouching over the back of the chair, elbow on his knee, right hand under his chin. His eyes met theirs.

They waited for words of inspiration, for assurance that they were not lambs to the slaughter. They wanted to hear him say they could win. They needed to know he believed it, because they still weren't sure they believed it themselves.

In such moments, when a team faces seemingly impossible odds, the urge to rouse them with emotional rhetoric can be strong. Years later, one of the men in the room would recall the team talk in vivid detail. Kiernan began, he said, by slowly invoking the names of Munster players of the past who had come agonisingly close to beating the All Blacks.

'Tom Kiernan . . . Jerry Walsh . . . Brian O'Brien . . . Paddy McGrath . . . Mick Lucey . . . Mick O'Callaghan . . . Phil O'Callaghan . . . Jim McCarthy . . . Gordon Wood. What do we all have in common? [Long pause, piercing eye contact].

'*We never did it!* We never beat the All Blacks. And *you* can.'

But, in fact, Kiernan wasn't nearly so melodramatic. At first, he said nothing at all. Half a minute passed, slowly. Now his head was bowed. They shifted uneasily in their seats, waiting for him to collect his thoughts. Another thirty seconds ticked by. Nothing.

After two minutes, they began to steal glances at one another, all thinking the same things.

'*When's he going to speak?*'

'*What kind of team talk is this supposed to be?*'

'*Someone say something, for Christ's sake.*'

Five minutes. Still nothing. They stopped looking around

them and withdrew into themselves. They felt isolated, cut adrift from the group. Alone.

Eight minutes. Now no one was moving. Some were breathing so deeply it was as if they were gasping for air. Others felt intimidated, nervous and, in a few cases, frightened.

'*Everyone else is concentrating. What's wrong with me?*'

'*We've had enough now.*'

'*Jesus Christ, it's like a boiling kettle in here.*'

Ten minutes and still not a word. He just stood there, still crouching, motionless. He had planned the silence, but it was a risk. He couldn't be sure about how they would react. What if one of them laughed, as one of the lads at Cork Constitution had done when he'd tried the same thing years before? But deep down he knew no one would laugh. They had given too much already for that. He just had to make sure the temperature was right, that they understood what he wanted from them: discipline, alertness, focus. He didn't want boot, bollock and bite, the traditional virtues of Munster rugby. He didn't want them to kick it up in the air and charge after it. Down that road was glorious failure and he was sick of that. Too many Munster teams had been acclaimed for effort against the overseas teams, instead of victory. In the end, it amounted to nothing.

What Kiernan knew about winning, he had learned from losing. As a boy in Cork he had kept a scrapbook detailing the near misses by Munster teams of the past. As a player he had faced the All Blacks four times – more than any other Munster man. Every match had been close, never more than a single score in it. He hadn't won any of them. All he was left with were hard-luck stories he had no mind to tell.

When it was announced that the All Blacks were coming back to play Munster for the sixth time, he had got to thinking. What if you could prepare a team not doomed to repeat the mistakes of the past, a team that had learned the hard lessons taught to Munster men down the years? Against the All Blacks, there was no margin for error. One bad mistake, one missed tackle and it wouldn't matter how much they might play above themselves: they would go down in history as gallant losers like all the others. He had come to understand that on days like these you could assume nothing. You covered every angle, anticipated every problem. And then maybe you had a chance.

He wanted his players to visualise the match and their part in it, to imagine it before it had happened. They had to be mentally prepared for whatever was thrown at them and they had to get there themselves, no matter how long it took.

After fifteen minutes he knew they were ready. He had already made sure they were physically fit enough to go eighty hard minutes: now their heads were in the right place. Over the previous six weeks he had brought them closer together than any group of Munster players had ever been. Now there was nothing any of them would not do for the team, nothing they would allow themselves to do that might hurt the team. Kiernan would never know anything of the uncertainty that had pervaded the room, because he was not like them. Focus was not something he switched on and off. Throughout his rugby life it had always been there. But what mattered now was that by isolating them for a short time he had made them stronger.

Finally he moved towards them, only a few inches, but they knew what was coming and they felt a sense of release. He began to speak, and in a few minutes he told them how they might beat the mighty All Blacks. A few minutes for a lesson that was thirty years in the learning.

What they needed to remember, he said, was that four

days before the first international of their tour the All Blacks would be playing for a result. They wanted to go out and get it over with, to move on an unbeaten team. But if the match started badly for them, the younger, less-experienced All Blacks would start thinking, 'What if we lose?' No matter what anyone said, they were human and they were beatable.

Munster weren't playing for a result. They were playing for glory, for everlasting fame. They were playing, too, for one another.

As the tourists' bus crossed the Shannon at Sarsfield Bridge and then crawled past the Munster team hotel, nobody on board had any idea that they would soon be facing not just fifteen players motivated like never before, but the force of history, and the driving influence of a man who understood its lessons.

Chapter Two

Limerick Rugby Miracle

Munster were always going to beat the All Blacks; it was just a matter of when. People think 1978 was the shock of the century, that it just happened out of the blue, but it was a long time coming. The single biggest reason was Munster's tradition. We believed we could do it because our predecessors had convinced us it was possible. All you had to do was look at the results. We were the lucky ones because it was Munster's time, but those guys helped make it happen.

Donal Spring, Munster forward in 1978

Limerick, 1905

Two days after beating Ireland with ease, the All Blacks left Dublin in a private compartment on the three o'clock express, headed south. They had fourteen matches left to play on their tour of Britain and Ireland, but people had already made their minds up: they were the greatest rugby team ever to set foot on a field. Every opposition had been beaten so badly that someone said they should be called by a new name: The Slaughterers.

They had achieved fame they could never have imagined. People stopped and applauded if they saw them in the street. Men would ask to feel their biceps. Sometimes, in the less well-heeled parts of town, women lifted their skirts in invitation. Newspapermen vied with one another to acclaim them as something more than human, masters of a form of rugby unheard of only weeks before. One of their backs was 'a cross between a greyhound and a flash of lightning'. Their forwards were 'Trojans of the scrum'. As a team they were 'as persistent as a lot of wasps; as clever as a lot of monkeys. They work together like the parts of a well-constructed watch.' It was as if they had come not from a distant land, but from a different planet.

People feared for Munster, their next opponents. The *Limerick Leader* challenged its readers to nominate the correct score, offering a prize of one guinea for the first correct entry opened. An optimistic soul from the Killeely area of the city guessed the score as Munster 3 All Blacks 0. His was one of six entries that favoured the home team; most of the rest, in enormous numbers, anticipated a massacre. A reader from Roche's Street was the most scathing about Munster's chances. His guess was an All Blacks win by fifty-five points to nil.

They had left New Zealand on the SS *Rimutaka*, twenty-five players, a coach and a manager. Emissaries for the wonderland of the southern seas. 'The Britishers are panting for those Ashes,' they were told. 'Don't let them get them.' But few turned up to see them off at Wellington: it was too wet, too cold, too much trouble.

Every day, up on deck, they ran, passed and scrummaged. Other passengers on the *Rimutaka* asked them if they would be good enough to take on the English and the Welsh, the Scottish and the Irish. They did not know. They hoped they would not let down their families back home, the loved ones who would not see them again for more than seven months.

After forty-two days at sea they saw Plymouth Sound in the half-light of early morning. England, the mother country. They started their tour known as the Colonials. Along the way they became the All Blacks, on account of their shirts, shorts and stockings. People said they could hardly be expected to beat Devonshire, the English county champions, in their first match. They won by fifty-five points to four. Newspaper subeditors, convinced the result was wrong, changed it to five to four. They soon learned. In their next ten games the All Blacks scored 353 points and conceded a total of three.

News of every great victory was telegrammed back home by George Dixon, the team manager. In the months they were away, one thousand Russian Jews were murdered in Odessa and the Wright brothers flew for thirty-eight minutes and three seconds, but in New Zealand no story was bigger than the deeds of the All Blacks. With each triumph the nation swelled with pride. The players vowed that, come what may, they would not – could not – lose.

They knew what to expect in Limerick; it was the same mostly everywhere they went. Hundreds, if not thousands, of well-wishers would cheer from the station concourse. A delegation of local nobs would meet them off the train. Young boys hoisted high on the shoulders of their fathers would ask questions . . .

'Which one's Wallace?'

'Which one's Stead?'

'Where's Dave Gallaher?'

. . . but rarely would they receive answers. Even though the men they had come to see were famous, few knew what they looked like. They could be black, brown, white or yellow.

The people of Limerick were not to know, for they had never before seen an All Black. 'Their skins,' one newspaper reported, 'are of an equable brownish olive tint.' But most of those waiting at the station did not read newspapers, or anything else. Newspapers were for the educated and the privileged. So was rugby, by and large.

For Arthur Budd, president of England's Rugby Football Union a few years before, the game's problems had begun when the working man took it up. Men like Budd wanted to keep rugby to themselves. They believed it was theirs to keep. And, for the most part, they succeeded. In Ireland the establishment aped the English way – not for the first time, or the last. Yet there was one place on the island where the spirit of rugby triumphed over the men who sought to marginalise it. In Limerick it became the game of the people, all of the people.

The classless rugby city: it has become a cliché now, forever to be wheeled out whenever Limerick's love for the game is talked about. Dockers and doctors side by side on Saturday afternoons. Old women arguing about loosehead props. The only part of Ireland where it is spoken of on the factory floor. But why?

'We've been hearing the same thing for a hundred years. I'm sick and tired of listening to it,' said Tom Kiernan, nearly three decades after his Munster team took on the All Blacks at Thomond Park. 'You ask people why it's a classless rugby city and they all say, "Because everyone plays it." As if that explains it. But nobody has a reason for *why* rugby became so popular there in the first place.'

The reason is because rugby saved Limerick. It lifted the city off its knees. It made its way into the worst of places and offered up a little joy. The love for the game so evident these days, the passion that feeds the legend of Munster and the All

Blacks, has its roots in misery. To find out why rugby means so much now, you must discover what the place was like then, just before it fell under rugby's spell.

The debt Limerick owed the game has been repaid many times over, but few have ever acknowledged that it existed in the first place. Misery has always been a touchy subject there. It gets people's backs up, puts them on the defensive and into denial. Such was the way back in 1876, the year Limerick's first rugby club was founded. When a citizen wrote to complain that the streets around him were full of filth, his letter was waved away with contempt. 'It must have been written by one of the disappointed candidates for the position of second sub-sanitary officer,' said one of the city worthies, Alderman Zachary Myles.

If you had strayed off the main streets and walked among the labyrinth of tumbledown lanes, it wouldn't have struck you that a game played by a handful of Protestant college boys was just what the city's underclass needed in 1876. In a garrison town, where the British Army commanded the open spaces, the have-nots were 'literally rotting in squalid dens', Charles Dawson, the High Sheriff Designate, wrote that year. From this desolation, the only escape was alcohol. There were 282 liquor shops, but only two dentists. Children were living under the same roofs as pigs. There were donkeys in back yards flooded with stagnant water and sewage, with barely enough room to move.

Dr O'Connor, from the workhouse fever hospital, believed that Fitzgerald's Lane was among the worst of all these places. He had fifteen patients from the lane; another had already died. In August 1876 he went to Fitzgerald's Lane and found a wall with a large hole in it. A man called Michael Kelly, who lived in the lane, told him that the excreta of five families was thrown through the hole and it stayed there for two or three months. The stench was unspeakable. Was it any wonder, Michael Kelly asked, that he had three children sick with fever? The doctor reported his findings to Zachary Myles and his colleagues on the Urban Sanitary Board. A few weeks later, they met to discuss his report.

'His statement was not proved,' said John Cronin.

'A mere statement is no proof,' said Stephen Hastings.

'Dr O'Connor has proved his case by evidence which would be believed in any court in the world,' said Maurice Lenihan, a local newspaper editor. 'I think we will agree that the state of things which was found to exist in Fitzgerald's Lane was most disreputable.'

'No, no,' said Cronin.

'You will not agree to that?'

'Certainly not.'

What John Cronin meant, perhaps, was that the lane was no better or worse than two hundred others.

The biggest problem in the lives of the people, Charles Dawson believed, was 'the want of a proper means of popular enjoyment . . . the total absence of any rational and harmless amusement'. Dawson could not have realised it then, but this 'means of popular enjoyment' was about to arrive. Rugby – introduced by the army and by affluent Protestants who had played it in public schools in Dublin and beyond – may not have been harmless, or even rational, but it was destined to fill the void.

Eighteen days after the meeting of the Urban Sanitary Board, Charles Burton Barrington stepped off the *Scythia* at the port of Queenstown in Cork, fresh from the Philadelphia Regatta. Within weeks, Barrington and his industrious friend William Stokes had rounded up the local bluebloods and formed Limerick's first rugby club. Barrington was an old boy of Rugby School in England, birthplace of the game. His grandfather had built a hospital for the city's swarming poor, constructed of limestone and designed to last centuries. His own contribution to local life appeared, at first, vastly more modest: he had drawn up twenty-three rules for a game nobody played, apart from a handful in his own privileged circle.

For their first fixture, Limerick Football Club travelled to Dublin to take on Wanderers at Clyde Road. They arrived the night before the match and stayed at the Gresham hotel, the finest accommodation Dublin could offer. When they took to the pitch, it was clear to all present that Limerick rugby had arrived. 'The presence of the Limerick men in their exceedingly neat uniform would alone excite admiration and a finer set of players never did battle for any club,' enthused the *Irish Times*. The match was drawn. Afterwards, both teams sat down to dinner at the Arcade hotel and, when it came to the toasts, they joined glasses and drank to the future success of rugby in Limerick among like-minded gentlemen.

Rugby's rise in the city was a strange kind of miracle. Barrington was no missionary: he did not venture into the lanes to preach his gospel. Others spread the word in a crumbling city fast being abandoned by the gentry; British Army soldiers, pig buyers who ruled the roost, but who liked to encourage the man on the street. Paddy 'Whacker' Casey, who was one of the founders of St Mary's Rugby Club in 1943, says the game's appeal in his grandfather's time was no different from what drew him to rugby as a boy in the twenties.

'It was all the excitement. Most fellas were showing off how tough they were. And it was a simple game then. Not like now. We played on a small little patch in Johnny Cusack's field. Rugby back then was street against street, parish against parish. The matches

we played were like faction fights – that's the truth. You'd see eight forwards running up the middle of the field with the ball at their feet and the crowd cheering. Any fella that tried to get in their way deserved a medal for bravery. He mightn't be able to play no more after that.

'Before rugby, people had nothing to play at all. They were livin' in big, high tenement houses and lanes. Limerick was full of lanes. If they had jobs they worked for the big people, all the nobs and the Protestant crowd. If you had one toilet you were lucky and that would be a dry toilet. You know what a dry toilet is? A bucket. They were all slums. You could smell the tar and the lime when you'd go in the door and then the backbone soup and the cabbage. It was a blessing to knock those places, but some fine men came out of them and rugby gave them something they enjoyed doing.

'The whole thing derived from the British Army. Back before I was born they took young lads in at twelve and fourteen. People were so poor they were only delighted to see them going in. "Join the army and see the world," that was the cry then. In peacetime the army played rugby above in the Bombing Field and below in the Island Field. They had regiments all over the city. Other fellas learned it from watching them and kept at it. They played anywhere they could, even in prison. The British were gone from the city by the time I was a boy but rugby was getting more popular all the time. We played hurling in the summer and rugby in the winter, but hurling was expensive at that time. You wouldn't be able to get a hurley, money wise. Half a crown for a hurley was a lot of money. If you lived in St Mary's parish, rugby was your game. All you needed was a patch of land and a ball. They'd go round collecting for the ball, going to all the houses in the parish, looking for a penny. Then we'd play away.'

In a city with no university, the game's upper-class roots withered in the ground. It grew anew, blossoming on barren land. The transformation took less than a decade. Eight years after Barrington's team emerged resplendent, two new clubs were born – Garryowen and Shannon – and along with Young Munster they would dominate the landscape for a century and more. Amid the boom new teams emerged everywhere, in the parishes and the schools, drawing their players from the lanes and beyond. They played for the Transfield Cup and the Tyler Cup and the Munster Challenge Cup, the greatest prize of all.

All the while rugby thundered ahead in Cork, its thriving university a nursery for the senior clubs. Every so often, the two cities came together under the Munster banner and triggered debates that would rage for a century. Why more Cork fellas in the team than Limerick fellas? Why the full-back from Constitution and not the Garryowen man?

After a succession of embarrassments, the club founded by Charles Barrington and William Stokes died in 1905. That was also the year it began in earnest for the Munster team, the birth of their great tradition of taking on the overseas teams. On a late November afternoon, at a ground that overlooked Fitzgerald's Lane, they became the first Irish province to face the challenge. And what a challenge.

When the New Zealanders' train pulled into Limerick station a gathering of local dignitaries, businessmen and rugby officials stood in line on the platform, their eyes fixed on the bald-headed, mustachioed man in his mid-forties who emerged first from the team carriage and moved towards them with the aid of two walking sticks.

'Welcome to Limerick, Mr Dixon!' they cried.

'Welcome to the All Blacks!'

When the crowd caught sight of the players, smartly turned out in three-piece suits with a silver fern attached to their lapels, every man carrying a heavy suitcase, they broke into wave after wave of applause, so prolonged and so enthusiastic that it startled Dixon.

'Three cheers for the All Blacks!'

'Three cheers!'

The tourists proceeded by bus to Cruise's Royal Hotel, half a mile away, with crowds lining the route. The next match in their marathon tour was due to kick off in nineteen hours' time, but the All Blacks were not ready to rest. In any case, they found the hotel unsatisfactory. Dixon's bedroom was small and dirty. There was a bath, but grime clung to the enamel and he could not bring himself to use it. He summoned his players and they left the hotel to stretch their legs, happy to talk rugby with the locals who followed them in droves. With such interest on the streets, Dixon speculated, the attendance at the match would be huge. That was good news: they had been guaranteed a healthy share of the profits.

The All Blacks were impressed that so much was known about their triumphant tour and taken aback by such a wide-spread interest in rugby. When asked about the challenge they were expecting the following day, they were respectful. Munster would be worthy opponents, they believed. Modesty was yet another of their traits.

In the *Limerick Leader* that day there was awe for the visitors, along with advice for their latest victims in waiting.

The New Zealanders are the men of the moment. Their visit has shaken up the dry bones of Rugby Football and created a revival in the game that will be felt for years to come. No one who has an atom of sport in him, even if he has never before seen a football kicked, should miss seeing them. What is the best game for the Munster men to play against them? Is it better to try to imitate their style . . . or to stick to the traditional Irish game and play it for all it is worth? The proper thing would be to play the ordinary game and put as much devil into it as possible. Try and smother them, and give them as few opportunities to pass as possible. Keep the ball on the ground and close to the feet and see how the typical Irish rush agrees with their methods of defence. Whenever there is a need for kicking, let it be always into touch.

On paper form, Munster has not a dog's chance against these bewildering players, and the question is only how many goals and tries they will score. But paper form is not always the best of guides, and the Munster players have a chance to prove it entirely wrong. If they play their game, and play it with a heart deserving of success, and not as men already beaten, then the match at Limerick will not be the easiest the New Zealanders have participated in, and Munster football will be more highly thought of in the future than in the past.

The O'Grady Delmege coach hire service took the All Blacks to the Markets Field. Once again a large crowd followed on foot. The Munster team was made up of eight Corkmen and seven from Limerick. There were plenty in Limerick who questioned that ratio, but the match itself put any argument into grim perspective. Those present witnessed rugby beyond their imagination. The performance of the men in black was especially satisfying for Mr John Egan, a member of the Shannon Rowing Club. His was the 137th envelope to be opened in the *Leader* office that night and on the coupon inside was written the correct result: Munster 0 All Blacks 33.

The following afternoon, the All Blacks were back at the

railway station to catch the return train to Dublin. With the engine running and his players all safely aboard, Dixon leaned against a carriage door and answered questions from a reporter on the platform. The silver timepiece tucked in his waistcoat pocket showed 3.55 p.m., the precise time of departure. There could be no delays, no disruptions to the punishing schedule they had set themselves. They were booked on the night boat to Wales and the international match against England at Crystal Palace was less than two days away.

'Mr Dixon,' said the man from the *Chronicle* hurriedly, 'do you have a message for the citizens of Limerick?'

'Nothing could exceed the kindness shown to us by the people of Limerick,' Dixon replied, in his measured way. 'We shall never forget your warm-hearted and real Irish welcome. On behalf of the team, I would like to thank you most heartily.'

'And will Limerick see the All Blacks again?'

'In any subsequent visit to these islands,' Dixon said, 'we shall be only too pleased to include Limerick in our tour.'

The guard's whistle sounded and a great roar echoed down the platform from some of those he had thanked. They were there in strength once more, perhaps convinced they would never again see such a team.

'A moment later,' reported the *Chronicle* man the next day, 'my affable acquaintance had entrained and his jovial and convivial conquerors were far down the permanent way.'

That morning Dixon had been handed a cheque by the Munster branch of the Irish Rugby Football Union. It was made out for £50, the smallest amount he had received thus far. By contrast, the match against Midland Counties had brought them £500 1s. and the game against Devonport Albion, in Plymouth, had yielded £404 7s.

Dixon may have been disappointed, but he was not surprised. On taking his seat before the match he had found that few, if any, of the hordes that had accompanied his team to the ground, and fêted them in the city the previous night, appeared to be present. There were between three and four thousand people there, 'all apparently better-class', Dixon wrote in his diary that night.

He concluded that the missing thousands 'did not possess the small amount necessary to gain admission'.

In the classless rugby city, people were still rotting in their squalid dens.

Chapter Three

All Blacks and Angel Rapers

Limerick, 1963

The triumphant tour of 1905 convinced the people of New Zealand that they might be rugby's chosen ones; the Second All Blacks left them in no doubt, winning all thirty-two matches when they came to the northern hemisphere in 1924. Every side that followed in their footsteps was aware of the debt owed to these men, knew they were part of a tradition far bigger than any one team.

It took them fifty-eight years, but the All Blacks kept the promise made by George Dixon to return to Limerick. The city that welcomed them back in 1963 was greatly changed: this time, thousands were not locked outside the big match for the want of a pittance. The decrepit lanes had been torn down, one by one. People no longer lived in habitual misery. Those who had been born in slums found there was a point to life, other than surviving it, and rugby played its part in this transformation. In the influence it now had on local life, the game had only one equal: the Catholic Church.

The 1963 match, like the one in 1978, was played at Thomond Park. It proved to be a seismic encounter, arguably the greatest rugby game seen in Limerick for the best part of a century. Its significance did not end there, however: there was a legacy. It convinced the thousands who were there – and one man in particular – that Munster had it in them to beat the All Blacks.

The Fifth All Blacks, led by their captain Wilson Whineray, arrived on the one o'clock train on the Monday after their international against Ireland, posing absently for a photograph on the railway station steps. Like their predecessors of 1905, the New Zealanders were billeted at Cruise's. The next day the word from the hotel waitresses was that they wanted raw eggs on top of their steaks and they wanted them for breakfast. The regulars at Angela Conway's, where the talk was mostly of rugby, also had it on good authority that a fellow called McPhail, some class of manager, had bitten the head off the head waiter after seeing the modest portions the hotel was serving his players for dinner. Miss Pat Cagney, manageress of the dining room, said her instructions were that the players should be offered the *table d'hôte* menu, not the *à la carte*. It seemed the Irish Rugby Football Union, who were footing the bill, had requested this particularly. Nonsense, said McPhail, they're to have whatever they want, and not in twenty minutes but *now*. And so the All Blacks had steak that night, as much as they could eat, and more of it in the morning. Or so they said at Angela's, lowering their last pints before walking out into the rain, up Athlunkard Street and off towards Thomond Park.

At the Dalcassian Bar in Castle Street, halfway between Angela's and the ground, Mick Crowe had opened his cavernous premises in mid-morning to a handful of regulars who sat on timber benches directly before him across the pine sawdust floor, nursing pints that rested on empty beer barrels topped with trays.

They were mostly from the parish of St Mary's; plasterers

and plumbers, dockers and dogsbodies. They handed over some of their wages at home and gave Crowe the rest. He was selling fourteen or fifteen thousand pints of stout a week. Many of the older men were refugees from the demolished lanes, living in the city's first council estate nearby, in houses made of mass concrete, not so much built as poured. Others had fathers and grandfathers who had endured the worst of the slums, men who had passed on a love of rugby to the next generation. There was hardly one among them who had not played the game. And they had stories, an inexhaustible supply, drawn from a folklore that sustained them as surely as porter. Had these men been around in 1905, they would have been among those who cheered the All Blacks at the railway station and then stood outside the ground while they destroyed Munster, unable to come up with the price of admission.

Most of Crowe's regulars had pet names: it meant they belonged, that they were characters. There was Socks Smith and Pigeon Roche, Paddy Eyepole and Skeff Sheehy, Coppa Storan, Gaw Wallace, Fongo Ryan and Wobbler Gavin. He had Buster Mac, Buller Mac, Gussie Mac and The Hammer Mac. There were the Fitzgerald brothers, Mikey and Yawdy; the Byrnes, Richie and Ned; and the Healys, Stephen and Sean.

If any two men characterised what rugby had come to mean to the city, they were the Healy brothers. In a city that had long been in thrall to the game, it would not have been easy to find two men whose lives had been as affected by what they felt for it. Their story was the story of Limerick rugby: they were hard and proud and passionate.

The Healys were plasterers by trade and prop forwards by inclination. Sean was the last of twenty children born to Dolly Healy but sixteen had died on her. Convulsions, they kept telling her – your child died of convulsions. She never really knew what it meant. Sometimes Dolly would visit the Robinsons in one of the other tenement flats on St John's Square and marvel at the wonder of their possessions, only for Jack Healy to snap that they had been bought with tainted money.

Plenty of men around St John's Square had fought with the Royal Munster Fusiliers in the war, but what marked Jack Healy out in peacetime was his refusal to accept a British Army pension. His brother had died in Flanders and Jack himself had sustained shrapnel wounds to the neck, but he renounced a handsome pension on the grounds that in victory the British had not honoured the freedom of small nations. After that Jack didn't talk so much about his days in the king's uniform.

That was the way things were in Limerick. Before the war the British Army had owned the city. They played cricket and the locals didn't care much for its strange rituals. They played rugby and it was a different story. Their influence on local life was profound. Join the reserve and the door at Cleeves or Stokes & McKiernans swung invitingly open. Decline and you were left to rot, for jobs were not so easy to come by in the first two decades of the new century.

For years after the garrison's demise the stigma of association touched almost every part of the city, so that for the most part people made out like it had never existed. Those who had fought on foreign fields, who had seen their fellow Limerickmen die lonely deaths, returned to a city that preferred not to recognise their sacrifices. In some cases the shame that others expected them to feel brought poverty to their own children.

But if the Healys had come up the hard way, the same could be said for most of those who followed rugby in Limerick.

'Rugby is a religion in New Zealand and it's the same for us,' Stephen Healy would say. Such an interest meant that when the All Blacks came to town, some businesses shut for the afternoon and others found their workforces decimated by phantom funerals and imaginary flu.

For years the Healys had idolised the All Blacks. They pored over accounts of their fearlessness, marvelled at their indestructibility. The 1963 team were reputed to be the biggest ever and the brothers knew how tall they were, their weights to the nearest pound, what they did for a living.

Together with their friends Colum McGrath and James 'Ter' Casey, the brothers had taken the train to Dublin to see the New Zealanders at Lansdowne Road. Three years in a row, back in the late twenties, Casey had made the final Irish trial and every time they had sent him back to Young Munster uncapped. For the men who drank in the pubs around the Yellow Road it was a travesty. It was one thing to overlook a Limerick flanker or wing, but something far worse to snub the city's best prop. Casey was a delivery man who drove a horse and cart for McMahon's timber yard. It was said he could carry as much lumber on his back as the horse. As the man from the *Daily Express* wrote: 'Had Casey been a University man, a bank clerk or a wearer of plus fours he would have got his cap without hesitation.' The boys down in Charlie St George's used to put it another way. The best horse, they would say, wasn't jumping the ditch. Eventually the selectors bowed and gave Casey two caps, enough to earn him a lifetime of respect in his home town.

At Lansdowne Road, the four friends had begun to think the unthinkable when Tom Kiernan, Ireland's youthful full-back, put his team 5–0 ahead with a measured conversion in the first half. But brute force and the kicking of their own full-back, Don Clarke, had given the All Blacks victory by a single point. Now, with the Munster match little more than an hour away, the big news from the All Blacks camp had seeped out. Don Clarke, whose celebrity transcended that of any rugby player who had ever set foot in the city, had withdrawn from the team.

His absence was both a good thing and a bad thing for Munster, Crowe's customers decided. Good because the All Blacks would feel the loss of his boot, bad because he might have struggled on a surface that was certain to cut up after the morning's hard rain. At more than seventeen stone, the one thing Clarke did not possess was speed around the pitch. It would not have been hard to picture him struggling to heave his heavy frame back and forth across the Thomond Park mud, and the Munster three-quarters surging on to the loose ball. And maybe it was idle dreaming, or the drink talking, but nearly every man in the pub had seen Munster come close against the touring teams often enough to cling to the hope that they might give the New Zealanders a game this time.

What chance did Munster really have against the might of the Fifth All Blacks, against a pack of forwards who weighed a stone a man more than their own? Not much, you would have said, if you had seen them lining up for a team photograph behind the stand shortly before kick-off. Seven of them were squeezed together on a small timber bench, their arms and shoulders pressed tight against each other, as if on a crowded train, their eyes conveying geniality rather than the promise of physical menace. The remaining eight stood behind, chests puffed out for posterity. You could have written the caption to the picture there and then: 'The Munster team that lost to the mighty All Blacks on 11 December 1963.'

Except, on closer examination, there was something unusual about the picture when it was published a few hours later on the front page of the *Limerick Leader*. Fourteen men acknowledged the camera (one even smiled; he became a politician). The fifteenth stared into empty space with eyes that saw nothing. Tom Kiernan disliked having his photograph taken at any time, but the minutes before a match was for him the worst time of all. If he allowed it to, the ritual would break his concentration, so he never did.

His dark, close-cropped hair was cut high across his forehead, emphasising a furrowed brow. His face was fierce with concentration, oblivious to the lens, his lips curled into a forbidding crescent. The others had come to play. Tom Kiernan was there to win. When he spoke to them before a match, the message never changed. The object of the game, he would always say, is to win it. He lived by that.

'There are as many bones in your body as there are in theirs,' he told the others in the dressing room. 'Just go out and play as well as you're capable of playing. That's all that's needed of you. Don't let them through you – you stand up to them. Any man that doesn't do that might as well fucking emigrate.'

It seemed to Jerry Murray, as he looked around him, that only one man in the room truly believed Munster's best would be good enough for victory. Kiernan was a good talker, but not that good.

Murray, a twenty-one-year-old second-row forward from Cork Constitution, did not believe that the object of the game, this game, was to win it. For him, it was about avoiding public humiliation. (Had Kiernan seen how many people were out there? Did he not realise that the Munster second-rows were conceding twenty-five pounds a man to their opposite numbers?) Winning did not come into it. Put a few points on the board. Keep their tries down to a minimum. Then shake their hands and get off the pitch, beaten but not embarrassed. Against the All Blacks, that was enough.

The rain was soft but unrelenting. The pitch had been off-limits to the locals for weeks and it was found to be sodden when the protective straw was removed.

'Kick everything down Herewini's throat,' Kiernan had told Mick English, as if there was ever a prospect of Munster's Number 10 doing otherwise. Targeting the visiting full-back was a kind of blood sport at Thomond Park and Herewini appeared to have the credentials of another victim. English, certainly, was equipped for the kill. He could kick like a mule, huge punts that soared into the stratosphere and allowed his forwards time to hare off in pursuit of the full-back underneath the ball. And, at this moment, the spectators knew full well what was expected of them. Eerily, disconcertingly quiet whenever a kicker from either team went for goal, they became a baying mob when the opposition's full-back was trying to steel himself under the dropping ball. And in that split-second, just before his hands touched the ball and his body felt the impact of the charge, could be found the essence of Munster rugby: the fusing of its players and supporters, a union of equals, so that every man, woman and child in the ground felt like a participant. In a setting as intimate as Thomond Park, it took a special kind of ability to handle such a bombardment of the senses.

Herewini handled it.

English kicked everything, kicked magnificently, and Kiernan asked many questions of his own, but Herewini answered them instinctively, catching every hoisted ball and lashing them back into the Munster half and into touch. The rain and the heavy ground didn't bother him: he played in the mud all the time back home. Mostly, he just skated across the top of it. But Herewini's problem was that the rest of the Blacks were being swept away by the gathering Munster storm. At the front of the stand, the noted New Zealand press correspondent Terry McLean could not believe how badly the All Blacks were playing. He wrote later: 'They trailed around like Brown's cows and were booted around as Brown's cows sometimes are when Farmer Brown gets out of bed on the wrong side at 4.30 a.m. and has to take it out on somebody.'

Blood was pouring from a cut to Mick O'Callaghan's head, the wound shaped like a horseshoe, but it was being washed away by the rain. The prop forward went off for stitches, and in his absence New Zealand scored twice – Herewini with a penalty and Ian MacRae with a try. O'Callaghan came back thirteen minutes later amid tumultuous cheering wearing a bandage, had that ripped off, left the pitch a second time, came on to another enormous roar with a fresh bandage and told his hooker, the smiling future politician Paddy Lane: ''Twas Horsley done it.' So the next time Ronald Hugh Horsley looked up at a lineout, and began to rise for a ball deliberately aimed over his head by Pat McGrath, O'Callaghan jumped across him and held his arm, and Lane drove a fist flush on to his jaw, a right uppercut that drew only a shake of the head from Horsley but another roar from Thomond Park.

Kiernan was charging into the backline, all mouth and menace, and when Henry Wall burst clear for a try after taking a quick lineout, bringing Munster within three points, Jerry Murray began to see in some All Black faces something he hadn't believed was possible. It was dread, so palpable that four decades later one of the sufferers could recall every detail of his abject day.

*

'I saw them looking at me and I knew what they were thinking. It was, "Hell, these guys aren't All Blacks at all – they're humans." As if they had suddenly discovered it. And the only thing on my mind was: "How am I going to get out of this bloody place? I want the game to end. Now. Now would be wonderful. Right now." I knew I was in real trouble. I didn't think we could hold out. They were demented, so close together, like swarming bees. It was, "Kick it up in the air Mickey English and we'll fucking well get under it." Misty rain fell all day. I wished to hell I had resin in my pockets because I was having trouble handling it. Any time I dropped a ball they were saying, "Hell, it's worth running at these guys." They put the grubbers through and every time English launched one of the up-and-unders the crowd went mad. You could hear them screaming. They were right in your face.

'Tell you the truth, I'd been relieved to see my name on the team sheet in the first place. Number 10: E. W. Kirton. They weren't playing me much. Not after Newport. When I got back home, any time I went near a bar, from the top of the North Island to the bottom of the South, they'd say, "There's that Earle Kirton, the bastard who lost us the game against Newport." It was my first time to wear the jersey. I was too young to cope. The next time they played me, four or five games later against Cambridge University, they said: "You'll be fine here. You're up against a twenty-year-old kid, for Christ's sake." And I was playing quite well until all of a sudden the fella attacked me, did a bit of step and ghosted past. Then he did it again. And again. Afterwards, someone told me his name: Michael Gibson.

'I knew damn well Munster weren't anywhere near as good as the All Blacks in terms of individual skills. But it wasn't a day for skills. It was a day for guts and English's angel rapers. And there was something about the crowd, the way they got behind Munster. I can't remember what the ground looked like. I don't think it was anything special. But I remember the crowd. I'll never forget the

38

crowd. Later on somebody asked me what it was like. I said that after playing at Thomond Park I now knew what the Christians must have felt like in the Colosseum. That's what it was like.'

Kiernan almost won it in the closing minutes, running thirty yards up the stand side and for once beating Herewini with a cross-kick, but an All Black reached the loose ball first, and then, with the wind blowing diagonally across the field, his forty-yard penalty to draw the match just missed right of the posts. As heroic failures went, it topped the lot.

'MUNSTER GLORIOUS' announced the evening paper. Even the Healy brothers, analysing the match in the Square Bar that night, could find little to fault Munster. By Christ, they had stood up to them, they said. It was true that Colin Meads was absent from the New Zealand team, but in all respects Munster's performance had been better than Ireland's on the previous Saturday. Who could have guessed that a provincial team would give the All Blacks a greater scare than the national XV? And if only Don Clarke had played instead of Herewini, they would have won. That, at least, was the Healys' view and it was shared by many of those who lowered pints long into the night at pubs the length and breadth of the city.

But for Tom Kiernan there was no consolation in 'if only' – only regret and the learning of hard lessons. The object of the game was to win it. Munster had lost. That was all there was to it. In his eyes, there could never be any glory in failure.

Chapter Four

He Was in the World Before

Cork, 2003

The white-haired man in his sixties stands in a reception room at his splendid home and says he has barely changed a light bulb in his life, so how would he know how to work a video recorder? He is holding a videotape and looking at it doubtfully. Someone has written 'All Blacks/Munster 1978' in red ink on the spine. The tape is placed in the machine, but the screen remains blank, so he picks up the telephone, punches in a number for his wife and begins repeating her instructions to the visitor. Soon the picture jumps to life and there is the rat-a-tat-tat sound of drums, distant at first, but growing louder, and fifteen men in black appear to keep rhythm by slapping their hands against their thighs, while a dozen photographers drift across the screen, pointing their cameras at the scene, and a voice announces that the All Blacks are 'doing their haka' for the benefit of the large Limerick crowd.

'Well, that, ehm, presumably states their intentions,' says the commentator Fred Cogley, as the All Blacks conclude by rising half-heartedly off the turf – no more than twelve inches – before jogging gently into position. 'Unbeaten on this tour so far, they come to Thomond Park strongly fancied, then, to beat Munster.'

Many years have passed since Tom Kiernan watched the fifteen minutes of footage that survive. He moves to the edge of his seat.

'Christ! You see that?' he asks. 'Could you have got a worse start?'

'Jesus, that was a bad kick, an awful kick.'

'Pity Ward didn't let it out just there!'

'Watch this now!' he says towards the end. 'I'd like to see that again. Don't look for Ward, look for Tucker.'

After a maul halfway inside the New Zealand half, with Munster back-pedalling, the ball comes back to Colm Tucker in a yard of space. He takes it three steps to his right, away from the massed ranks of bodies, who are expecting him to drive on, for everyone knows that ball-carrying is his stock in trade. Just as the giant All Black Andy Haden comes across to nail him, Tucker checks his stride and in the fraction of a second available to him he pops the ball back to Tony Ward, four yards away on his right shoulder, and so precise is the pass, so soft the hands, that Ward has to pluck it out of midair before letting it fall virtually in the same movement, and as his right boot flashes through it the All Black out-half Eddie Dunn realises what is about to happen, but he is too late, far too late.

'It's over!' Cogley shouts. 'Tony Ward has done it!'

'You see Tucker there?' Tom Kiernan says. 'You get that chance once in every three years. It's the sign of a fella at the top of his game, doing the right thing in the right way at the right time.'

It is not surprising that he still finds something majestic in Tucker's simple pass, for it was a snapshot of everything he ever stood for on a rugby pitch. As the Munster coach that day, all of his preparations had been aimed at producing such sharpness. He had fallen silent at the team meeting before

41

the match, silent for a very long time, because he had wanted his players to think for themselves. To think of what they might do in any circumstances that arose. He compares it to a story he once heard about the golfer Nick Faldo, leading the British Open with one round left to play, hitting balls on the practice range before teeing off on Sunday afternoon. Rather than hit dozens of shots with one club before moving on to the next, Faldo had imagined himself on the golf course, hole by hole, shot by shot.

'I don't think I ever put so much into a match,' he says quietly after the tape has run its course. 'The silence in the team room was the culmination of everything.'

What of the beginning? When did it start? Some say it began five weeks before, when the Munster players came together for a short tour to London, but they are wrong; wrong by thirty years or more. He walks into another room and pulls out a large and sturdy purchasing ledger, a relic from another era, inscribed with the autographs of Irish rugby men such as Jack Kyle and Karl Mullen. The pages of the scrapbook are dry and musty now, and the fiery boy who kept it has mellowed, but the passion forged in boyhood still burns. On the opening page, carefully clipped from the *Sunday Independent* of 14 March 1948, is a report headlined:

AMAZING SCENES AS IRISHMEN WIN RUGBY CROWN AFTER 49 YEARS – DELIRIOUS THOUSANDS MOB TEAM

The following year brought another Triple Crown and another rich harvest of cuttings. The boy who kept the scrapbook would soon learn, however, that the days when Irishmen were chaired off rugby pitches in triumph were few and far between. Nobody could have known back in 1949 that it would be another thirty-three years before the Triple

Crown was won again, and that the future architect of that triumph had yet to celebrate his tenth birthday.

Young Tom, with his scissors and paste, kept a record of those lean years. There was gallantry and disappointment, near-misses and thrashings, heroic effort and bitter defeat. But the scrapbook was more than a record of battles past; it was an expression of a boy's love for a game, a childhood affair that shaped the rest of his life.

Michael Kiernan left his native Westmeath in 1925 and moved south to Cork, second city of the new Irish state, where an up-and-coming civil engineer could find a job with prospects. He was twenty-five years old, earnest and hard-working, private yet decisive. He was appointed general manager of the South of Ireland Asphalt Company, on a large salary. He could see where he was going and it pleased him: marriage, a big family, four decades with the same firm and a comfortable retirement. For twenty years his life followed that path, until tragedy threw it off course, not once, but twice.

While still in his twenties Kiernan married Eileen Murphy, the daughter of a pig-buyer from the Curragh Road, beside Musgrave Park on the outskirts of Cork city. Eileen was a vivacious girl, a chain smoker seven years younger and far more outgoing than her husband. Before leaving the midlands Michael had never laid eyes on a rugby ball, but such ignorance was never going to survive marriage to Eileen Murphy. Three of her brothers – Matty, Timmy and Neddy – played for Cork Constitution and Munster and she supported them avidly. She was rugby royalty in Cork. Her first cousin, Noel Murphy, had won eleven Ireland caps. An uncle on her mother's side, David Desmond, had captained the first Con team to win the Munster Senior Cup, in 1905. If there was going to be a rugby player among Eileen's offspring, the genes would be from her side.

In the early summer of 1945, the couple conceived their sixth child, but three months before Eileen gave birth it was discovered she had an inoperable tumour. Her baby, a girl, lived only for a few days. Eileen died soon after. She was thirty-nine years old.

Of her five surviving children the youngest, Tom, had just turned seven. In his grief, Michael threw himself into the biggest engineering project of his career: the construction of the runway at the new airport in Shannon, County Clare. At weekends he found particular comfort in the companionship of his youngest child. The boy's aunts and uncles were struck by his maturity. There was, they sensed, something different about him.

'He was in the world before,' they would say.

A few weeks after his wife's death Michael took Tom to the Munster Senior Cup final between Cork Constitution and Garryowen. The game was held at the Mardyke, the epi-centre of sporting life in Cork, on to which the Kiernans' home backed. The contest between the two great Munster clubs was a hard and intoxicating spectacle, with forwards to the fore, but the young Tom Kiernan's eyes were drawn mostly to the busy and bossy scrum-half wearing white. In his last big match for Constitution, Neddy Murphy played a blinder.

From that day on, Neddy's nephew threw himself into the game of rugby with an intensity that would never fade. In 1947, the first overseas team to visit Munster since the 1905 All Blacks came to the Mardyke in Cork. Australia had just defeated Ireland with ease. People thought Munster would be cannon fodder. In injury time, Munster led 5–3.

A month short of his ninth birthday, young Tom was

overwhelmed by the commitment of the men wearing red shirts. And then it happened. The pass to Australia's John Hardcastle was at least three yards forward but Ossie Glasgow, the Ulster referee, could see nothing wrong with it. Hardcastle scored in the corner.

GALLANT MUNSTER PIPPED AT THE LAST

And so it went on. When Tom was rising thirteen, South Africa came to Limerick and were hanging on at 6–6 with twenty minutes to go when Munster's Jim McCarthy took a pass inside his own half and bolted for the line, with Mick Lane in support. As the cover closed in, McCarthy shipped the ball to Lane on his shoulder, who scored. From the halfway line came a shrill blast from Ossie Glasgow's whistle. Forward pass this time, Ossie reckoned. Thus reprieved, the Springboks scored a try, and that was enough.

UNLUCKY MUNSTER RUE DISALLOWED TRY

Two years later, on a bitterly cold day at the Mardyke, Munster were seconds away from a famous draw with the All Blacks, the score 3–3. Enter, stage left, the New Zealand wing John Tanner.

LAST-MINUTE HEARTBREAK FOR BRAVE MUNSTER

In these defeats, the young Tom Kiernan would find several morals. He would come to believe that referees were not to be trusted when the chips were down. You had to let them know you were there, watching them every time they put the whistle to their lips. Wherever possible, you reffed the match yourself.

His brother Jim was already making a name for himself at Presentation College and Brother Athanasius took one look at the latest Kiernan and knew he had a natural. The boy never had to think about what to do. Athanasius started him off as a scrum-half and that suited Tom fine, because he was perfectly positioned to make the referee's decisions for him. One day he went too far, said too much, turned the air too blue.

'In crooked, ref! Fucking crooked!'

The reprimand had long been coming and Athanasius moved to deliver it.

'Look, Tom, that won't do. That won't do at all.'

'What? What?'

'That kind of foul language.'

'What foul language?'

'Listen to me now. Maybe in future time you might be playing in front of thousands of people. That kind of behaviour wouldn't be acceptable now, would it?'

'No, brother.'

Athanasius's lecture, meekly accepted, ultimately went unheeded. The young Tom Kiernan was unable to prevent these outbursts because he cared too deeply, if such a thing is possible in sport. Sometimes he snapped and snarled at the other boys and in the early fifties fellows weren't used to being bawled at on the sports field. Who needed that? The smarter boys at Pres, or maybe the less sensitive ones, respected his dedication and his will to win. Others saw it differently, and in time they took their revenge. The boy who would go on to captain his university, Cork Constitution, Munster, Ireland and the Lions was defeated in a vote for the vice-captaincy of his school. Whether or not that slight mattered to Tom Kiernan, nobody could tell. On the pitch, he remained his old self: the lack of a mandate did not silence him. Off it, he never betrayed emotion. You could look at it another way. Where rugby was involved, he was strident and outgoing; his mother's son. But there was another side to him, which said that no matter what happened in life, good or bad, you didn't make a bloody fuss; you just got on with it.

It was the part of him that came from his father.

1 November 1952

Tom was in a wood, ten yards behind the setter, and the dog had frozen in its tracks, tail held straight out, nose pointing towards a bush straight ahead, front paw off the ground.

'High cock!' Tom shouted.

The setter sprang forward and the pheasant broke cover, its wings whirring.

'Mark out!'

The game was thirty yards from Michael Kiernan's gun, right in the kill zone. He squeezed the trigger.

'Bird down!'

More than any other day in the year, Michael Kiernan looked forward to the opening of the shooting season. You could take a man out of the midlands, you could make him president of the most famous rugby club in Cork, but that didn't mean he had to love the game. But put a double-barrel shotgun in his hands, with a bird clawing at the winter air in his sights, and the few seconds before he pulled the trigger were total enjoyment to him. Long ago Michael had accompanied his father to a remote stretch of farmland in Dunmanway, west Cork, and it was to the same spot he had now driven, two eager setters in the back, his thirteen-year-old son alongside him in front, the lackey boy he had once been.

It was Tom's responsibility to manage the dogs and flush the game for the guns. As a beater you were serving your apprenticeship until the day you were handed a gun your-self. The season continued until the end of February and every Saturday and Sunday Tom was by his father's side. Sometimes they were joined by another gun, Sonny Horgan, who had a pub on the banks of the Bandon. On a good day the setters might retrieve six or eight birds and they would pack up and drive back towards the city, the Kiernans breaking their journey at Horgan's. A small Jameson was Michael's tipple. Over a wood fire, they would discuss the day's kills and the ones that got away. Sometimes Tom's dog flushed a bird but it was still in the air after the shot rang out from Sonny's gun.

'You missed!' Tom would say. 'How did you miss that one?'

'Jaysus, I gave that bird a couple of grains,' Sonny would counter. And there he would have wished the conversation to end, but maybe the boy just had better eyesight.

'Well,' he would say, 'I didn't see any feathers falling.'

Rugby players were not the only ones in his firing line.

23 September 1955
Shortly after 6 a.m., fire burst through the windows of Number 1 Redclyffe, a guesthouse, and began to spread next door to Number 2. There were seven people in the guest-house. Mr and Mrs James from Carmarthen, who were returning to Wales that morning, fled in their nightclothes, taking only their sailing tickets. They ran to the front garden and watched the flames destroy their possessions. The Jameses were soon joined by three other guests, leaving two people trapped inside.

Donal O'Connor, a guesthouse employee, finding his way out blocked by fire and smoke, opened his first-floor window and climbed on to the ledge. From there he jumped to the

48

ground fifteen feet below, where he lay semiconscious. At the rear of the house, on the second floor, Rose Fitzpatrick was also on a window ledge, twenty-five feet off the ground and terrified.

From next door Tom Kiernan, aged sixteen, went to assist her. He climbed on to the roof of a coalhouse underneath and told her to drop – not jump – from the windowsill. He reached out and broke her fall, bringing her on to the coalhouse roof, so that she suffered only an injured leg. Convinced the boy had saved her life, she later wrote to him expressing gratitude and enclosing a £5 note. She also wrote to the lord mayor of Cork, urging him to recognise the boy's bravery in some official fashion.

By chance, a reporter from the *Cork Examiner* was passing and he summoned a photographer for the story of the damsel in distress rescued by the plucky teenager. The photographer arrived and sought out the hero of the hour. The hero of the hour said he would not pose for a photograph under any circumstances. The reporter, seeking at least a quote to dress up his story, was told he was making a big thing out of nothing. Other than that, the hero had no comment to make.

Not your average sixteen-year-old, the reporter considered.

When he received the letter, Cork's lord mayor made contact. He asked the boy to pay him a visit, so that he might show the city's appreciation for an act of such selfless bravery.

No thanks, said Master Tom Kiernan.

30 January 1960
Two years in a row Ray Hennessy had been full-back in the final Irish trial and both years he had blown it. The selectors had had no choice but to bring old Noel Henderson back from centre, but now Henderson had finally packed it in and

people figured Ray only had to turn up and the green jersey was his.

Hennessy was a star full-back for Cork Constitution and Munster and he was named in the Probables team. For the Possibles, the selectors chose a student who had come to their attention three weeks previously in an appearance for the Irish Universities. No doubt about it, Tom Kiernan looked one for the future. Problem was, Ireland needed somebody for now.

The way some people saw it, the trial was a lose-lose proposition for Hennessy. With his record, only bad could come of it. After all, he was the man in possession, the only provincial full-back available. In two weeks Ireland would face England at Twickenham. What were the chances of them blooding a raw kid there?

Maybe that line of thinking seduced Hennessy. In any case, the night before the trial he announced that he had pulled a muscle in his leg. Nothing serious, but enough to prevent him from playing the following day. Kiernan was thus promoted to the Probables XV.

He knew it was going to be one of those days when his kick at goal at the Wanderers end struck the left-hand upright and bounced into the hands of his cousin, Noel Murphy, who scored under the posts. After that, he could have closed his eyes and kicked the ball over the bar. The Probables won in a canter, and everybody was happy, except maybe Ray Hennessy. Old Ray never did get to wear that green jersey.

WHITES 27 BLUES 3

The most satisfying aspect to Saturday's final trial was the splendid display of full-back Tom Kiernan, for this 20-year-old Cork student never put a foot wrong . . .

As soon as the news came through they told Michael Kiernan that his son had been chosen to represent Ireland.

'Tom got his cap!' they cried.

'Tom got his cap . . . Tom got his cap . . .' he replied, over and over.

He had no idea what they meant. Three years previously, after Michael had turned fifty-seven, doctors had diagnosed premature senile decay. His father's decline coincided with Tom's university years, but if it was a burden to him he did not show it. 'He was wonderful to him, absolutely wonderful,' his sister Anne recalled, forty-five years on. 'It was hard for him, because the bond between them was huge. They were very, very, exceptionally close.'

26 December 1960

Because it was Christmas, Michael's nurse was away and so Tom brought his father breakfast. For nearly a year, he had been confined to bed at Redclyffe and life had ceased to have any meaningful quality for him.

Tom hit the road. He had a game to play. The previous year a club had been founded in Abbeyfeale, County Limerick, by the local doctor and his wife. George and Betty O'Mahony were fierce rugby people and they had two sons – Slick Mick and Billy – at university in Cork with Ireland's star new full-back. The match between the new club and an Invitation XV was intended as a message to the world that rugby had made it to Abbeyfeale.

They told him the news as he came off the pitch. There had been a phone call from Cork. His father had died in his bed.

He was shivering from the cold when he turned the key in the ignition of his Renault 7CV. No matter how many times he tried, the car's rear engine would not come to life. It was kind of the Abbeyfeale people to take him home to Cork, kinder still that to a man – and woman – they were there at his father's funeral two days later.

25 January 1967
Three years and two months after Munster's epic defeat to the All Blacks, he puts eight points on the board against the next tourists to turn up in Munster: Australia. Thirty seconds left and Munster lead 11–8. They have it won. And then the Australians are awarded a penalty, out on the left, ten yards outside the twenty-five. Most people think they'll kick it: they can draw the match. But they don't want to draw against Munster, they want to win. They launch a high ball under the posts. He's the full-back: he calls for it. But Pat McGrath doesn't hear, or maybe he does, but anyway he drops it. Scrum under the bar.

The ref is Ray Gilliland. A Belfast man. He knows the way referees think. Here you are, end of a match, a fella knocks on a ball – you bloody well blow for the scrum. You're not inclined to think about the final whistle. Not unless somebody thinks about it for you.

They form the scrum, Ken Catchpole prepares to put in. Kiernan walks up to the referee.

'How long to go?'

'It's over.'

'Well blow the fucking whistle then, if it's over.'

So Ray Gilliland blows his whistle.

16 January 1973
Different with the All Blacks. You can get on top of them, sometimes, but that's never enough. You must drive a stake through their hearts. Ten years and thirty-six Ireland caps after first encountering them he's still there, captain of his country and of Munster. There's been talk that, at thirty-four

and with a Lions captaincy and thirteen international seasons to his name, he's no longer worth his Ireland place. But you won't hear this at Musgrave Park, not among his own people and certainly not now, with the All Blacks a beaten team at last. The eighty minutes are up; only a minute of injury time remains. Thousands of supporters are about to scale the perimeter wall. The score is Munster 3 (B. McGann, pen.), All Blacks 0.

Right at the death, there's a ruck thirty-five yards from the Munster line and Phil O'Callaghan is caught with his hands on the ball, preventing it from coming out on the All Blacks' side. Penalty. In the stand, Kiernan's cousin Noel Murphy rises from his seat and makes his way down the steps. Murphy, the Munster coach, is not unduly worried. It crosses his mind that the referee has only awarded the penalty because he believes it to be unkickable. In a moment, the ball will drift wide, or fall harmlessly into the arms of Tom Kiernan, historic captain of the first Irish team to beat the All Blacks.

Trevor Morris, the New Zealand full-back, retrieves the ball. Nobody has ever heard of Trevor Morris.

Number of Test matches played by Trevor Morris during tour of 1972–3: 0
Number of attempts at goal by Trevor Morris against South Western Counties at Redruth, two weeks previously: 7
Points scored by Trevor Morris against South Western Counties: 0

Trevor Morris puts boot to ball and a few seconds later Kiernan's boys have made history. They are the first Munster team to draw with the All Blacks. The score is Munster 3 (B. McGann, pen.), All Blacks 3 (T. Morris, pen.).

In the home dressing room, Murphy calls his players to attention. Of the fifteen men in red jerseys, four will never wear the green of Ireland or see a day like this again. Forty-one caps for his country, eight for the Lions, Murphy has long since made his mark. He raises an arm and positions his index finger over his thumb, allowing a sliver of space between them. 'Lads,' he says, 'ye were *that* close from being famous.'

20 January 1973

Lansdowne Road, four days later. The All Blacks watch the Ireland captain jog into position for his fifty-second cap. But when they get up close they don't see Tom Kiernan, full-back of international repute; they notice only that almost every hair on his head is grey. 'Won't be seeing this fellow again,' thinks Bryan Wilson, the flying machine from Auckland.

These All Blacks have already beaten England, Wales and Scotland. They want a Grand Slam, badly. In almost seventy years of touring, no New Zealand team has achieved one. Eighteen minutes into the second half they are on course, leading 6–3, when Alex Wyllie takes a pass from Bob Burgess at full pelt and sees that only the old man stands between him and the line. It's no contest. Kiernan comes to tackle and Wyllie blasts past him as if he doesn't exist. Game over. Or so it seems.

With seven minutes remaining, something extraordinary happens. This is the way history recorded it: veteran full-back Tom Kiernan, sensing that his final opportunity to lead his men to victory against the mighty All Blacks is slipping away, suddenly turns the match on its head and gives them something to remember him by. He bursts out of his own twenty-five and knifes through the cover. A weaving run takes him thirty yards upfield. The old stadium shakes with approval. In an instant, Ireland are a team transformed.

And this is what actually happened. Veteran full-back Tom Kiernan sees his opposite number Joe Karam slice a kick for touch. The ball travels further infield and Kiernan comes to catch it but it dips before he gets there. In desperation, he puts out a leg and attempts to trap the ball, but fails. Mortified, he bends down to pick it off the ground and, when he looks up, two All Black forwards are right in front of him. Their eyes meet and time stands still. It is by far the most embarrassing moment of his career. They're waiting for him to kick it and he's thinking, 'There's only one thing I can do and that's run. There's nothing else.' So he runs and makes – at most – fifteen yards. Far enough.

Two minutes later Barry McGann kicks a penalty, then Tom Grace scores a try in the corner, diving on the ball just before it goes dead. Bedlam. Ten-all, conversion to come, no coming back from here. Out on the touchline McGann arcs his heel into the turf, places the ball, steps back, thirty yards from the posts and a stiff wind in his face. He strikes it and it's perfect, high and mighty, dead centre. When it's halfway there McGann hears the first cheers directly behind him, getting louder until they are reverberating around the ground. And then the wind catches it and blows it off centre and it drifts towards the left upright and sails over the top. And for the next thirty years people come up to McGann and tell him they were there when he had that kick to beat the All Blacks and they *swear to God* it went through the posts, which is what he thought himself at the time, and what he thinks now, but the flags stayed down and that was the end of that.

'Only for you, McGann, we'd have been famous,' the debutant Kevin Mays said in the dressing room afterwards. Mays had reason to be rueful; in a few months his brief international career would be over. And by then also, the axe had fallen on Tom Kiernan. They called him to the phone at his in-laws' place on a Sunday, two screaming children in his arms, a reporter on the line.

'Sorry to be the bearer of bad news but they've just named the team to play Wales. You've been dropped, Tony Ensor's in at full-back. Is this the end of the road for you?'

He was one cap short of the international appearances record held by Colin Meads, of New Zealand. It had been one of the great Irish careers.

Soon he was telling Maree, his wife: 'That's it. I'm finished now. All over. You'll be seeing a lot more of me.'

And he meant what he said, he really did.

They had five children, all under seven. Their eldest was mentally handicapped. Maybe Maree believed him, maybe she didn't, but at the time it was good to hear him say it.

Turned out, it wasn't true.

Rugby came after him again, calling in a debt. And perhaps he *had* taken more than he'd given. People reckoned that someone like him, with all he'd achieved, it wasn't right that the game should lose him just like that. He was the kind of man who could carry a torch. They asked him to take over as Munster coach and he said fair enough, he'd give it a go, see where it took him. Maree understood, knew only too well what rugby was to him. And maybe he was trying to justify it in his own mind, but it wasn't as if he was down at the local drinking ten pints a night and staggering home. At least he was always *doing* something.

He stepped in and nothing much happened. They won some, they lost some. They played the All Blacks in his first year as coach and were outclassed. Other than that, they didn't trouble anyone who kept a scrapbook. Off the pitch, the pressures kept building.

Maree gave birth to another child. They now had six under eight years old.

The company he worked for, Moremiles, was in expansionist mode. That meant he had to travel all over the place on business.

He was Cork Constitution's representative on the Munster branch. That meant he had to attend meetings at far-flung hotels on dark winter evenings, where such matters as improvements to the toilets at Musgrave Park and the cost of insuring schoolboys against injury were discussed late into the night.

He felt under terrible pressure and something had to give. He was thinking, 'Christ, I've had enough of this.' He walked away from the coaching job and they appointed him president of the branch, one of the youngest men ever to hold the post. Old before his time.

After a year, his successor as Munster coach decided he didn't fancy the job much. It was unfortunate, but they couldn't very well come back to him. He had done his time, paid his debt. It wouldn't have been fair to ask him.

They asked him anyway. They flattered him by saying there was nobody else. They said maybe he could take it for a year and bail them out of trouble.

There were a hundred reasons to reject it and one to accept.

He accepted.

He took it because the Eighth All Blacks were coming. A match against Munster had been fixed for 31 October 1978 at Thomond Park. When he thought about it, Munster didn't have a bad bunch of players. They were limited, it was true, but they were honest. They had a handful of internationals and others – such as Gerry McLoughlin, Colm Tucker, Moss Finn and Christy Cantillon – who were knocking on the door.

57

The *Cork Examiner* broke the story of his return, but many would have missed it. They gave it four paragraphs at the foot of an inside page, below the news of a golf outing by a group of local motor mechanics.

In time, the All Blacks match would become an obsession with Kiernan. Among the Munster players he could call on, he would find that one in particular felt the same way as he did about beating the All Blacks. It seemed that McLoughlin, the prop forward from Shannon, was on a mission all of his own.

Chapter Five

Locky the Warrior

Limerick, 1977
The Christian Brothers of Sexton Street had no love for rugby. Hurling was their game. In their eyes it had many fine qualities, but the one which stood apart was its Irishness. They saw it as their duty to nurture, to show the boys in their care that magic could be made with the ash wand. For young lads who dreamed of being the next Mick Mackey or Eamonn Cregan, this was their academy. For years rugby was unheard of at the school, until the day a new economics teacher showed up in the staff room. Gerry McLoughlin was his name, but mostly people called him 'Locky', and it didn't take the brothers long to find out that rugby was at the centre of his universe.

He played in the front row for Shannon, but he hadn't been blessed with a prop's physique. In the early days he'd looked like a back-row forward; a little under six feet tall and barrel-chested, but with long, thin arms and a perfectly distinctive neck below a mop of red curls. Good prop forwards weren't supposed to have necks you could see, because in the front row necks could be broken. Lack of size was never going to stop Locky, however. What he lacked physically he made up for mentally. The power he could summon was disproportionate to his physique and there was a wildness about him and an eagerness to learn that made him stand out.

He was a regular for Munster and he longed to wear the green of Ireland, but the years passed and the call did not come. It didn't help that Munster were going nowhere, or that Shannon were still living in the shadow of their illustrious local rivals Garryowen, the boys in blue, the blue-eyed boys. Some said it was because he was too light, but he had worked hard on his frame, lifting weights and taking the bodybuilders' protein powder, the yellow stuff that promised maximum muscle-building nutrition. He would bounce into the school staff room, telling anyone who would listen that he'd had steak for breakfast, a big juicy one, just like the All Blacks and the Springboks, and he'd soon be the size of those fellas. But, outside of Limerick, nobody noticed the difference.

The way the lads who drank with him in Jerry Flannery's pub in Catherine Street saw it, they were sick to death of it, the way their pal Locky barely got a mention in the Dublin papers, the way they talked up the likes of Ned Byrne, who played for Blackrock College in Dublin, which was why he was in the Ireland team. The powers that be were biased against Shannon men like Locky. In their heart of hearts they knew he would scrummage Ned Byrne off the pitch at Thomond Park, over the wall and into the stand. With a pint of plain in his hand and a few more inside him he would say so himself.

'There isn't a prop in Ireland who can send me backwards, lads! Not one!'

Phil Orr the lads could accept – there was no shifting him – but not Ned Byrne, nor Mick Fitzpatrick, nor Tom Feighery. Maybe Shannon weren't exactly renowned for their thrilling brand of rugby – people worried that their backs might get frostbite – but the power of their forwards was a sight to behold and it was a different game then, a time when all you needed was ten men with the right stuff. Locky could play both sides of the scrum, and yet every time there was a vacancy up front the Irish selectors would put another Dublin joker in the pack. Not that it did them any good: the wooden spoon beckoned when England beat them 4–0 on the first Saturday in February, in a spectacle that made Shannon look like the Baa-Baas on full throttle.

For the boys at school, Monday morning was the best time to have him walk into class. 'That's a fine shiner you have there, sir,' a boy might say. 'How did you get it?' And if they were lucky he might tell them to close the books for a while and they would hear the story of Shannon's latest triumph – some spellbound, others just pleased to have been spared the laws of supply and demand, or five hundred lines for having no homework done, or maybe a more painful punishment, for it was a time when most boys took a beating every now and then.

Because of his efforts, rugby took a foothold in the school and before long there were plenty of boys who preferred it to hurling. This did not please the brothers, but with the senior rugby team in the semi-finals of the Munster Schools Cup, they had no choice but to swallow it.

The game had come a long way in a short time at Sexton Street and the man responsible for its rise had ruffled feathers along the way. Things had got off to a bad start, what with the unfortunate business over the Clint Eastwood film. The brothers blamed Locky for that fiasco and they had a point. It had, after all, been his idea.

To get the school team up and running he had been given the go-ahead to screen films on Friday afternoons in the school hall, with the admission money set aside for jerseys and balls. The brothers agreed to this venture on the assumption that nothing would be shown which might compromise the virtues of the youngsters in their charge. Give us the boy, they would say, and we'll give you the man. In the Ireland of the 1970s they saw themselves as moral guardians, standing firm against the rising tide of filth and smut.

To begin his film club Locky had chosen *Coogan's Bluff*. It was an action movie suitable for twelve-year-olds, the brothers were given to believe by their new economics man, and when the lights went down the hall was packed solid with eager schoolboys. Some of the brothers sat in the front row, while others roamed the hall with torches and hissed words of warning.

'No messin' now lads. Just watch the fillum.'

It wasn't long before the brothers at the front were shifting in their seats, with Coogan (played by Eastwood) first being soaped down by a married woman and then charming his way into the apartment of a pretty probation officer. When they saw Coogan fighting his way through acid-addled dancers and kissing lesbians in a New York nightclub they began looking desperately at one another. They were out of their seats by the time an exotic go-go dancer began a slow descent from the rafters on cable wire.

Too late. Long before she reached the floor every boy in the hall could see she was completely naked. When her swaying breasts nearly knocked Coogan's cowboy hat clean off his head, the boys erupted. With his very first offering, Locky's film club was delivering beyond their wildest dreams. They roared, they jumped up and down, they caused such pandemonium that the brothers knew it was useless trying to shout them down and they started running, now, thunder-faced, towards the projector. The plug was pulled just as a serious-looking artist was daubing paint on to the nipples of a woman who already had the word 'Peace' painted on her left buttock and the stars and stripes on her right.

'Home!' shouted one the brothers. 'Go home! The fillum is cancelled.'

Locky was standing in a corner as they filed out, muttering something they couldn't quite catch as the brothers surrounding him waved their arms about.

'Will there be any more movies?' a first-year boy called Andy Malone asked when he walked into class on Monday.

'I don't know,' he said, tamely.

'Well,' said young Malone, 'if there are, make sure they're excellent like the last one.'

For the brothers, there was the bitter irony that the teacher responsible for this debacle had sat before them as a boy in these same classrooms a dozen years before. There was also the disconcerting fact that the very same Gerry McLoughlin had once walked around Limerick wearing a soutane and collar. He had once been one of their own.

At fifteen, Locky had barely held a rugby ball in his hands. He was away to be a Christian Brother. A recruitment officer wearing a dog collar had come to Sexton Street, flourishing photographs of the most recent intake, every boy smiling for the camera.

'Now, lads,' he had said, 'somebody in this room might have a vocation. Tick the box if you're even slightly interested, you can talk to me in confidence.'

Bridget McLoughlin thought it was a fine idea. Nobody could say for sure whether her boys had a vocation, but she knew they'd be getting an education. So she sent Gerry to the brothers and Mick, eighteen months his junior, to the

Redemptorists. The Reds would make a priest out of Mick. Everyone said Bridget had done well by her lads, for it wasn't cheap sending them away and Bridget had another son and daughter at home. Her husband, Mick McLoughlin Snr, was a bus driver with CIE and ordinarily that meant it wouldn't be possible to send two sons to boarding school but Mick was on the tours for six months of the year and his passengers looked after him once he had taken them up to Connemara and down to the Ring of Kerry. The Christian Brothers and the Redemptorists were paid out of the loose change of American tourists, £120 a year for Gerry and £90 for young Mick.

Even when her boys eventually told her that they weren't cut out for the lives that lay ahead of them, Bridget McLoughlin considered the money well spent. How could you put a price on the education they had had?

Two and a half years away with the Christian Brothers had not changed Bridget's eldest son. Naivety was part of his skin. His circle of friends, a bunch of lustful altar boys from the parish of St Michael's, saw this as fair game, convinced him that the best opening gambit where girls were concerned was an arm around the shoulder followed by an immediate request for a date. Thus did Gerry McLoughlin first feel the sting of rejection.

Down by Pillar Lane they congregated, thirty-strong, boys from Denmark Street and Ellen Street, Robert Street and Punch's Row, kicking a football up against Boyd's gate for four or five hours.

'Lads,' said Eamonn Ryan, who was also known as The Rabbit, 'did ye ever think about playing rugby?'

The Rabbit had some friends, like the Ellen Street barber John Joe Ryan and Paddy Steff Walsh, who had once been part of a defunct inner-city rugby club called Presentation, and they started thinking about re-forming Pres. So he marched the lads down to Ellen Street, where you hardly saw a car all day, and showed them how to bind in a scrum and jump in a lineout. The Rabbit needed some bigger men too and it so happened that Locky and his best friend, Gerry Ryan, knew a couple of likely candidates.

Flash Mulconnery and his brother Michael were in digs with Gerry's mother, whose guesthouse was located over a bookie shop in William Street. The Mulconnery brothers must have liked their landlady's cooking: they stayed for twenty-two years. Until The Rabbit got hold of them, they had never played rugby, but they were hard men, lorry drivers from the wilds of Clare. Locky was a regular visitor to the guesthouse. He liked to eat the buns meant for the guests and challenge Flash and Michael to one-on-one scrums. These were usually resolved in his favour, but only after two or three tables laden with the Ryans' best crockery had been upended in the dining room. For Locky, the sight of grown men going backwards when confronted by his power confirmed what he had already begun to suspect: rugby would be the making of him. He had found his true calling. The intensity of the front row, the physicality of it, the opportunity to grind another man into the dirt; these were grist to his mill.

When the lads called for him at Roxboro Road, they found him in front of the television, eyes on the screen, arms extended and jerking back and forth, a plastic bag in each fist full to bursting with cement.

'I'm going to play for Ireland,' he told them.

As well as hanging around The Rabbit, he had also joined Shannon. His house on Roxboro Road was in the outer regions of Young Munster territory, but Shannon had been his father's club and you did what your father did. From the beginning, he knew where he wanted to go. When the reconstituted Presentation Rugby Club met to choose a captain, he told them: 'I'm the best player, so ye either make me captain or I'm not playing with ye any more.' The Presentation boys took this on board and elected Pat Powell. Locky went back to Shannon and stayed for twenty years.

Two honours in the Leaving Certificate were enough for a place at university. He went away to Galway and came back a teacher. To the boys at Shannon, that was a good one. Locky, a teacher? The same Locky who complained that their lineout code – odd number for the first jumper, even for the second, nought for the back – was too complicated and had to be changed? Brendan Foley, who had left school early for a job at the Good Shepherd Convent, had a problem with this particular grievance and he, more than anyone, knew how to rise Locky. The lads reckoned Foley was like the guy playing the flute and Locky was the snake.

'It's your fault.'

'What do you mean, Brendan?'

'Gerry, you can't hold anything in your head! I don't know how you ever became a schoolteacher. They must've given it to you on compassionate grounds. Lads, can anyone tell me, how did this fella get out of college?'

'How did he get *out* of college? You mean how did he get *into* college? How did he get past his fuckin' Inter?'

And Locky would scratch his red head and say: 'I dunno . . .' They loved him for that. Sometimes they felt like hitting him, other times they did. But there wasn't a man among them who didn't accept that what he gave them was unique. Because there wasn't anyone around like Gerry McLoughlin, not by a long chalk.

When he walked into the classroom he would write 'NEVER DO TOMORROW WHAT YOU CAN DO TODAY' on the blackboard. The older boys did not call him 'sir' or 'Mr

McLoughlin'; to them he was just 'Gerry', or sometimes 'Locky'. They knew of his desire to play for Ireland, especially those he had converted to rugby, but they knew also that he was ambitious for them, and if his interest in their progress was more obvious on the rugby pitch than in the classroom, they weren't complaining. None of them was planning on becoming an economist. He covered the curriculum, he enjoyed his work, but as a teacher he was at his best when rugby was the subject. Even though he was a married man with young children, he found time for them three nights a week, running every lap alongside them in training. For the boys in the front row there was specialist advice and, caught up in the language of man-to-man combat, he didn't hold back.

'Get your retaliation in first! Let him know you're there!'
'Never – *fucking ever* – take a step backwards!'
'Never let the opposition see you have a weakness!'
'Take the punishment and come back twice as strong!'
'Anything you can get away with, get away with it!'
'Hold on to the ball at all costs! Hide it!'
'Don't give it to the backs! You're strong enough to win any match on your own!'

Sometimes he grabbed the ball and challenged them to take him down and they hung off him as he drove on, dragging the whole lot of them along with him, through the near-swamp that was the back pitch of Thomond Park in wintertime. When those evening sessions finished he told them to be sure to get to bed early, because rugby players needed their rest.

He urged them to avoid the charms of the Presentation convent girls next door, who would hang around outside the City Theatre after school, passing cigarettes between themselves and maybe offering a drag to the boys that took their fancy.

'Stay away from those women! You'll go nowhere in rugby if you're messin' around with them. Wait until you can show them your medals.'

Come the week of the semi-final, the economics went out the window completely. Locky stood at the blackboard, chalk at the ready, detailing the lineouts and sketching his instructions to the out-half Frankie Brosnahan; how he wanted the ball kicked into touch, or into the 'A' section or the 'B' section, and no fancy stuff or they'd hear him in the next parish.

'Stop leavin' out the fucking ball!'

Brossy, as he was known, knew that to throw a flamboyant ball out to the wing was to invite trouble, that even if the team conceded ten tries in a landslide defeat, that one pass would have cost them the match in Locky's eyes.

'Put it ahead of the forwards!' he was told. 'Only give it to the backs if you can't do anything with it yourself. Keep it simple! Hang on until the forwards get to you. Any questions, lads?'

It was, in all respects, the Shannon way. He needed a decent lineout jumper and when a big lad called Brian Spillane came to the school he recruited him for rugby and watched him soar so high he would play more than a dozen times for Ireland.

But sometimes, when he lost his temper in the classroom, it was as if he was going into a maul, and when he got the notion that someone wasn't concentrating the chalk would fly.

'Pay attention! This is important!'

In the semi-final they were up against Tom Kiernan's alma mater, Presentation Brothers College of Cork, bastions of the establishment with seventeen Senior Cups to their name. He knew they had some useful backs, but backs wouldn't be much use to Pres if his forwards did their job. In the economics class they pushed their desks aside and created enough space for a scrum. They wheeled it this way and that, barging into the desks, and somewhere in the middle of it all he could be heard exhorting them to arch their backs and drive for all they were worth.

'I don't want to see you scrummaging with your head down like a bird! Always look up, never down.'

'Bind high on him and then bring your elbow inwards, like this. You'll bottle him up and take the strength out of him.'

'When the push comes on, drop your shoulder a bit. Like this, see? He won't be able to budge you!'

On such days, when a big match was close at hand, those boys in the class who had no involvement in rugby were told to get on with the economics, while he took his players into the corner of the room and fired questions at them, one after the other, until he was satisfied he could do no more. He had spent four years getting them ready. They believed they were unbeatable, that Pres would roll over when they turned on the power. That was what Locky had said, after all.

As chance would have it, the match clashed with Munster's most prestigious outing of 1977, a visit to the Arms Park to face a Cardiff team so powerfully equipped that they could leave Gareth Edwards on the bench in favour of the rising Brynmor Williams. As usual Locky was chosen for the front row, so that left the Sexton Street boys on their own.

For three seasons Munster had been coached by Tom Kiernan but they had little to show for it and in a matter of weeks Kiernan would walk away. He'd had enough. There was more to life. Who needed this? The first he saw of his players was at half past five on the evening before the match. Against a side of Cardiff's calibre, it was suicidal. Of course, he didn't get to pick the team – that was the selectors' job.

And in the history of bad preparation for rugby matches, this one took some beating.

After a brisk runaround in the fading Cork light they piled on to a bus – along with a couple of dozen alickadoos – and made for the ferry port. Given calm conditions, the overnight sailing to Wales would take ten hours, but calm conditions were no given. As it turned out, half the team couldn't sleep and so they played cards until the sun came up and the *Innisfallen* docked at Swansea. Then it was back on to the bus and off to Cardiff for lunch before the afternoon's battle against one of the top club teams in world rugby. Back down to Swansea then and across to Cork on the overnight boat.

The brains behind this trip – the gentlemen from the Munster branch – could see nothing wrong with it. Far from it: they regarded the fixture as a triumph. As was the way with these things, Cardiff had promised to return the compliment. Their visit to Munster the following year was a cast-iron money-spinner, and nobody could deny that the branch needed money.

That was why the boat trip was a masterstroke. Not only was it cheap, but it meant they didn't have to put the players up in a hotel. Two birds with one stone – what was wrong with that? Some didn't like it – such as the players – but they didn't have access to the full facts. Did they realise how much it cost the branch to put twenty fellas up in hotels?

Mike Knill and Barry Nelmes were the Cardiff props – internationals both. They couldn't budge Locky, but that was a small detail lost amid the slaughter. When a reporter asked the branch president if the boat trip had been a mistake, given the fact that a jaded-looking Munster had lost by thirty-eight points, he was soon put straight.

'The important thing is that the fixture is under way,' said the branch man cheerfully.

If anything, the Sexton Street boys felt stronger without their absent coach. They wanted to prove they could do it by themselves. The pitch at Musgrave Park was a quagmire: in other words, it was perfect. They were togged off in the dressing room, clacking their studs off the floor, when word came through that the match was off: Pres had complained about the state of the pitch.

It killed them, knocked the stuffing right out of them.

On Monday, Locky tried to rally them in class but they knew they could never be so fired up again. And Locky wasn't feeling too great himself, what with the latest hammer blow to his international prospects. The Sunday papers had not spared them and now the *Limerick Leader* was twisting the knife.

MUNSTER HUMILIATED IN CARDIFF

CARDIFF 51 MUNSTER 13

By Charlie Mulqueen

Nothing can excuse the complete collapse of the Munster side at the Arms Park on Saturday. After actually leading 9–6 with twenty minutes played Munster came apart at the seams and stood idly by as an average Cardiff side did just as it pleased and strolled to an almost unbelievable victory.

For many years Munster teams have stood up proudly to the might of the major overseas sides. Alas, too many of our representatives in Cardiff either forgot or never really gathered the implications of their heritage. Gone was the pride, the sense of honour, in wearing the red of Munster.

Later that week a Pres boy called Declan Kidney kicked Sexton Street out of the Cup and that was the end of their adventure. Years later, when the team captain, Kevin Flannery, saw the film *Dead Poets Society*, the story of an unorthodox teacher who urges his students to 'seize the day', he was reminded of those times, of how his own teacher had instilled in him a lifelong love for rugby. Most of all it brought back to him what it was like to be a part of something so special that nothing else in the world mattered.

'He made our lives fabulous,' Flannery recalled more than twenty-five years on. 'Our only interest was in what he had to say about rugby. He was our king. Maybe we were lucky to pass our Leaving but if it all came back again, knowing what I know now, I'd do the same thing. We turned out all right. Most of the good things that ever happened to me at that school were down to him.'

Soon after the semi-final defeat to Pres the brothers disbanded the rugby team at Sexton Street. They had been left with no alternative, they said. There had been an unsavoury incident on the pitch . . . They had the good reputation of the school to think of.

There wasn't so much rugby talk in the economics class after that. Gerry McLoughlin still turned up on Monday mornings looking like he'd gone a couple of rounds with Larry Holmes, but there were no more lineouts drawn on the blackboard, or scrums formed in between the desks.

Shannon finally got the Garryowen monkeys off their backs, grinding their way to a Munster Senior Cup victory that reduced hard men to tears of joy, but the Ireland selectors could still find no place for Locky in their front row. One day he made the replacements bench and when Willie Duggan injured his shoulder they told him to warm up. Ireland had already sent one forward into the fray. They had no choice but to summon Locky.

'You're going on now,' Noel Murphy told him. 'Are you ready?'

Ready? They had no idea how ready he was to run on to that pitch. His heart was pounding as he pulled the zip down his tracksuit top.

Murphy told Duggan to come off. The doctor told him. The referee told him. But Duggan wouldn't come. He walked over to the touchline, where Locky was waiting.

'I'll break your neck if you come on this field.'

And that was the end of that.

In the wider rugby world, the Springbok tour of Great Britain and Ireland was pulled for political reasons and when the All Blacks stepped in at late notice to fill the void Gerry McLoughlin stared hard at the newspaper when the details of their itinerary emerged. There it was, the fifth match of the tour.

Oct 31: v Munster, Thomond Park, Limerick

It was a stage with a spotlight, a chance to do damage, maybe the last chance. He didn't care who the All Blacks put up against him. The only thing that mattered was that the other guy went backwards.

Chapter Six

The Politician

Cork, 7 September 1978

It could be said of Bill O'Brien that he was living his father's life. Sixty-five years old, he had attained a seniority denied to Tom O'Brien, whose premature death gave rise to the two legacies that shaped the son's future. The first was his position of honorary secretary to the Munster branch. For forty-one years Bill controlled the game in the province from his gentleman's outfitters in MacCurtain Street, Cork. The shop, Lawson's, was leased from the adjoining Metropole hotel, whose grand Victorian edifice lent Bill's place a refined, upmarket air. It was the second legacy.

The older O'Brien had been known as 'Tommo' and there were some who called his son and heir 'Billo', but not many, for it suggested affability, and Bill O'Brien was not an affable man. Rugby consumed him, but it didn't interest him particularly. His concerns were purely administrative. That there was an end product, that the branch existed so that rugby might be enjoyed by those who played it and watched it, was not something at the forefront of his mind. In his eyes, the branch was rugby and rugby was the branch. It was its own *raison d'être*.

Although he had the build of a front-row forward, nobody

"ALL BLACKS"

15. B. J. McKECHNIE.
14. S. S. WILSON.
13. B. J. ROBERTSON.
12. J. L. JAFFRAY.
11. B. G. WILLIAMS.

10. ~~━━━━~~ E. DUNN
9. M. W. DONALDSON.

1. B. R. JOHNSTONE.
2. J. E. BLACK.
3. G. A. KNIGHT.
4. A. M. HAYDEN.
5. F. J. OLIVER.
6. G. N. K. MOURIE. — CAPTAIN.
7. W. G. GRAHAM.
8. A. A. McGREGOR.

MUNSTER

V

NEW ZEALAND

THOMOND PARK, LIMERICK
31st OCTOBER, 1978 - 3.00 p.m. PRICE 20p.
Hon. Secretary.

Team news:
Eddie 'Hands' Dunn comes in at
out-half in the All Blacks line-up

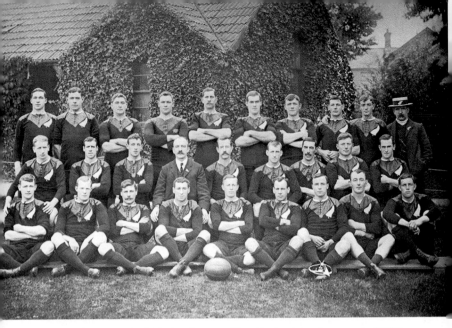

The original All Blacks: the great New Zealand touring squad of 1905.
Manager George Dixon is in the second row

Bloody hero: Munster's bandaged prop Mick O'Callaghan moves to block
in the titanic 1963 match at Thomond Park

Headquarters:
Bill O'Brien's shop,
Munster rugby
central for decades

Stout fellows:
the Healy brothers,
centre stage as usual

(*Below right*)
Hadah Sweeney's house,
first home of St Mary's
Rugby Club, Limerick

Tom Kiernan: (*above*) aged
twenty and still uncapped;
(*right*) the Grey Fox twelve
years later

Shannon boys:
Brendan Foley and
Gerry McLoughlin

Locky's warriors:
Gerry McLoughlin (in suit) and his CBS Sexton Street rugby team, 1977

Just dandy: Seamus Dennison

The golden boy: Tony Ward

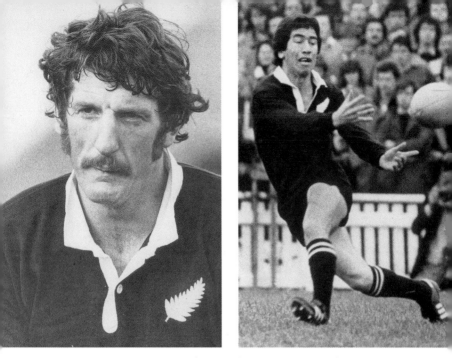

Mourie and his men: (*clockwise from top left*)
Graham Mourie, Eddie Dunn, Brian McKechnie, Stu Wilson

(*Above*) Dan Canniffe: immaculate as ever

(*Left*) Double act: coach Jack Gleeson and Mourie test the wind in Swansea, a week before the Munster game

Shooting the breeze: Kiernan (*left*) with Olan Kelleher, Christy Cantillon and Tony Ward the day before the match

Enter the Eighth All Blacks: arriving at Shannon airport, unbeaten

Munster immortals. Back row: Johnny Cole (touch judge), Gerry McLoughlin, Les White, Moss Keane, Donal Spring, Colm Tucker, Pat Whelan, Brendan Foley, Corris Thomas (referee), Martin Walsh (touch judge).
Front row: Tony Ward, Christy Cantillon, Moss Finn, Seamus Dennison, Donal Canniffe, Greg Barrett, Jimmy Bowen, Larry Moloney

could remember him playing the game, or even watching it much. Price or Paparemborde, Irvine or Ensor, the Young Munster blindside flanker or the kid from Cork Constititution – he could not be moved to express a preference. Ships were his thing. He had been born in 1913, two years before the sinking of the *Lusitania* off the coast of Cork, an event that gripped him in a way rugby or commerce never would. Fate had made him a businessman but nature had not equipped him for the life. He was the kind of proprietor who believed the customer was seldom right. His true calling might have been chief radio officer on an ocean-going liner, or some function where absence of personality was no bar to progress, but over the years the branch had become an alternative vocation for him. It was his fiefdom.

At best, he tolerated players, if they did not get above their station. At worst, he was infuriated by them. They could be an unendurable nuisance. In 1961 a player had arrived in Cork from England and joined the Dolphin club. He whizzed around the city in a white Triumph sports car, as if he owned Cork. Of course Bill had heard of Tony O'Reilly – who hadn't? – but to him O'Reilly was just another player. That he had played ten Tests for the Lions, scoring a record six tries, was neither here nor there. But one Monday morning O'Reilly had the temerity to telephone the shop and complain about the state of the pitch he had played on at the weekend. It was a disgrace, he said; it had made a mockery of the game.

Bill put the phone down and seethed at the insult to the branch. 'That upstart! Who does he think he is?' he asked his loyal assistant, John O'Keeffe. 'Coming down here trying to teach us about running the branch! We got on grand before he ever arrived.'

For weeks, O'Reilly's insolence was a talking point in the

small office at the back of the shop, where he spent the majority of his day, discussing branch matters with Noel Murphy Snr, Tim West and one or two other stalwarts. Soon after, O'Reilly scored a hat-trick of tries for Dolphin and was fêted in Monday's *Cork Examiner*. But when the match ball was handed in to Bill's shop that morning (most branch property was dispensed by and returnable to him) he noticed that it was a size four ball, intended for schoolboy rugby, not a regulation size five.

'No wonder O'Reilly scored all the tries,' he announced when Murphy arrived in the afternoon. 'Sure he wasn't playing with the right ball at all.'

Due to a paucity of passing trade, and the perception that only doctors, solicitors and other white-collar professionals were welcome as customers (in Bill's case, perception equalled reality), Lawson's was slowly going under. The shop sold Magee suits and Van Heusen shirts, Hortex ties and Bond slacks. Bill would not hear of stocking jeans or casual clothing. They would lower the tone and have his father turning in his grave. Who knew what kind of degenerates might darken his door in search of denim? If anybody walked in who did not look sufficiently prosperous, he would all but chase them out of the shop.

'Can I help you?'

'No thanks, I'm just browsing.'

'That's an expensive shirt. What exactly are you looking for?'

'Do you think I can't afford it or something?'

'Look, are you buying it or aren't you?'

To everybody's surprise, he had got married late in life, to the head receptionist of the Metropole, a woman with enough personality for the both of them. 'For God's sake, Bill, who's going to buy anything in here, with that miserable puss on you?' she would say on her visits from next door. But it was no use: misery became him. There would never be an heir who might ease him gently aside and turn things around, so he continued to steer the ship towards the rocks.

Even though he had been taken on in 1954, O'Keeffe felt he had to begin every day as if it were his first. Conversation was impossible. The younger man could see the business falling away, but his attempts to revive it by taking advantage of the shop's unique position at the heart of Cork rugby were doomed by his employer's gun-barrel straightness. Occasionally O'Keeffe pointed out that one of the local clubs was going on a foreign tour and might be a customer for a batch of commemorative jumpers. What about if he went down there and suggested it?

'We can't do that,' Bill would say crossly. 'They might think we're looking for business.'

'But Bill, we *are* looking for business.'

'I mean, they might think we're doing badly.'

There was no answer to that.

Not long before, a Munster player had been forced to play in a red T-shirt because one of the jerseys from the previous season had not been returned and the branch had balked at buying another one. There had been a request for a new set of jerseys for the All Blacks match, an order from which the shop would take its cut as supplier, but Bill wasn't so sure. The shop's profit would be the branch's loss. Bill had a duty to see that the financial affairs of the branch were in good order. In his book, that meant minding its money as carefully as if it were his own. His father would have expected that of him and a sense of obligation to Tommo had accompanied Bill throughout his life.

Could a set of new jerseys be considered a necessary expense? Hardly, at least not in the same way as a set of medals, say. He could tell you without consulting his minute book how much the medals for the Munster Senior Cup were costing the branch that year (£387, plus VAT). Gold did not come cheap, but there could be no skimping on tradition.

At the start of the year he had been hopeful that gate receipts from the match against the All Blacks might see the branch through, but now he wasn't at all sure. Not since he had given in over the London business.

The whole London thing was Tom Kiernan's idea. After a year's absence, during which he had served as the youngest branch president in living memory, Kiernan had just been appointed Munster coach for the second time. He had told the branch he only wanted the job for one season and people figured he only had one reason for taking it on. As soon as the All Blacks match had been announced, Kiernan's mind seemed to be on it. As branch president, he had insisted that a trip to London five weeks before the match would foster team spirit and now here they were, faced with the ruinous cost of it.

Ordinarily, Bill would have dismissed out of hand the thought of sending twenty players and more than a dozen officials out of the country for four days, just to play a couple of friendly matches. It was extravagant to the point of absurdity. These fellas had jobs to go to. What was the point of it? Team spirit? The branch didn't have the money for team spirit. Team spirit was the selectors' business. And anyway, what was the big deal about the All Blacks? A bunch of bloody professionals, that's all they were. How did he know this? Because a crowd of them had come into his shop five years previously, traipsing after some rep from Adidas, who was determined to give them free boots and tracksuits. Handed them over, just like that. He'd had to turn away, the thing was so upsetting.

He discussed the tour with Tom Collery, honorary treasurer of the branch for more than twenty years. Collery was a Young Munster man, from Limerick. He differed from Bill in that he had actually played rugby. Matter of fact, he had lined up alongside the great Tom Clifford, even captained him. It followed that the treasurer would come from Limerick, since the secretary was from Cork. The branch considered itself to be even-handed when it came to these things.

The two of them spoke regularly on the telephone, always about the affairs of the branch, and if that meant some young fella from Christian Brothers College whose mother had sent him in to be measured for a new school jacket had to wait for half an hour, then it couldn't be helped. The boy would be measured when Bill was good and ready. It wasn't as if his mother could send him anywhere else: Bill had the contract for uniforms at Christians, his alma mater. It sustained the shop.

Sometimes, a Munster player might come in to claim the tie he was entitled to after playing for the province in the previous season. Bill had the contract for Munster branch ties, too.

'Your name?' he would ask, reaching for the book he kept expressly for such visits.

A mere name, though, was no proof of eligibility.

'Matches played?'

When he had satisfied himself that the player was not an impostor, the tie would be handed over and the player made to feel he had benefited from an act of reckless generosity. But any player who thought he might be entitled to a free ticket or two for the big match against the All Blacks was gravely mistaken.

Younger members of the branch would hesitate before

entering Bill's shop; they would cower at the doorway, waiting for a sign from O'Keeffe. A shake of the head meant you turned on your heels, a nod and it was relatively safe to enter. Just so long as you weren't looking for another bloody hand-out.

'Where do these fellas think we're going to find the money?' Bill would say to Collery, whenever the latest demand on the branch's funds was made. And face to face with such irritants, the honorary treasurer could be scathingly abrupt, particularly when their proposal involved putting fellas up in hotels for no good reason. It was a familiar routine, but it had served the branch's officers well over the years.

The first part involved a question.

Why would we want to do that?

Then came a challenge.

Where are we going to get the money?

Next, a decree.

We can't afford it. Over my dead body!

And Tom Collery would suck on his pipe and walk away.

But Kiernan was different. He didn't crumble. He had fifty-four caps for Ireland but that cut no ice with Bill O'Brien. Four, fourteen, fifty-four, it made no difference. Players were players and Kiernan had been like all the rest of them, a drain on the branch's coffers. He had been educated at Pres, not Christians, and that counted against him in Bill's eyes. What's more, he had once had the impertinence to have a newspaper delivered to his hotel room at the branch's expense. But then that was quite a few years back and Bill had to accept that things had changed somewhat. Kiernan was on the inside now. He had served on the branch for four years.

On this, the first Thursday in September, as he looked around the conference room of the Kilcoran Lodge hotel in

Cahir, Bill could see that Kiernan would be absent when the full horrific cost of the London tour was revealed to the branch.

There were eighteen members present, and Bill began the meeting by opening a red minute book, four or five inches thick, so voluminous that a quarter of a century later it would still be in use. The third item in the minutes of the previous meeting was headed 'LONDON TOUR' in the left-hand margin. 'It was agreed,' Bill read, 'that the following would be the official party to London on 21–24 September: four officers, twenty players, five selectors, one coach, one team secretary, three committee members. Total: thirty-four.'

A few minutes later, Jim Turnbull, the team secretary, told the meeting that the estimated cost of the tour would be £4178. He was aware that such a figure would cause a shudder, but he wasn't too concerned about that. The trip had been agreed back in April and there was nothing any-body could do about it now.

What was preoccupying the team secretary was the second contribution he was due to make, a suggestion so radical that it was guaranteed to cause consternation. Once again, it came back to the All Blacks match. And once again, it was Kiernan's doing. The rest of them would guess that much, surely, for even though Turnbull had long since nailed his colours to the mast as a players' man, an attitude that made him almost unique on the branch, nobody but a complete revolutionary could have dreamed up what he was about to put to the meeting.

The branch was well aware, he began, that the All Blacks match was scheduled for 3 p.m. on Tuesday, 31 October. In the normal course of events, the team would assemble on the day before the match but on this occasion he, as team secretary, was suggesting that they meet up *on the Sunday morning.* This would enable the team to prepare thoroughly for the match. Unfortunately, it would necessitate an additional night at Jury's hotel, thus making three in all, a regrettable extra expense. But nonetheless . . .

Some of those whose eyebrows shot upwards when Turnbull came out with this were not much more than forty years old, men who considered themselves progressive, up to a point. Ralph Murphy had never heard of such a thing, couldn't believe the audacity of it. The protests from the old guard were not long in coming.

'What in the name of God would ye be doing there for three days?'

'Drinking pints – that's what they'd be doing.'

'Jim, with all due respect, this is totally uncalled for. We never did anything like this before.'

Jim Turnbull was not a fool and he knew he had lost the battle before it had been joined. But he knew also that Kiernan was a man who tended to win wars. He had decided that an extra day with the players might make a difference and nothing was going to stop him from getting it. Kiernan would be making the next move and Turnbull didn't know of any man in Cork who was more adroit at getting his way. Many years later, another of the branch members present that night in Cahir would reflect that Kiernan's most brilliant trait was his ability to create the illusion that he was not an arch-politician. He was, said Young Munster's Joe Kennedy warmly, the most perfect, most brilliant politician he had ever known.

As Bill O'Brien called the meeting to a close at the Kilcoran Lodge, Kiernan had fifty-four days to prepare a team that could do what he had never been able to manage himself: to beat the All Blacks, once and for all. To write a page of history for the scrapbooks, not another hard-luck story.

Chapter Seven

London Mauling

25 September 1978

Under a bright blue sky, Kiernan made his way to Cork airport. He and his Munster players were bound for London, where the team would play two warm-up matches. Kiernan was never late. He would imagine the worst-case scenario and allow extra time on top of that. All his life he had believed that in order to perform, it was necessary to prepare. In his playing days he had bought a new pair of laces for every match. The ritual of threading them into his boots helped him to focus on what lay ahead. He had bought new woollen socks routinely because he hated the way they shrank, the way old socks felt against his skin. His boots were always immaculate, polished without fail. In this respect, he was the opposite of Gerry McLoughlin, who would walk through the dressing-room door and toss his gear bag into the corner, dried mud caked to his boots.

McLoughlin, along with the rest of the Limerick contingent, had hit the road at dawn. No surprise that the Cork guys had an extra hour in bed, he figured. It didn't matter that the airport there was a glorified barn by comparison to Shannon, twenty minutes from Limerick city. The same logic had them training in Fermoy, another easy spin for the Cork brigade, the road to hell for the rest of them.

Still, times were changing. The nightmare boat trip to Wales was still fresh in the mind, but in London they were to stay at a four-star hotel in Knightsbridge. The two matches on their itinerary were three days apart and neither was being taken very seriously. The words 'team-bonding' had been mentioned. All in all, it had the makings of a first-class piss-up. Nobody wanted to miss it and some travelled even though they were injured. One player had a broken thumb, which he neglected to mention to Kiernan.

Early in his rugby career McLoughlin had been regarded as too light to be a prop forward of high class. He had once put four pounds of lead in his jockstrap in order to make fourteen stone for an Irish trial, convinced that the selectors would dismiss him if he touched the scales at thirteen-ten. Now, at twenty-six, he believed the stakes were higher for him against the All Blacks than for any of the other Munster players.

In Limerick, they knew he was ready. He had proved his worth on the biggest day of the year in Munster rugby and that was good enough for them. Before their eyes he had grown from boy to man.

1974: His first Munster Senior Cup final. Garryowen to beat. He's already broken into the Munster team, mixed it with a bunch of filthy Argentinians a few months before, showed them what he was made of. Now here's a chance to catch the eye of the Ireland selectors. So what if Garryowen have twenty-nine Senior Cups and Shannon have only one? No need to look back. He reckons they can take them up front. In Limerick, Garryowen are the white-collar wonders. A nice number at the bank, something in insurance, a cut above the rest but careful not to get too uppity.

This Garryowen team have earned respect in spades.

They're a class, class act, probably the best in the country, as good a rugby team as Limerick has seen in fifty years. Hell of a backline, beautiful to watch them throwing it around, but there's steel at the core. The tighthead is Tom Carroll, spends all day humping bags of flour around at Ranks. The hooker is Pat Whelan, months off his first cap, as aggressive as they come. At Number 8, the Deero – Shay Deering, a vet from the south side of Dublin, newly capped and soon to be a legend in Irish rugby, spoken of with uncommon reverence. In the centre, Seamus Dennison, a teacher from the sticks, first cap the previous year, softly spoken, hard as nails. Shannon haven't got a cap between them. In their entire history, they've had one international player: Brian O'Brien – first cap 1968, last cap 1968. But Locky isn't bothered about that. He's thinking, what good will Garryowen's backs be to them if they don't see any ball?

Garryowen win 29–0. No team has been beaten so badly in any previous final going back to 1886. Men against boys, as far as the Dublin papers are concerned. And as for the international ambitions of Shannon's flame-haired prop, let's just forget about them. Force his way into the Ireland team? Let's see him force his way out of a paper bag first. Put him up against Ray McLoughlin and you'd better make sure there's a spare bed at the nearest hospital. He's not big enough. End of story.

Shannon are one-half devastated, the other half mortified. At ten to six, when they're sure the coast is clear, three of them exit Thomond Park and head for town on foot. They walk into the Bailey Bar and make for the snug. It's empty. Thank Christ. They call three pints and close the door behind them. They don't want to talk to anybody; they want to hide. The door opens and a woman pokes her head around it. If she is not seventy-five, she is eighty.

'Ye were a feckin' disgrace,' she says, slamming the snug door hard.

The Shannon boys got together soon after and vowed: 'This will never happen to our club again.' The way Locky saw it, if Shannon didn't get their act together he wouldn't hold his place for Munster and if he wasn't playing for Munster he could forget about his green jersey. Brian O'Brien drove them hard over the next three years, and sometimes Locky broke his heart, he was so incorrigible. No one was more committed than the coach himself, but utter devotion to the cause did not spare O'Brien when his tighthead prop gave vent to his frustrations.

After one outburst, the air was so thick with accusations that O'Brien ripped the jacket from his back and answered the charges with his fists, giving as good as he got until he and Locky were dragged apart. When there was a row after training over the pack's failure to perform to Locky's satisfaction, O'Brien told him they'd sort the problem the next night. No, said Locky, they'd sort it out tonight. Few could resist the force of his ambition. The forwards were dragged out of the shower and back into the rain and the mud for another session with the scrummaging machine the team captain Bob McConkey had built with his own hands. On such occasions, only the pack was required to do over-time. For Locky, for a whole generation of Shannon forwards, the backs were always a necessary evil. Why let the ball out when they could win any match on their own?

Two things he believed, above all others. First, the prop who could send him backwards had not been born. Second, as he put it himself, usually after standing bolt upright in a scrum: 'Lads, if I'm not right, the rest of ye are bollixed.'

One day Shannon were playing Bohemians, their next-door neighbours at Thomond Park. The Bohs hooker was Pat O'Donnell, one of his best friends and the kind of competitor who would hook the ball with his head if his feet were unavailable.

'I'm telling you,' Locky told him halfway through the match. 'Don't bring down the scrum. You're doing it all day.'

But Pat O'Donnell tended not to take too much notice of what Locky said.

'Fuck off, Locky.'

'Right, I'm warning you now, Pat. If you bring it down one more time I'll take your head off.'

Even though the promised violence did not prove necessary, remorse at such a threat to a close friend brought him to the Franciscan church on Henry Street. At the confessional, he found the priest in an understanding mood, which was not a surprise because the priest's name was Fr Brendan Scully and he played on the wing for Shannon.

'But did you really mean it?' the priest asked.

Really meaning it was what made Gerry McLoughlin good on a rugby pitch. It was his greatest strength, but it could also be a weakness, because the ferocity with which he attacked his opposite number sometimes shook the foundations of his own pack. Shannon wanted to work a nice, comfortable ball back to Eddie Price, the Number 8; he wanted to work the loosehead opposite him up and down, before dispatching him into the care of the St John Ambulance. No point in telling him to do it another way.

'Fuck you, I'm doing it my way.'

1977: his second Munster Senior Cup final. Garryowen again. Tony Ward has landed in Limerick. Twenty-three years old and looks like a film star. No caps yet but that means nothing: at this moment, on this spring day, he might just be the best out-half in the world. Good job he doesn't play for Shannon. Locky has the game plan: 'We'll take them up front.' The extraordinary Shannon flanker Johnny Barry takes care of Ward and the pack does the rest. They murder them, 6–3. When the whistle goes, and the Shannon supporters start pouring over the pitchside wall, the first guy Locky sees running straight at him is Pat O'Donnell, who he once promised to break in two. The embrace is deeply felt.

Early next morning a car pulls up outside St Joseph's Church, where half-seven mass is in progress. Inside the car, the McLoughlin brothers wait for the newspaper vendor to set up his stall and then they emerge, first in line in all of Limerick to buy the Sunday papers. Locky gets the *Independent*, Mick buys the *Press*. They read the match reports once, twice, twenty times. Three years down the road and the Dublin reporters are starting to change their minds about Locky.

That summer he headed for Pat Phelan's gym in the Irishtown, a converted shed with holes in the floorboards, and pumped iron during the school holidays. A year passed. Shannon beat Garryowen in the Cup final again, with the same pack. And Gerry McLoughlin remained unfulfilled. Tighthead for Shannon, loosehead for Munster, not at the races for Ireland.

Locky was a certainty to play against the All Blacks. That meant he could drink as much as he liked in London. Others travelled with a mission in mind. Olann Kelleher, the third-best scrum-half in Munster, was hoping to come out of the London weekend as Number 2, thus securing a place on the bench at Thomond Park. The first-choice scrum-half, Donal Canniffe, was unable to make the London trip but was sure to face the All Blacks. Kelleher was hoping to play his way on to the bench by starring against Middlesex in the first of the tour games and suggested as much to Vince Giltinane, one of the five Munster selectors. Giltinane was a Dolphin clubman. So was Kelleher. Sometimes you got breaks like that. Sometimes the other guy did.

'Listen,' said Giltinane quietly, 'you must be off your game. The last thing you need is to play against Middlesex.'

'Why not?'

'Because we'll probably get hammered.'

'You mean?'

'You won't be a sub against the All Blacks.'

Maybe it was better to wait for the second tour game, Kelleher thought to himself.

It was a scorching day in London, the traffic into Knightsbridge backed up for miles. The plane had landed an hour late and so once their bus had reached the hotel it was almost time to turn around and head north towards Sudbury, home of Wasps. The rushed atmosphere was anathema to Kiernan: the trip had started badly. It would get worse.

Middlesex were coached by a New Zealand dentist who had history with Munster. Fifteen years after his nightmare at Thomond Park, Earle Kirton was settled in London, with a very fine All Blacks career behind him. It seemed to some of his players that he still carried baggage from the old days, that the humiliations endured in that 1963 tour had clung to him, convincing him that he always had something to prove. He had four England players in his team – Andy Ripley, Chris Ralston, Dave Rollitt and Bob Mordell – though none would play another international. He also had two All Blacks, the wing Terry Morrison and Paul Sapsford, a prop.

Ripley had played against Munster only a few weeks before in a friendly for the Wolfhounds. Munster had not been impressive, and speaking to a handful of their players afterwards it was obvious to him that the sum of their knowledge of Middlesex was close to zero. 'These guys haven't got a clue about us,' he told the others as they changed. 'Let's show them what we're about.'

It was never a contest: Kirton's boys tore Munster to pieces, snapping at their heels like rabid dogs. If the Munster players regarded the fixture as anything other than an inconvenient run-out in between drinking sessions it did not show. There was no desire, no heart, no evidence that they would not be destroyed in five weeks' time. Middlesex won 33–7 and the scoreline flattered the visitors. If the game had lasted another ten minutes, Middlesex would have put fifty points on the board. Ralston dominated the lineout, Ripley tore giant holes in the defence and Morrison, a former national sprint champion of New Zealand, was not seen for dust. In the *Limerick Leader* the next day, Charlie Mulqueen did not pull his punches.

Munster rugby stands numbed and shocked this morning as followers assess the effects of last night's 33–7 drubbing by Middlesex in London. This was an abysmal display by Munster, whose problems at scrum-half, in midfield and front row were cruelly underlined by a highly efficient Middlesex XV. The forwards, lifeless and disjointed, were beaten to a frazzle. Heads will surely start to roll.

Munster's biggest problem was in the front row. Alongside McLoughlin and Pat Whelan, Ted Mulcahy was out of his depth against high-class opposition. It was obvious to Kiernan that he would need to find a more robust prop or the All Blacks would take a wrecking ball to his scrum. The one Munster player who came out of it well was Kelleher, who watched the slaughter from the sidelines. Picked at scrum-half, Colm Murphy was brutally exposed.

At the end, Noel Murphy, Munster's chairman of selectors, walked over to Kirton and grimaced.

'Jesus Christ, thanks for that. That was supposed to be a little warm-up for the All Blacks match, not a bloody hiding.'

'Well, you won't get anywhere near them if you play like that,' Kirton said, which was the most diplomatic thing he could think of at the time. That was also the theme of the three Irish newspapermen covering the tour. Kiernan, they reported, had just five weeks to turn his abject team around. If he did not do so, the consequences would be both predict- able and dire. There would be another humiliation and – much worse – Munster's proud tradition against touring teams would be defiled.

Kirton was among those who believed the challenge was beyond any mortal. A few weeks later he would receive a phone call from the All Blacks coach, Jack Gleeson, and during the course of it reveal what he really thought about Munster. After fifteen years, his memories of Thomond Park were still painfully sharp, but he did not – could not – associate that experience with the ragged bunch his Middlesex team had cut a swathe through. It did not seem conceivable to him that the human spirit was capable of such a transformation in so short a time.

'Jack,' he told Gleeson, 'you won't have any problems. All you've got to do is up the pace. If you play at a clip, they won't be able to live with you. You'll blow them away.'

From his principal British-based informant, Gleeson also sought opinions on certain individuals, among them Tony Ward, the new prince of Irish rugby. In Limerick, they had long since been transfixed by the swagger of his gait and the explosive impact of his jink. Now Ward was in his prime and news of his brilliance had spread after an electrifying first Five

Nations tournament earlier in 1978. But if Gleeson had expected a eulogy, or a warning about the damage Ward could do, he was talking to the wrong spy. Kirton believed that Ward did not send his backline away often enough because of a singular failing in his own game.

'Sure he's good, Jack,' he conceded, 'but he doesn't run on to the ball. He takes it standing still and then he does a little sidestep or a shuffle. The silly bugger would be a tremendous fly-half if he ran on to it. I don't think he'll cause you too much trouble.'

Kiernan was disappointed by his team's performance, though he knew it was in large part down to poor conditioning. There was plenty he could do to put that right. He intended to push them on the training field as never before. He restricted his post-mortem to a single remark, but the growling manner in which it was delivered spoke volumes. 'Get the maps out, lads,' he said. 'We're going back to Fermoy.'

The first training session at Fermoy would take place the following week, but there was no time to lose, so at 10.30 on the morning after the match Kiernan gave them a taste of what was to come. At St Paul's, a public school in Hammersmith a short distance from their hotel, he ran them so hard that the session lived in the memory of many who endured it as by far the most gruelling of their lives.

The spectacle was watched by a couple of passers-by taking their dogs for a walk and for them it was a pitiful sight. One of those who looked on was John Reason, the most distinguished British rugby writer of his era. He lived one hundred yards from the front gate of St Paul's and was in the habit of taking a stroll with his bull terrier along by the school grounds. At first he did not recognise the players. Then he began to pick out a few. The big man was unmistakably Moss Keane. The one with the long hair looked like young Ward. It struck him that the forwards looked desperately small. This bunch, he considered, looked an even bigger shambles than the previous night's result had suggested, if that was possible. Even if they ran like dingbats all day, it was unimaginable that they could compete with the All Blacks physically. Experience had taught him that Irish teams seldom looked anything on the training field; that once they got out on the pitch they often fizzed out of the bottle. But this lot? He couldn't see it. As the sun beat down on the banks of the Thames, Reason walked on.

The reserve hooker Gerry Hurley, a hard country boy from Bantry, was the first to throw his guts up. 'This isn't worth it,' he muttered when the order came for him to go on, but still he obeyed it. One by one they neared the point of physical collapse and still the session continued, the temperature climbing as twelve o'clock came and went. Mad dogs and Irishmen, out in the noonday sun.

Les White, the English prop forward drafted in by Kiernan because of his Munster roots, started lapping them. White had reason to believe that he might get called up for the All Blacks game, but he stood there and told the rest of them he was wasting his time bothering with Munster: they were so unfit the New Zealanders were bound to embarrass them.

When their bodies screamed that another hundred yards might be the death of them, Kiernan decreed that they would finish with a half-mile, to be timed. The backs had to run it in less than two minutes and twenty seconds, the forwards in three minutes. Even though some of them were already bent over in pain, nobody dared to put up a protest. He commanded too much respect for that, and, besides, they could see there was no point in moaning. Kiernan wasn't in the mood for mercy.

Sharing a room with Ward, the wing Jimmy Bowen went to bed at six o'clock that night. Sleep came easily. He had never felt so tired in all his twenty-one years. For Kiernan, the session was satisfactory. In itself it was useful, because it was depressingly clear that his players were a long way short of the fitness level required against the All Blacks, but more than that its intensity was a wake-up call, the second inside twenty-four hours. Kiernan was saying to them: unless you are fit enough to last eighty hard minutes, you are of no use to me. One of the lessons he had learned against the All Blacks was that in order to compete against them, you had to be mentally alert throughout. Lapses of concentration late in the game had been the undoing of vanquished Munster teams. Tired players threw matches away. There was nothing he could do about the fact that he had a group of players who, by his standards, were notable for their limitations as much as for their strengths. But some things he could influence and he launched himself into the task. The following day, he took them back to St Paul's and ran them until they dropped again.

Kiernan might have hoped for an improvement for the tour's second match, against an Irish Exiles XV at Sunbury, but there was none. On the Saturday night before the match, half the squad hailed taxis outside the Rembrandt hotel on the Brompton Road and instructed the drivers to take them to Soho. That was where the sons of Catholic Ireland generally made for when they found themselves in London.

In the hotel that night there was a singsong and Kiernan and the selectors joined in. Brian O'Brien, the Shannon representative, was persuaded to sing his party piece, a song he had heard sung by such notables as Frankie O'Flynn, front-row forward in the famous Shannon Cup team of 1960, when Kiernan and his fellow college boys from Cork had been beaten in a replay at Thomond Park and bonfires burned all over the parish of St Mary's.

> *How's it done?*
> *You ask me, how's it done?*
> *I've got a trainer man*
> *Who taught me all I know*
> *Sure feels good to have him in my corner*
> *Hear his voice a-whispering low*
> *Big boy, remember*
> *You must remember*
> *Stand up and fight until you hear the bell!*
> *Stand toe to toe, trade blow for blow!*

In the early hours of Sunday morning several senior members of the Munster team were standing up, but only just. They walked the streets of Soho looking for a cab to take them back west. It was hopeless. They walked for hours, and it was bright outside when they stepped inside the lobby of the Rembrandt. Some say Kiernan was coming down the stairs for breakfast when he ran into them. Perhaps he was, but in any case he said nothing. He had imposed no curfew, believing that the trip was largely about the bringing together of a group of players he hoped might have it in them to make history. He wanted them to enjoy one another's company, but there were limits to his laxity. The second match of the trip was now only hours away. To prepare in such a way was a betrayal of everything he had stood for as a player. There would be consequences, but they could wait until the weekend was over.

Over breakfast he called out to Moss Finn, one of the bleary-eyed revellers, a university student with the pace on the wing to take him a long way.

'Moss, the Irish selectors are going to be at this match,' he said. 'They'll be watching you.'

Theirs was a wasted journey: Munster were shockingly bad. Three strikes from Ward gave them an early 9–0 lead but by the end they were hanging on at 15–15, against a team playing for the second time in twenty-four hours, a team with more than its fair share of journeymen.

'How in Christ's name have you so many on the Ireland team?' one of the London Irish alickadoos teased Kiernan. It was a fair question and one the Irish selectors may also have been asking, as they considered their options for the first international of the season, against the All Blacks on 3 November, four days after the Munster game. On the evidence before them, they dismissed Finn from their thinking and drew a line through some other names, among them Gerry McLoughlin. That was no big deal for Locky: he had come to expect rejection. All it meant was that the stakes on 31 October were bigger still.

Back in Cork, Bill O'Brien followed the tour in the *Examiner* and rued the day he had been persuaded to part with £4000 of the branch's money when seemingly the only return was humiliation. Kiernan, though, considered it well spent. It gave him a starting point, something to work with. His team might have lost, but they had lost together. If the branch had a problem, he was prepared to fight his corner.

There was, however, one outstanding piece of business to be seen to.

Soon after the squad's return, in a demonstration of ruthlessness more befitting of the All Blacks, Whelan was quietly relieved of the captaincy. Into his place came Donal

Canniffe, the scrum-half from Cork who played his rugby in Dublin. Canniffe had been absent from the crime scene in London, unable to travel because of injury. There were those in the squad who believed the punishment was unnecessarily harsh, that Whelan's ardent brand of leadership was just what they needed on the big day. That view held little currency among the selectors. If Kiernan disagreed with the decision, he did not raise a voice against it. More likely, in Canniffe he had the captain he wanted. A thinker, not a shouter; an organiser, not an agitator; a leader in his own image.

The press corps of the day were not in the habit of probing into such matters. They telephoned Kiernan at Moremiles when they needed team news and he was good enough to take their calls and throw them a few morsels. Decisions like the one to jettison Whelan as captain were prefaced with the words, 'In a surprising development . . .'; the press boys rarely went beyond that.

Had Gerry McLoughlin been offered the captaincy he would have accepted without surprise. Self-belief was not something he was short on. At Shannon, long after he had established himself in the front row, he once asked O'Brien if he had been selected for a match.

'You have,' O'Brien told him.

'Where?'

'Out-half.'

It was a good joke, but Locky didn't get it. He just nodded in agreement and walked on, as if the selectors had hit on something.

When October came he began thinking of the All Blacks and what he might do to them, what they might do for him. He thought about Gary Knight, the Test match tighthead more likely than not to face him at Thomond Park. The hardest player in New Zealand, so they said, with the scars to prove it and a cauliflower ear to match his own. This much he knew: if Gary Knight took him out by the roots, he could forget about the green jersey for good.

Chapter Eight

Worst Dump in the World

'What's the story about Fermoy?' one of the younger players had muttered in London, after Kiernan had said his piece.

'Fermoy,' he was told, 'is the worst fucking dump in the world.'

It wasn't the town itself they hated, but the training pitch just outside it. Nobody had more loathing for it than the handful of players living in Dublin. They had to leave work early to get there and it was two or three in the morning before they arrived home, cursing the place. On 4 October, a week before the All Blacks party left New Zealand, the Munster players came together for the first time since the London trip. The match was now less than four weeks away.

They met at the Grand hotel, which overlooked the River Blackwater in the heart of Fermoy, and changed in the ballroom. From there they traipsed out to the lobby in their socks and got back into the cars for the short journey to the field, the sight of which sent a shudder of dread into their hearts. There was something grimly appropriate about the training ground set back from the river's northern banks. Here was a place where, for generations, military men had been whipped into shape, occasionally by means of the cat-o'-nine tails. Here was where men had once learned the importance of accountability to one another and to a shared purpose. Not that any of this occurred to Kiernan's vanguard. To them, the place was just a dump where they couldn't see their boots for high grass.

Long ago, there had been two active barracks in Fermoy, and they held the town in their massive shadow, guarding the cut-stone bridge across the Blackwater. The first was built in 1806; the second, on the site of the rugby pitch, three years later.

In 1834 a company of infantry commanded by a Captain Markham arrived at the barracks. The captain accepted an invitation to dine at the mess of the 92nd Highlanders, but found himself insulted in a discussion about the Peninsular Campaign by a Colonel McDonald, who had lost an arm at Busaco in 1810. A duel was fixed for six o'clock the following morning on the exercise ground of the West barracks.

Twelve paces were measured and soon a single shot rang out from Captain Markham's pistol. It missed. The colonel's gun had failed to discharge.

'Fresh pistol,' the captain instructed his second.

'What!' said the colonel. 'Is Captain Markham going to fire at me again?'

'I did not come here for child's play,' said the captain, with his last words. At the second time of asking, the colonel's aim was true and his pistol deadly. Markham died where he fell, in front of the vast barracks, on a patch of ground that was still in use as an exercise facility one hundred and forty-four years later, only not by soldiers. It was here that Kiernan took his men, here that he ran them into the ground, again and again.

The massive façade of the burnt-out West barracks ran the length of the pitch. The hulking structure was disfigured by more than a hundred gaping holes where there had been windows. The once imposing centrepiece, over which a clock was set at the building's highest point, was now barely visible, scarred by dense ivy and home to a scattering of birds. The building had been set on fire by a mixture of petrol and strong whiskey during the Civil War in August 1922. A detachment of soldiers loyal to Eamon de Valera had been temporarily stationed there and when the order came for them to move out before the arsonists set about their work, one of them took aim with his rifle and fired three rounds at the clock high above him. Time had stood still on the site ever since, and by 1978 it was considered a dangerous structure. In a matter of months it would be razed.

Lights had been mounted high on the crumbling edifice and these, allied to the headlights of the selectors' cars – left running in the four corners of the ground – made training possible on winter nights. One of these vehicles had once acted as camouflage for Larry Moloney, the stylish Garryowen full-back who hated training. He had fallen to the ground behind a car one night when the players were lapping the pitch under Kiernan's gaze, and stayed prone on the turf until the rest of them came round again. Kiernan hadn't noticed him rejoining them, or at least if he had he let it go.

As at St Paul's School, there was little science in Kiernan's training methods. For much of the session he stood alongside the selectors and watched the players running laps of the pitch, all the while shouting what could loosely be described as encouragement. He told them to form a vertical line and keep running, with the player at the back sprinting to the front and taking the ball from the man there, a process which was repeated over and over, until they dropped.

'Faster! Pick it up!'

'Keep going! Two more laps!'

'Do you know how fit the All Blacks are going to be?

They'll be fitter than any team you've ever seen! Keep going!'

He knew that, man for man, any team he might put out could never remotely be the equal of an All Blacks XV, but that didn't mean they couldn't win. With the right spirit, they could be far more than the sum of their parts. With the right strategy, he could conceal their weaknesses and make the most of their strengths. When all was said and done, that was the whole point of rugby. But he reasoned that without a high level of physical conditioning, without the ability to survive eighty punishing minutes, any tactical strategy he might conceive was a waste of his and their time. He drove them hard because he needed hard men. He hadn't come for child's play.

Kiernan liked his training sessions to start on time and finish on time, to be conducted wholeheartedly and precisely. When he brought them to a halt, the players headed back to the hotel for a shower. Before they went their separate ways, the Munster branch stretched to some sandwiches and a cup of tea. Once the plates had been emptied, there was no point in asking for more. There were strict limits to the branch's benevolence.

After the first session, Brendan Foley noticed that even the milk for their tea was poured as if it was the last drop in the house. Given free access to the milk jug the previous week, they had seemingly abused the privilege, so that now the hotel waiter did not let it out of his hand. The hotel would have reasoned that such parsimony was only to be expected, given the meagre sum the branch was paying them for the players' refreshments.

Foley might not have had much growing up, but nobody had ever rationed the milk in his tea. He had been capped by Ireland two years before, a van driver among accountants and solicitors, and the one Limerickman in a team thrashed by the French at Parc des Princes.

To Kiernan he was one in a million, blessed with the kind of robustness that reminded the coach of Willie John McBride. He had first come across him at a Munster training session on the back pitch at Thomond Park four years before. He had told Foley then to go down on the ball while the other forwards rucked the skin off his back for forty-five minutes. The big man had just taken it, without a word of complaint.

He had learned his rugby with St Mary's, the junior club in the parish. Limerick junior rugby could be a brutally tough apprentice ground for a boy of seventeen. Men twice his age had tried to intimidate him at the lineout with digs into ribs, and worse, but he had held his own. There was no choice. If you didn't show them you could take it, and sometimes give it, you didn't survive.

Among Limerick rugby people, those drawn from the city's working-class strongholds and beyond, Foley was loved. He had been reared in St Mary's Park, a council estate on the slide towards anarchy. People knew that when his time was over he would be there alongside them, supporting the next generation. He was all heart, the soul of Limerick rugby.

History would repeat itself in years to come. Foley's son Anthony, five years old in 1978, would grow up to become one of the greatest of all Munster players. Like his father, he would be cherished most on the terraces.

In Kiernan's Munster team, Brendan Foley was the player the ordinary supporter identified with more than any other. Locky was Locky, a law unto himself, a one-off. In Foley, they saw themselves.

Chapter Nine

Brendan Foley's Story

The first years of my life were spent in another family's parlour on the Quarry Road in Limerick city. My family rented the room for four shillings a week. There was me, my brother Gerard and my father and mother, Anthony and Rosaleen Foley. In the autumn of 1952 we were given a two-bedroom house of our own in Ballynanty Beg, a new Corporation estate that overlooked Thomond Park. I suppose it came not a day too soon. My mother was heavily pregnant with her third child.

She hung a new pair of curtains and pulled them across on the night she felt the baby coming. They preserved her dignity and helped to drown out the clatter of builders working late into the night. It was seven o'clock and dark outside. There were twelve days to Christmas Eve.

My father went to fetch the doctor, but he couldn't be found. He eventually turned up shortly after a local nurse had helped my mother give birth to another boy. Afterwards, everybody said it must have been a very busy night for that doctor because he was hardly in the door when he was walking back out again. Half an hour later, at half past eight, my new brother was dead. Nobody ever found out what the cause was because at nine o'clock my mother was dead herself and they buried her without giving my father an explanation; buried her in a nun's habit alongside my dead baby brother, Michael. Nobody in Ballynanty asked questions, because who was going to give them answers?

Some said it might have been because my mother had been so good to her own mother, taking care of her when she had suffered a stroke and gone childish, forever lifting her on to the toilet and back into her favourite armchair in the corner of her parlour on the Quarry Road. Maybe the strain had been too much, they said. But the next thing they knew, it wasn't really their business any more because once the funeral was over my father closed the front door behind him and he never came back again.

After the burial in Mount St Lawrence he made his way through the Christmas shoppers in William Street, hand in hand with Gerard and myself, and out to his sister's house in St Mary's Park. Madgie McNamara had agreed, at the funeral mass the night before, to take us in and raise us as her own. Hospitality was the only thing she could offer us. Her house had three bedrooms, including a box room. She had four children of her own and her husband, Fred, was out of work more often than he was in it. On occasion he helped to clean the turbines out at Ardnacrusha power station and sometimes he made a few bob up at St Mary's Church, mowing the grass and ringing the Angelus bell when Willie Bartlett, the parish clerk, wasn't around. But mostly he didn't do much.

The night we arrived my father looked my uncle in the eye on the doorstep. 'Thanks, Freddie,' he said. 'Thanks very much.' Some nights my father cried and called us over to comfort him, and Uncle Fred would say, 'Look, Tony, enough's enough now.' But all this I didn't find out until later, much later. When it happened, I was two years old.

The McNamaras had once lived in Sheep Street, but the house collapsed one summer's evening after heavy rain and they were relocated to 59 St Munchin Street in the Island Field. There was a small vegetable garden at the back, and a spot where they kept a few chickens. My aunt was a great woman for baking apple tarts, rhubarb tarts, griddle cakes and soda bread. My father paid for our keep, bought our shoes and our schoolbooks, and told us that Madgie was our mother because our mammy was dead. He was a labourer for Molloy's, a famous building firm in Limerick. He was tall and thin, rakishly thin. He had gone bald early in life.

When I was still a young boy my father got married again and moved out of the McNamaras' house. He would call to see us once or twice a week on his bicycle and take us for a spin, Gerard on the metal seat behind him, me on the timber square in front.

At the Christian Brothers school in Creagh Lane, it was quite rare to own a pair of football boots. The school had a big bundle of old-style boots and you went through them and found a pair. I was one of the first in my class to have my own. They were new but they were on sale in a second-hand shop for a pound. I looked at them for weeks, hoping nobody would buy them. Eventually my aunt took me in and we got them. I was ten.

Every day after school we played soccer on a small patch of grass opposite Eddie Price's house. Sometimes forty or fifty of us kicked a ball up and down the street, from boys of ten to men of sixty. We played hurling with broken sticks scavenged from the Gaelic Grounds and we skinned orchards.

One day, when I was fourteen, five or six of us went down to the Scouts Field, where the St Mary's rugby club trained. They were only too delighted to see us coming. Throughout their history the Saints had been thrown off every pitch they ever trained on. They would take a chance on a new field and somebody would come along. 'Out!' If they had nowhere to go they would run the Island bank, often in the fading light, taking care not to hop off a passing horse. The only bath or shower they had was the Abbey River, or the contents of a zinc bucket.

They were formed in 1943 by a fella called Whacker Casey and their headquarters then was a broken-down house in Glueyard

Lane owned by a character called Hadah Sweeney. Most nights he stumbled in drunk singing his song, 'Ireland Mother Ireland'. There were no chairs, just a couple of timber benches and a fireplace. He had no electric light, just a paraffin lamp, so they paid for it out of God knows what. Then they got him a bag of coal a week to keep the place warm.

By the time I joined, Saints had bought an old timber hut from Shannon airport and put it up directly in front of Hadah's house. This became the new clubhouse. They called it the Casbah. There was a potbelly stove inside, where Peter Hayes would boil oxtail soup. Between Hadah's and the Casbah was a piece of waste-ground, about fifty feet long and twenty feet wide. That was another of our training grounds. It was such a cramped space that fellas had to throw lineout balls from inside Hadah's house.

Next to Glueyard Lane was Flag Lane, home to the famous Hayes family. The one who started me off in rugby was Mick Hayes. He was a labourer up at CIE, the railway station. The older men who played with him for Saints called him the Red Fella, said he was a fabulous player. He told us if we backed away from anything on the field, we were cowards, not fit for rugby. If you got on the wrong side of him, even once, that was it for life. At training, my attention would wander over to where Star Rovers were playing a soccer match. If they were a man short, I'd ask Mick if I could fall on. He didn't like that. He said I was always dragging myself together. He didn't mince his words.

'Brendan – you're lazy! You've always been lazy. The others are making a laugh out of you. There's a young kid there and he's up first. You're last. Every time there's a loose ruck, you're last. You're not putting it in, Brendan. You don't want to put it in. And if you don't want to put it in, Brendan, there's only one thing for it. Chuck it up.'

After training, myself and Mick and a handful of others would go walking, the length and breadth of Limerick, and I'd hear all the stories about Saints. Mick saw something in me, he thought I had potential. I was long and lean. When I was seventeen we won the Junior Cup, for the only time in the club's history. I joined Shannon then, the senior team in the parish. They had a few promising young players, including a fella with red hair who talked a lot. Gerry McLoughlin was his name. By then I was working at the Good Shepherd Convent, driving a van. I've always loved open spaces and the open road.

After serving my time in the Shannon pack I was picked to play for Munster. I knew if I could play well in a big match, against one of the overseas teams, the Irish selectors might notice me. In 1976 the Australians came and we gave it a real go, should have beaten them. The following Sunday morning I heard my name being called out on the radio: picked for Ireland against France. Straight away my friend Thady Coughlan drove me into Shannon and we had a party in the clubhouse. My father was very proud, but he wasn't a drinking man so we had to make up for him. I was the first Shannon man capped in ten years and only the second ever. For people like Mick Hayes, and the lads I'd grown up with in the Island Field, it meant the world. My friend John Ryan said, 'To think that one of us could be picked for Ireland, after comin' from our stable.'

The following year I lifted the Munster Senior Cup at Thomond Park, one of the best moments of my life. Three of us were picked for Munster against the All Blacks. For the other two lads, Locky and Colm Tucker, it was their chance to show the Irish selectors they were good enough. Maybe having three Shannon fellas in the Irish team was too good to be true, but we thought we were good enough. Not too many teams got the better of the Shannon pack.

Chapter Ten

Enter the Friendly All Blacks

New Zealand, October 1978

Shortly before they departed on their tour of Britain and Ireland, the men who would become known as the Eighth All Blacks played a three-Test series against Australia. The New Zealanders were a team in form and it was suggested by some that their neighbours might use violence as a means to contain them. In such circumstances, for as long as anyone could remember, the response from the men in black was predictable. They fought back. They hit harder. The lesson that nobody took liberties with the All Blacks was handed down amid a hail of punches. But suddenly, all that was past.

'No rough stuff,' said Jack Gleeson, the New Zealand coach.

'You mean,' said the lock Frank Oliver, 'that we can't have a go at them when they come the rough stuff on us? And we are All Blacks?'

'That's what I mean,' said Gleeson. 'No rough stuff, today or ever.'

On the night before they boarded the plane, Gleeson's choice as captain for the eighteen-match tour reaffirmed the pacifist message.

'We are aware that we, as a team, need to project a good

image,' said the twenty-six-year-old Graham Mourie, a farmer from Opunake.

The Eighth All Blacks were travelling as ambassadors for the game of rugby. Not only would they play fair, they would play with flair. Talking to John Hopkins of the *Sunday Times* before leaving for England, Gleeson promised: 'My team will play fifteen-man rugby. We had an overall look at the game and said, "Let's make it more inviting and entertaining, so everyone is involved." You people in Britain, because you have concentrated on forward play, have neglected back play. With the modern laws, backs have got to complement forwards if you wish to score tries. We have made a complete turnaround in our style of play.' That Gleeson believed his approach to be effective as well as aesthetically pleasing was clear. 'We are hoping to win all eighteen of our matches,' he added.

Tall and lean, his somewhat unkempt fair hair parted to one side, Gleeson was manager of the Empire Tavern in Feilding, the third generation of his family to make a living from the pub trade. He had recently turned fifty and was in his second year as All Blacks coach. Recognition of his abilities had come late, but not too late, and he threw himself into the job. There was much to do, for the All Blacks were in the doldrums, living on past glories.

Rugby, he believed, was a game of thought, of strategy. At its best, it was played at pace by men encouraged to run the ball from anywhere and everywhere. Almost single-handedly, he began changing the face of New Zealand rugby.

The British & Irish Lions tour to New Zealand in 1977 convinced him that scrummaging techniques in the British and Irish game had moved on to another level and he went about matching them. Although he was by nature a private man who shied away from confrontation, he was occasionally prepared to make an exception. At a seminar he attended early in his reign, the legendary All Black prop Ken Gray began preaching the gospel of the front row, using methods perfected long ago.

'Ken,' Gleeson interrupted, 'you can't teach that sort of thing now. Ideas have changed. This is what we want.' As Gleeson demonstrated the new techniques, Gray stood and watched. And then he left.

A progressive attitude had served Gleeson well, but man management was the greatest of his gifts. 'People are different,' he would say, 'and so are rugby players. So you've got to treat them differently for best results. Take a horse trainer with twenty or thirty in his string. He doesn't set them all the same work. Some need to be taken gently, others to be given plenty of work. Same with rugby players.'

But deep down, Gleeson knew results were what it was all about. No matter how many plaudits his team might receive for the quality of their rugby, it was far more important that they win. Four months and seventeen days after their departure from Wellington, with the zip of their earlier triumphs beginning to fade, the 1905 All Blacks had succumbed by three points to nil to Wales in a match infamous for a disallowed try by the New Zealander Bob Deans. On an exhausting tour, it was their only blemish in thirty-six matches.

In the hours that followed, thirty-five thousand telegrams were dispatched by Cardiff Post Office. The average for a normal Saturday was eight hundred. As one newspaper put it, 'the quickest road to fame is to play the New Zealanders'. When the *Rimutaka* dropped anchor in Auckland on 6 March 1906, twenty thousand people were at the harbour to welcome them home. They were national heroes, one and all, and what they had done would never be forgotten by their countrymen.

None of the 1905 team's six successors had managed to defeat all four nations on tour, so when Jack Gleeson boarded an Air New Zealand DC-10 at Auckland airport seventy-three years later, the mission was clear as day in his head. They would win a Grand Slam. They would return undefeated.

The bespectacled, silver-haired little man at his side as the jet flew to London via Honolulu and Los Angeles had a rather different objective. 'We want to enjoy ourselves and make friends,' said the tour manager Russ Thomas. 'I believe sport is the hope of the future.'

Noble they may have been, but Thomas's words had to be viewed in context. And the context for the tour of the Eighth All Blacks was the tour of the Seventh All Blacks.

Keith Murdoch hated a lot of things but more than anything he hated journalists, and maybe with good reason. Before he had set foot in England in the autumn of 1972 they had him down as a wild animal, a psychopath let loose among polite society. A newspaper cartoonist depicted him being taken out of the All Blacks' plane in a steel cage, snorting with rage. Some said he was indeed mad, those close to him insisted he was misunderstood. On one thing there was near unanimity: he was the hardest, most ferocious rugby player in the world, a prop forward of immense, almost supernatural power. In Limerick, they would have loved him unconditionally and stood him drinks for life.

A writer chronicling the All Blacks' tour, having made himself known to the other players, approached Murdoch when he judged the moment to be right. The more co-operation he could get from the players, the more vivid his account would be, and already Murdoch had the makings of a leading character.

'My name is Wallace Reyburn. I'm doing a book on the tour.'

'Fuck off.'

Wallace Reyburn did as he was bid.

Not long afterwards he observed a cartoonist from the *Daily Mirror* circling the All Blacks in the bar of the Britannia hotel in London. The players posed helpfully as he completed his sketches, until he reached Murdoch, who made it abundantly clear that the cartoonist's attentions were unwelcome.

'If you try to do a fucking drawing of me I'll fucking well break your fucking hand.'

Murdoch was a cartoonist's ideal subject. More than any other player he satisfied the desire for satire and a sense of exaggeration. He weighed more than seventeen stone, but the features that commanded attention were his penetrating eyes and a sinister moustache, jet-black and stretching as far as his jawbone. The cartoonist at the Britannia, Ralph Sallon, was seventy-three years old, but seniority did not save him. Murdoch seized the hand in which he held his pencil and began bending it back. Sallon's pain was only eased when other players pulled Murdoch off him.

Nobody much liked the Seventh All Blacks. When their first match kicked off in Gloucester, the crowd started murmuring. 'What about the haka? They've forgotten the haka!' But they hadn't forgotten. They had just decided they weren't going to bother with it.

Wherever they went, beds were broken and hotel doors were ripped from their hinges. When their manager, Eric Todd, lectured them about their conduct on the second night in London, he succeeded only in uniting them in contempt for him. Their boisterousness increased. Had things not gone further, history might have been kinder to them. But things did.

At the Angel hotel in Cardiff, in the early hours of the morning after Murdoch scored the only try in a win against Wales, a waiter had a pint of beer poured over his head. Murdoch, who was responsible, then upended a tray of empty glasses carried by another waiter, after being told the bar was shut. He followed the waiter into the kitchen and mayhem ensued.

Four bouncers attempted to restrain Murdoch, who quietened down only after the intervention of other All Blacks. It seemed the storm had passed, but it had only just begun. One of the doormen, Peter Grant, provided the following account:

> As we were coming out of the kitchen Murdoch shouted at me, 'You IRA bastard!' I'm not even an Irishman. I come from Nuneaton. Then I was out near the bar talking to one of the other players. I thought Murdoch had gone by then. But all of a sudden – clock! He struck me from behind a pillar with a right-hander. I'm reasonably big [in fact, he was four inches taller than Murdoch] but this bloke had hands like shovels and his arms and wrists make mine look like matchsticks. I was dazed but ready to have a go back at him. Fortunately other security men held me back. They probably thought all hell would break loose if they let me go.

Or maybe they thought Grant would leave the hotel in a body bag. He failed to press charges.

Todd told the press he had given Murdoch 'a bloody good talking to' but then named him in the team for the next game. Opprobrium from outside the touring party saw that decision reversed. Much against the will of the other All Blacks, who continue to paint him as the victim of a newspaper witch-hunt,

Murdoch was sent home in disgrace, stripped of the jacket bearing the proud silver fern. Rather than subject himself to another media scrum in New Zealand, he jumped plane at Singapore and then disappeared, forever more, into the Australian outback. His own version of events remains untold.

Other tales of misbehaviour emerged. One concerned an alleged visit by several players to a girls' school, one of the many public relations exercises typically performed by touring rugby teams. After listening to his team-mates entertain the girls with well-received niceties about life as an All Black, the final player addressed the gathering thus: 'Everyone else has said what I was going to say, so all I would like to add is that the first girl up here with her knickers in her hand gets a big prize.'

The 1978 tour, Russ Thomas was determined, would be different. These All Blacks would restore the favourable image of New Zealand rugby. There would be no doors forced open by shoulder charges, no opportunity for the Fleet Street newspapers to heap shame upon the men in his charge. He himself would set an example. On 12 October, when the squad landed at Heathrow airport, Thomas, Gleeson and Mourie were taken to meet the British media. Thomas worked the room, a friendly and dapper presence, both buttons on his blazer done up, a smile chiselled on to his face. He shook the hand of every journalist present, which both surprised and flattered them, and reiterated the friendly spiel from the farewell party: 'We are aiming to make this tour enjoyable for the players and we are looking forward to making new friends. We are very conscious of the need for good relations with critics in Britain.'

When one reporter attempted to reopen old wounds, Gleeson stepped in. 'We haven't come here for a war, we've come to play rugby,' he said.

The following day's headlines were everything Thomas had hoped for. 'Friendly All Blacks Arrive' they read.

A few hours after the All Blacks' plane touched down in London, Tom Kiernan got in his car and drove to Tipperary. There was one thing to be said for driving thirty-five miles to a Munster branch meeting on a Thursday night in October: it gave him a chance to think. If there was something he could say for himself, it was that he thought things out more than other fellas. They just didn't have the same interest, or the time. They might consider something for three hours; he'd spend three days thinking about nothing else. With most things in life, he found, it was just a question of how much interest you had and how much you hadn't. If you agreed to take something on, something important, then you did your best. You put everything into it. Everything.

With rugby teams, it was all a question of balance, of trying to get all the strands together, and that was hard. When facing the likes of New Zealand, Irish teams depended on everything coming right on the day. If you got enough lucky bounces and they got none, if you took your chances and they blew theirs, if all fifteen of your men played above themselves and half of theirs had stinkers. If, if, if.

Some people reckoned there was only one way to prepare a Munster team against overseas opposition: you sent them on to the pitch with fire flaring from their nostrils. You told them to tear into the touring team like a pack of crazed wolves. And in truth, Munster had been doing pretty much that against the All Blacks for years. What had it led to? Failure. You needed more.

Could he prepare a team to beat the All Blacks? He could try his best: it might be good enough and it might not. But unless they put everything into it, he knew they'd get nothing out of it.

What would it take? How did things stand now, nineteen days before the match? He weighed things up.

First, it was a virtual certainty that any Munster team he sent out would play with spirit and passion. In itself that would not be enough, nowhere near enough. But it was necessary and it was a start.

Second, he had some very good players. Every one of them was brave. They would also be physically fit – the Fermoy sessions were seeing to that. And they would be mentally right – he'd make sure of that.

Third, they would need to pick the right team. It would be named in two days' time, after the final trial. That was the selectors' job, but . . . put it this way, he knew who he wanted.

He reached Cahir and pulled into the Kilcoran Lodge hotel. There were twenty-one members of the branch present. Blazers, people called them. Among other things. Fellas who hadn't seen the branch's working from the inside were inclined to criticise and complain. The players had heard he wanted them to meet up two days before the match. It was all the talk after training in Fermoy and they knew it was causing consternation.

'The branch fellas think he's off his game.'

'Three nights in the hotel! They'll never agree to it.'

'They'd have to give us another meal on the Sunday.'

'A prawn cocktail and a steak maybe. I'll have a cut off of that.'

'They'll never pay for the Limerick fellas, though. We'll have to go away home. They won't put us up in the hotel.'

'They wouldn't give you the steam off their piss.'

Kiernan had a somewhat different perception of the likes of Bill O'Brien because for four years he had seen the branch's workings from the inside. His uncles, the Murphy brothers, had never sat on a Cork Constitution committee in all their years at the club. Like most people, they found it easier to sit in judgement from the outside. But that wasn't his way. It was better to be pragmatic about it, to bend the ears of the people who mattered while on the inside. Thus he had persuaded O'Brien and Tom Collery, with a quiet word away from the committee room, that the extra night was necessary. When he put his mind to it, he usually got his way.

Billo brought the meeting to order and the London tour was the first item on his agenda. The final bill for the trip had come to £3604 and Kiernan knew he would have to convince the branch it had value for money. He had with him a neatly typed three-page document. He knew there was no point in pretending that Munster had been anything other than lamentable against Middlesex and his report did not spare them.

'It appeared to the writer that at least three players were carrying injuries into the game and that the fitness of a number of players left a lot to be desired.'

The sixth conclusion, however, was a defiant one: 'There is little doubt in the writer's mind that such tours are of considerable benefit.'

The conservative elements on the branch could grumble as much as they liked. When it came to preparing a team, he didn't care what any of them thought. He knew he was right. Every penny had been well spent.

The meeting continued into the night. Driving back to Cork later, he thought about the All Blacks again, but the mental picture was blurred. There were few survivors from their last tour and he had only read about the new breed, such as the flying wing Stu Wilson. Teams were being destroyed by the rapier thrusts of the deadly Wilson, cutting and slashing his way to the try line. With the ball in hand he looked sensational.

He had grown up in Wairarapa, farming country bordered by the Tararua Mountains on the bottom of the North Island. When he turned nine, a local farmer was called up for an All Blacks trial and then selected for the 1963 tour to Britain and Ireland. He made a bit of a name for himself overseas and that got plenty of nine-year-olds back in Wairarapa thinking. What would it be like to wear the black jersey with the silver fern, just like Brian Lochore?

Young Stu Wilson wasn't among the daydreamers, though. He was too busy playing soccer and hockey and his father's game, golf. When they roped him into playing rugby, he was bored by it, didn't understand what was going on, just ran around in the wake of the bigger boys who hogged the ball and wouldn't allow a little kid like him near it.

'What did you do today, son?' his parents would ask.

'Played footy.'

'Who won?'

'We did.'

But it was years before he felt anything for rugby, before he began to see that it was a team game, that it didn't matter how big or how small you were. And then, suddenly, he wasn't such a small kid any more. He grew up, filled out. He began to believe that maybe rugby might be the game for him after all.

In his early days, people sensed that he craved involvement, that he needed to be in the thick of it, and for a while he thought he might make a centre. In the middle of the park, a guy didn't have to go looking for work: it was there.

In the end it was Gleeson who provided reassurance, Gleeson who made him realise that his vocation was for

119

the wing. He had chosen him for the New Zealand Colts two years previously, and then taken him on the tour to Argentina, blooding him in the black jersey.

'The game is for fifteen players,' Gleeson would say. 'We will offer every member of the team a game of rugby, not just a presence on the field.'

Gleeson had been a wing himself, so he knew what it took to beat a man, knew the thrill of running full tilt at the last defender knowing you could take him. He told Wilson it was best to beat his man on the outside and the kid took that to heart.

Speed was Gleeson's game and Wilson had the legs and the quickness of thought to play it. Recalling his first trip to Europe, to play the formidable French in 1977, Wilson reflected that Gleeson wanted 'speed to breakdowns, speed at set-pieces, forming quickly, releasing quickly, thinking quickly. Two-man lineouts. More two-man lineouts. Quick, quick, quick – keep those big bastards moving. Bewilder them. Exhaust them. And then kill them.'

From there, things only got better for Wilson and he arrived in Britain as the most lethal wing in world rugby. According to the newspapers, a try he had scored against Australia the previous month required skill, speed and super-human power. The crowd at Lancaster Park had gone wild.

There was no point in Kiernan merely telling his boys to 'keep an eye on the blond fella'. He'd have to do better than that. He'd have to find out more about Mr Wilson, find a way to stop him from tearing Munster to shreds.

Chapter Eleven

Stu Wilson's Story

I was twenty-three years old and a Test winger for the All Blacks. All I needed was the ball. Come on, guys, just give it to me. I reckon I could dance around this guy here with my eyes closed. Shit, guys, just give me the ball! If I haven't got the ball, I can't dance.

Mostly, we wingers were like dogs chasing cars. We stood around waiting and waiting to get a touch. And then every once in a while we got to chase. I knew straight away if the chase was on, if the kick was a good one or a bad one. I could tell by the way the ball left the stand-off's boot, the trajectory over the first few yards. As soon as he hit it, and it was right, I'd say to myself, 'That's good, that is EXCELLENT. That gives me time to get there and hustle their guy going for it.' As I ran, I'd be thinking, 'Yes! I'm back in the ball game. God, this is great!' But if it was too long or too short my excitement level would just drop straight away: 'Oh! That's no good. It's a waste of time even chasing that. It's too far.'

I was there to score tries. And for me, a good try was poetry in motion. How can I describe how good it feels to score a try in the black jersey? Maybe by saying that there's no high in life quite like it. Out on the wing, I could see everything unfold. If there was a move on, I knew I would be the last man in the chain. I would have to finish it. And finishing, that's what I was good at.

I preferred the ball from a lineout – you get a little bit more room to move. If I saw Andy Haden go up and get a ball in the lineout and he took it nice and clean and it came down to Mark Donaldson, the scrum-half, then I knew the call was going to involve me on the end of the chain. And I got quite excited about that. We were up and running. The gatherer had got the ball. Now it was over to us to operate the move.

I could see each link slotting into place. I talked to myself, calling out the names as the ball was moved from one set of hands to another, as the decoy runners took out one or two of their tacklers. There's a little bit of trickery in the midfield, what we call a wraparound, and you've got to factor that into your thinking on the move. I counted down the links as I ran. I knew the exact point at which I would get the ball, if it all worked out right. I'd be thinking, 'X marks the spot. I've to hit that X, I've got to be there.'

Three more links and it would be me, then two more, and then it was just, 'This is it! This is what I've been training all year for, on wet, horrible grounds. This is what I've lost jobs for, just to make sure I could still be an All Black. This is fantastic. Now just give me the ball. GIVE ME THAT BLOODY BALL!'

And if I could beat a couple of guys on the way to the try line, by either going inside or outside, well that was the ultimate. If he was coming across flat, I could drag him with me and then just step inside him. If he was holding back, if he had a little bit of space to work with and I knew he was quick, then I'd work him straight at me and go in and out. That's always the classic. You've got to have a bit of speed to go around your guy. I'd drag him in, I'd go on his left-hand shoulder if he was coming across, just to stop him in his tracks and get him to come directly to me, to move him away from that tackle zone, because if he's good he knows exactly where he wants to nail me. He'd have to change his angle and that would slow him down. Straight away, I'd try and gas it, hit the burner and go outside him. And that's the classic.

In and out. It sounds easy, but it's hard to do. It's a lot easier to sidestep inside a guy off your best leg.

As soon as I hit the line, the crowd's up. Even in hostile territories the crowd will still roar, because it's a try. And all you hear is the roar. You're feeling pumped. And if you've beaten a couple of guys to the line, you can justifiably get up and say, 'Wow, that's not bad Stu, that's pretty damned good, son.'

Even if it's just a straight run with an overlap, where there's nothing to beat and you just have to run the try in, it's still a good try, because it's a try for the black jersey. But if you have to work for it, if there's a bit of work on, a bit of physical contact on the goal line, you've got to be strong enough to beat the tackle and go over. Your instinct takes over. 'Will I have to go low? Is that tackle, that flying tackle, going to be high? Then I'll go low. I'll skid along the ground to get over the goal line that way. Or do I have to dive over on top of that guy?' That's when you have to start working. For the best tries, you have to do a little bit of work to get there. Anyone can run straight to score.

Some of the moves we used in the first four matches of the tour – the ones before the Munster game – were so simple but they always worked. We couldn't believe it. The simplest move was the best one you could pull out. It was just so bloody wonderful to do. If I could do the job at the end of the chain then I would wander back to halfway, tap Andy Haden on the back and say, 'Well done, big fella. That one's for you.' Because without those guys you've got nothing.

Sometimes, when you think everything looks perfect, it just doesn't work out. I'd get so excited and all of a sudden you'd see someone come up and smash the living daylights out of the midfield and the move would break down. There might be a little bit of hesitation with the pass from the second link to the third, or maybe the dummy runner would be too slow and not quite get there, or the conditions might make the ball a little bit messy and slower to move to me. My excitement would get up and up and up and then I'd go, 'Ohhh! No, it didn't happen.' It's like surfing. Sometimes you get on a good one and sometimes you miss the best wave, because it just didn't happen.

Before we left New Zealand, the day we landed in London and every day after that we were told we had to be ambassadors for New Zealand rugby. On the previous tour the All Blacks made through Britain, they had some big, big boys with them and they had a reputation, those boys, of being a little bit boyish. They were not slow to push doors when they said 'pull'. That was their style.

We stayed in some of the same hotels as the '72 All Blacks and some of the staff were still there. I could see it in their eyes: 'Oh God, the All Blacks are back. How many doors and TVs are they going to break this time?'

Jack Gleeson and Russ Thomas told us that if anyone broke even one glass, they'd be sent home. They said, 'We will not have another Murdoch affair on this tour.' The British journalists following us around were waiting for something to happen, but we gave them nothing. We thought we were better than that. We wanted to be smart, intelligent rugby players. We didn't need to be physically violent off the field. You can put your mongrel dog on the pitch, but don't let him loose off it. It wasn't long before the management realised that the thirty guys they had picked were different, that they didn't need to keep telling us to behave ourselves. We just wanted to play rugby.

Jack told us to play at pace and pass the ball. That suited me just fine. It meant I was involved, that I could hurt teams. It meant I could score tries and that's what I was there to do. And even though we were a long way from home, we could feel the expectation on our shoulders. We knew people were getting up at four in the morning to listen on the radio or watch us on television.

The All Blacks change the mood of the country. Only two things can do it – either an election or the All Blacks. And if we won, *everyone went to work happy that day. If we lost, we knew there would be a dull ache around the country and that questions would be asked, because when you're an All Black failure is not acceptable. When they give you the jersey – when you join the exclusive club – they remind you about the teams that went before you. They tell you about the 1905 Originals. They tell you the Invincibles of 1924 were away on tour five months and never lost a game. They say, 'Do you want to come home a hero like those guys, or do you want to come home, get off the airplane and walk through the exit like a failure?' It's hard. It's ruthless. It's the way it was, the way it is, the way it always will be.*

We wanted the Grand Slam, because no New Zealand touring team had ever done it. We wanted to win all of our eighteen matches. We wanted to be the new Invincibles.

Chapter Twelve

Horses for Courses

Cork, October 1978

The news item in the sports pages merited only a single paragraph. It was, after all, of only marginal interest to most rugby people. The Welsh referee Corris Thomas, it said, would officiate at the Munster v All Blacks match on 31 October. Touch judges would be appointed in due course.

Corris Thomas? Kiernan had never come across him before. But one thing was certain: he would know all about him before the match. For Kiernan, doing your homework on the referee was as important as finding out about the opposition. It was part of what you did, if you were playing to win.

He picked up the phone and called a friend in Wales.

'What can you tell me about Corris Thomas?'

'What do you want to know?'

'Everything – I want to know who he is, what age he is, how long he's refereed. I want to know what he does for a living, what's he like as a ref, what he has for breakfast. Everything you can find out about him.'

'I'll put something together for you.'

The information arrived through Kiernan's letter box soon after.

*

For breakfast before a game Corris Thomas insisted on beans on toast, with two cups of tea, not coffee. He never had lunch. This detail was not included in the briefing received by Kiernan, but he learned plenty. Enough to get him thinking.

Thomas was, like Kiernan himself, a chartered accountant and a former full-back. His playing days had not amounted to much and after suffering concussion in a match he turned to refereeing. It was soon clear that his talents were more suited to the whistle than the ball and he rose swiftly up the ranks. In his eighth first-class game he found himself shaking hands with Ian Kirkpatrick, captain of the Seventh All Blacks. He had arrived. Thirty-one years old and already in the big time.

He was different, everyone said so. He had his own way of interpreting the laws of the game. The only problem was that some people said he didn't apply them, he opted out. The higher he rose, the more the older referees in Wales bad-mouthed him.

'Corris Thomas refuses to give penalties!'

'Corris Thomas is letting them away with offside all day!'

'Corris Thomas is playing God with the laws of the game!'

And Corris Thomas, who also possessed a university degree in law, pleaded not guilty to all charges.

It was true that he awarded fewer penalties than any other referee in Wales – half as many as the next man, according to the statistics. But at least when he blew his whistle the players knew why. They didn't say, 'What the hell was that for?'

When people accused him of being lax, he would reach into his lexicon of legal phrases and quote them the one closest to his heart.

'Their bloke was miles offside ref!' a coach might protest.

'*De minimis non curat lex*,' he would reply. 'The law does not recognise trivialities.'

And then he would put it into plain English for them.

'Suppose I go into the middle of Cardiff at two o'clock on a Monday morning and I park on a double-yellow line. I'm not allowed to park there, twenty-four hours a day, but nothing will happen. I am breaking the law, but it has no effect and the police will sail past, happy to ignore it.

'If I park there six hours later, the first policeman to arrive will book me. I haven't done anything different, but this time it's had an effect. It's the same in rugby. Did that guy being offside have any effect whatsoever? No, it didn't. If there isn't a problem, why bother to enforce the law? I simply apply the way the laws of the land are administered to the laws of rugby. Okay?'

That usually shut them up. They didn't always agree, but they came to understand that he was not for turning, even the Welsh Rugby Union member who took him aside and warned: 'You've got to give more penalties. It doesn't matter what for, just give more.'

Corris Thomas told him to get lost, said he either did it his way or he was giving up the game, and his way meant he gave penalties only when he absolutely had to.

In Cork, Kiernan began thinking of how this resistance to whistleblowing might be made to count in Munster's favour.

Two days after the New Zealanders' arrival in London, he drove to Musgrave Park in Cork for the Munster trial match. Once the final whistle blew, the selectors were due to go into conclave in order to select the team to face the All Blacks. In the vast majority of cases, their minds were already made up. In reality, the match between the Probables and the Possibles was not so much a trial as a run-out for the chosen ones. They were expected to reward the faith shown in them by winning in a canter.

Hugh Condon, a twenty-three-year-old medical student who played for London Irish, had been named in the centre for the Probables XV. For months he had been looking forward to the All Blacks game. He had been part of the team so badly beaten by Middlesex, but he had scored the team's only try that evening and if there were going to be scape-goats, he believed he was well down the list.

Wearing black jerseys, the Possibles led 10–3 at half-time. The Probables played as though they were the Certainties, as if the contest offered them only the chance of being injured and forced out of the big match. The forwards were lifeless and ponderous. The back line had no thrust, with Tony Ward effectively shepherded by Johnny Barry, his old nemesis from Shannon. If Jack Gleeson had been sitting in the stand, he would have seen how his players might approach the task of containing the new star of European rugby. He could have told one of his men at Thomond Park: 'Today, you must play like Johnny Barry. You force Ward back inside every time he tries to come off his left foot. Take Ward out of this game and they're beaten before they start.' But, of course, he wasn't there. He was at Twickenham, watching England scrape a draw against Argentina and seeing nothing to worry him. Still and all, it was Ward who pulled it out of the fire for the Probables, dropping a goal in the last few seconds to draw the match 16–16.

In their own minds, a few Possibles became Probables and one or two Probables feared they were Probably Nots. One of the last to leave the dressing room, Condon overheard two of the senior players talking about the likelihood of changes. 'There'll be one at most,' one of them said. The possibility that it might be him did not cross Condon's mind. He went upstairs to the bar with Les White and ordered a cup of tea. At half past seven there was still no news from the selectors' meeting room and Kiernan walked in, looking like he was in a rush. He was off to the Cork Opera House.

He walked over to where Condon and White were sitting and caught Condon's eye. 'Lads,' he said, 'it'll be horses for courses against the All Blacks.' Condon thought nothing of that until the following morning, when he bought a newspaper at Cork airport and read that the selectors had made one change. He was out, not even named among the substitutes.

		Age	Height	Weight
15	Larry Moloney (Garryowen)	27	5.11½	12.11
14	Moss Finn (UCC)	21	5.11	14.7
13	Seamus Dennison (Garryowen)	28	5.8½	11.12
12	Greg Barrett (Cork Constitution)	21	6.2	12.5
11	Jimmy Bowen (Cork Constitution)	21	5.11	12.5
10	Tony Ward (St Mary's College)	24	5.8	11.7
9	Donal Canniffe (c, Lansdowne)	29	6.0½	12.7
1	Gerry McLoughlin (Shannon)	26	5.11	15.0
2	Pat Whelan (Garryowen)	28	5.10½	13.4
3	Les White (London Irish)	34	5.11	15.7
4	Moss Keane (Lansdowne)	30	6.4½	17.1
5	Brendan Foley (Shannon)	28	6.2	16.9
6	Christy Cantillon (Cork Constitution)	22	6.0	14.4
7	Colm Tucker (Shannon)	26	6.1	15.5
8	Donal Spring (Dublin University)	22	6.4	14.7

Reserves: Micky O'Sullivan (Cork Constitution), Olann Kelleher (Dolphin), Barry McGann (Cork Constitution), Gerry Hurley (Sundays Well), Ted Mulcahy (Bohemians), Anthony O'Leary (London Irish).

Two decades on, the name of Greg Barrett – and not Hugh Condon – would be carved in stone on a plaque at Thomond Park, along with the rest of the Munster team. Seventeen days after the trial, at around five o'clock on a Tuesday afternoon in London, Condon walked out of a tutorial room and someone asked him if he had heard the news from Limerick. He felt numb when they told him. The pain of it would never completely leave him: there would be too many reminders for that.

Kiernan was not in the room when the team was picked but he wasn't expecting any great surprises from the five wise men. They knew who he wanted. Sometimes fellas moaned about bias against this club or that, but he never bothered listening to any of it. The way he looked at it, Noel Murphy might personally like one guy and hate another, but the bottom line was that he'd prefer himself. He would carry the can for any team he selected, so he would pick his worst enemy if he thought it would help him win the match. People just didn't appreciate that.

The side the selectors finally came out with was, above all else, solid. Nine were internationals. Against that, eleven of them had been on the team murdered by Middlesex, but, as Kiernan had told the branch, that match counted for nothing. He believed that a handful of them were high class and the rest would do. On a personal level, he had time for every one of them, which was unusual. He knew what they could do and what they couldn't, knew that if they tried to play the All Blacks at their own flamboyant game they would lose by twenty points, minimum. There was no point in asking them to do what they weren't cut out for. He would take them as he found them, conceive a game plan that played to their strengths, as he perceived them.

*

The All Blacks played the first match on the following Wednesday, the fixture against Cambridge University regarded as the gentlest of openers. The gates at Grange Road were shut well before kick-off and supporters locked outside began climbing the roof of Selwyn College for a vantage point, so many of them that the gates were re-opened for fear that the college roof might cave in. The All Blacks coasted into a big lead but then for no apparent reason they began unravelling, dropping balls, missing tackles and losing lineouts as the students answered the urgings of their dynamic young captain, the Irish scrum-half John Robbie. In the end the winning margin was twenty points, but the manner of it impressed no one. Had not the 1905 team won their first match by fifty points? Ever since, their successors had been expected to open in a blaze of glory. Why else play a bunch of students first off?

'We won, didn't we?' Gleeson said when reporters asked for an explanation. The negativity of their questions annoyed him. He left Russ Thomas to do most of the talking and wandered away. He knew it had not been an impressive beginning. He didn't need any journalist to tell him that.

'What is it that is causing you to make mistakes?' he asked the players later. 'Is it lack of concentration? Or is it fear?' Hearing this, or rather half-hearing it, Terry O'Connor of the *Daily Mail* reported it as, 'Or is it too much beer?'

Gleeson went to work on them. For the first time on a tour, he introduced tackle bags – six feet high – in time for the next match three days later. And so the All Blacks entered Wales in fighting form and put Cardiff to the sword, in front of 43,000 at the Arms Park. Wilson scored two exhilarating tries, the second with the kind of verve matched by Terry McLean's description of it:

As the *pièce de résistance*, thirteen minutes before no-side, BeeGee [Bryan Williams] subtly sidled from his post on the left wing as Loveridge again set the backline running, going right. By the time Osborne had the ball in his hands Williams was outside him, his dark eyes so fiercely fixed on Camilleri that the little man, like a moth darting at the flame, closed in on him. That left Wilson with the ball in hand, Rees standing sentinel ahead, the cover racing madly across, the goal line beckoning, twenty metres ahead. Nearing Rees, Wilson held the ball out to him in both hands, inviting him to pluck at it. It was a masterly touch to set a man back on his heels. Then Wilson squirmed rather than swerved and with an heroic dive thrust himself at the goal line just inside the corner flag. It was, simply, a great try, a very great try . . . beyond criticism in construction and execution.

Wilson, impetuous and impatient for the ball, was not content to hold his position on the right wing and wait for it to come to him. It was a time when wingers ran up and down their track and strayed no further. Not Wilson. In that game, and in the next, before another 40,000 baying Welshmen in Swansea, he dashed across from the wing on to the opposition's outside centre, forcing him into a decision: would he stay on his man or desert him for Wilson? From these seeds of confusion came tries, glorious tries.

'This is the fifth Test as far as we're concerned,' Gleeson had said of the West Wales match, the third of the tour. With his players gathered in a circle around him before kick-off, Ray Gravell led the Welsh into song, while the All Blacks stood together, not singing, not even talking, but watching as Mourie traced an index finger around the silver fern on his shirt. The message was unspoken but unmistakable: 'This is what we are here for. The silver fern on our shirts makes us special. We must protect it at all costs.'

For the second game in a row, Wilson scored two tries, and again the second was the pick of them. It bore a strong resemblance to his classic against Cardiff, with Williams again causing havoc by joining the line from the left wing and finding Wilson. Nobody laid a hand on him as he flew across the line. The best defences in Wales, the strongest of the home nations, had no answer to Wilson. It seemed he could break the opposition as he pleased. When the team to play London Counties three days later was announced his name was missing from it, along with those of his fellow wing, the deadly Williams, and the dominant Mourie at flanker. All three were being rested until the tour's fifth game. The one against Munster.

Meanwhile, Kiernan's players were getting fitter by the week. A few hours after the All Blacks had taken care of West Wales, they headed for Fermoy once more, some of them snarled up in Dublin's evening traffic, listening to bulletins from Swansea on the radio, others bundling into cars in Limerick, closer to their destination but cursing it just as much.

Seamus Dennison stood at the door of his bungalow in Roscrea, County Tipperary, a gear bag slung over his shoulder. He waited for Lally, his wife, to return from work in the car they shared. She was four months pregnant with their first child. She kept the engine running when she pulled up beside him and he threw his bag into the back, kissed her hello and goodbye and got behind the wheel. Kiernan didn't appreciate people being late.

Like his great friend Larry Moloney, the Munster full-back, Dennison was a country boy who had been introduced to rugby at boarding school in Limerick city. Standing a fraction

134

over five feet eight, bearded but almost bald on top, he didn't look much like a rugby player but he was, in fact, one of Munster's key men. He had speed and great hands, and he could read a game better than most. Above all, he was brave – too brave, some said, usually when he had been knocked senseless after a huge tackle in midfield.

He had no fear of the All Blacks, for he was one of the survivors from the 1973 team denied victory only by the last-minute penalty kicked by Trevor Morris. He had been immense that day, not missing a single tackle in eighty minutes. He didn't need Kiernan to tell him that more of the same would be required against Mourie's men, that if he didn't stand up to them, the All Blacks would feast on Munster mince.

Chapter Thirteen

Seamus Dennison's Story

We saw them coming out of the cinema in Abbeyfeale, togged out in all kinds of different gear. I was nine. I didn't know who they were or what they were at.

'Who are those fellas?'

'They're rugby players.'

'Rugby players! What were they doing inside in the cinema?'

'Puttin' on their togs.'

'In the cinema?'

'They've nowhere else to change, shur.'

'Where are they going now?'

'Off up the road a couple of miles. They've a field up there. That's where they play the rugby.'

'I didn't know there was rugby in Abbeyfeale.'

'There wasn't. But these fellas are after formin' a club.'

'What's rugby like?'

'Couldn't tell you, never seen a match. But they say it's very rough altogether.'

'Are Abbeyfeale good at the rugby?'

'Not by the look of of them. But shur, they're only startin'.'

'Maybe we'll go up and have a look.'

Abbeyfeale is a country town on the Kerry border in west Limerick, thirty-nine miles from the city. People supported the

Limerick hurlers and the Kerry footballers. I grew up playing Gaelic football. Back in 1959, there was some kind of a falling-out in the GAA club and the local doctor and a few more guys started a rugby club in the town. At first, they had only their field. No goalposts, no lines, nowhere to change, no nothing. They were fellas from Abbeyfeale and fellas who would be associated with fellas from Abbeyfeale. The first time I ever saw a rugby ball was up in that field. We didn't know what they were doing. They didn't either, but they got the hang of it eventually. Every now and then some crowd from the city would come out to play them. That would be a major occasion.

My father, Danny Dennison, was a tailor by profession. We had a drapery shop in the town. At home, we kept greyhounds. My father travelled to every coursing meeting going, north or south, east or west. He had a dog that won the Kingdom Cup, a big thing in Tralee, but mostly he was a roaring gambler. He travelled everywhere with Johnny Moriarty, a bookmaker from Listowel. When he won, he could arrive home with anything: rugs, coats, a washing machine, half a cow. He knew people at all the stalls and he bought whatever was going. When he lost, I'd be sent down to the pub to ask him to come home.

When I was twelve I was sent to a boarding school in Limerick, Mungret College. By then my father was ill with a heart problem, but he still took himself off to coursing meetings and my mother was petrified he mightn't come back at all. Two years later he died of a brain haemorrhage.

Things were different in the city. For a start, they played rugby at Mungret. It wasn't exactly a stronghold, but it was good enough. I was always small and light but I took to it straight away, loved it. Forty years on, nothing has changed. Lally, my wife, says rugby is like oxygen to me.

In my second year the whole school was taken to Thomond Park to see Munster and the All Blacks. They did the haka and the *whole shebang. It was something else. To be that close to it was an unbelievable experience. Tom Kiernan was Munster's captain. I was right behind the goal-line when Henry Wall scored their try. What I found out when I started playing for Munster afterwards was that it didn't matter if you were in the crowd or on the pitch, the feeling you got was the same. The overseas teams were going to get a match – everybody made sure of that. It was obvious the All Blacks were far bigger men that day, but Munster got stuck into them. It made a huge impression on me.*

In 1967 we went down to Cork to see the Australians. Jerry Walsh was playing in the centre for Munster. He was my hero. He was only a small fella, but Christ could he tackle. I'll never forget the guy tackling fellas three times the size of him and he absolutely devoured them. If you hit them right, the big fellas will go down. Jerry Walsh was the living proof of it that day. He was like a beacon to me. I knew I was never going to be a big fella. Jerry Walsh showed me I didn't have to be to get on.

My best friend in rugby was – and still is – Larry Moloney. We were in the Munster back line together and we played our club rugby with Garryowen. People said Garryowen were the fancy boys. Maybe we were. No matter where we were on the pitch, the ball went from hand to hand. We scored more points from getting the ball inside our own twenty-two than we ever did outside it. But our boys were well able to look after themselves. They could mix it all right. With Young Munsters, you knew you were going to get the shit kicked out of you as soon as you went out. You either stood up or you might as well not bother showing up. When it came to one Limerick city team playing another, that was expected. If the crowd coming down from Dublin beat you, that didn't matter. Dublin was only a crowd of fancy dans. But by Jesus you had to beat the local crowd. It honed our competitiveness. And when they gave you a Munster jersey, you knew what it meant. You knew who you were representing.

Early in 1973 I played for Munster against the All Blacks. We should have won that match. Even back then we were training in Fermoy, an awful frigging hole of a place. Noisy Murphy ran us until we got sick and when we did, that was enough, that was great. Great session. At the time some people thought we'd be shitting bricks over meeting the All Blacks, but I never saw it that way. I was never going to be scared of them, but until Kiernan spoke to us I thought we were in danger of getting properly stuffed. Kiernan was the bee's knees as a motivator. He just had it. Whatever he said, it would get you going. There was nobody within an ass's roar of him.

My mother listened to these matches on the radio, always in fear that something bad would happen to me. I suppose she knew what I was like, even though she didn't understand the first thing about rugby. My father never saw me play. It took my mother ten years to come to a game. It was later in 1973. Munster were playing Argentina; a brutal, brutal match. She was in the stand at Thomond Park with Lally. This hoor hit me late, half an hour late, a centre big enough for the second row. I never saw it coming. I was knocked out cold, stretched out on the pitch. My mother never came again after that. It was probably just as well she didn't come to see me against the All Blacks in '78. She wouldn't have been able for what happened in that. She would have been carried out of the place.

Chapter Fourteen

Tickets And Tape

26 October 1978
The All Blacks were starting to click, much to the relief of their coach. Tension had been evident on Jack Gleeson's taut face ever since the departure from Auckland and sometimes the responsibility of his post felt like a dead weight on his shoulders. It was said of him that he had the face of a man who had to raise $20,000 by Tuesday to stave off the bailiffs. The defeat to Australia in the third Test back in September had shaken and deflated him, but after the third victory of the tour, against West Wales, he allowed himself to relax a little.

Gleeson walked into the press box that day in Swansea and talked nineteen to the dozen. He knew it had been a thoroughly convincing performance, full of attractive rugby. As he spoke his excitement was obvious, but it was mixed with another emotion: relief. When one reporter looked down he noticed that Gleeson's hands were trembling.

The report in *The Times* the next day made pleasant reading for those in the All Blacks' corner.

ALL BLACKS' OLD-FASHIONED STYLE WINS 'FIFTH INTERNATIONAL'

WEST WALES 7   ALL BLACKS 23

The field of St Helen's was no place for faint hearts yesterday afternoon. The New Zealanders scored three tries to one and so vaulted, with emphasis and style, as stiff a hurdle as any touring side might care to face at this point in a tour. Increasingly, it seems that this team might well achieve an invincible record.

The first Test match of the tour, against Ireland at Lansdowne Road, was now just ten days away. First, they had to deal with London Counties at Twickenham and then travel to Thomond Park to take care of Munster. In the New Zealand camp, the feeling was growing that they had what it took to become the new All Black Invincibles.

Early that morning in London, Dinah Maxwell-Muller, a secretary with the Hamlyn publishing company, picked up the telephone and heard a man's voice ask for Brian Busteed, her boss.

'Whom shall I say is calling?'

'Tom Kiernan.'

The previous evening, Kiernan had supervised the last of the Fermoy training sessions and the sharpness shown by his players had pleased him. Physically, they were now in good shape. The mental preparation was next and he would have the best part of three days with them to work on that, a luxury unimaginable to him or to his players only a few months before. Before that, he had some important business to take care of.

Kiernan was calling his old friend from university because something told him there might be a problem with the arrangement they had made. In any case, he never left anything to chance.

Busteed picked a small package off his desk. It wasn't supposed to be there. It was supposed to be on its way to Kiernan in Cork.

'I'm looking at it, Tom. No sign of him. He must have forgotten to pick it up.'

Kiernan cursed down the line. It was typical: you just couldn't rely on people. They would promise to do something and then make excuses when it wasn't done.

'What can we do, Brian?'

'I'll think of something.'

Kiernan felt immediately reassured. Busteed, he considered, was a rare breed. He would trust him with his life.

Busteed called his secretary into the office. 'I need to get this package across to Ireland today,' he said. 'Can you get yourself on the next plane?'

'Of course,' said Dinah Maxwell-Muller, for she was an adventurous woman. 'What's in the package?'

'A videotape.'

'How exciting! What's on it?'

'A rugby match.'

'What's so urgent about that?'

When Busteed told her Kiernan was anxious that his players should get a good look at the All Blacks before playing them she wondered if she was being sent on a fool's errand, but she was happy to do her bit for the Munster cause. The next plane to Shannon left in two hours and had seats to spare. Busteed paid for the ticket and Kiernan arranged for someone to collect the tape at the airport.

'What will he look like?' his secretary asked.

'He's six foot two and he'll be wearing a red jumper. I think you'll find one another all right. He'll be looking out for a slinky blonde.'

Because Heathrow was nearby, she had just enough time to rush home and pack an overnight bag. The only flight back to London that day was full. It was a nuisance, but she would make the best of it.

In years to come, tales of the scarcity of tickets would spread, the mythology of Munster and the All Blacks inviting them. But the tickets were not, as would later be claimed, 'like gold dust'. On this Thursday morning, five days before the match, you could have bought as many as you'd liked.

No one asked Brendan Foley if he could lay his hands on one as he made his morning calls to pubs and shops around Limerick, taking orders for lemonade.

Behind the counter of the Allied Irish Bank in O'Connell Street, Larry Moloney fielded no inquiries for tickets. Had anyone asked, he could have told them to walk fifty yards down the street, where Nestor's sports shop had them in hand.

Up at the Christian Brothers School in Sexton Street, no one plagued Gerry McLoughlin for a ticket. Even if they had he could have told them that the Munster branch's combined allocation of complimentary tickets to the players and substitutes was zero.

At Lawson's menswear in Cork, the branch's spiritual home, Bill O'Brien had tickets for sale – but not to just anyone who walked in off the street. His view on tickets was that, in principle, they were to be reserved for the alickadoos of his acquaintance. Sometimes the shop's better customers, the ones keeping it afloat, fell victim to this policy.

'I don't see why he should get one,' Bill would scoff to his assistant John O'Keeffe, 'he was never at a rugby match before! The rugby people must get them first.'

A short distance away, at 15 Alfred Street, where a sign read 'W. D. WALSH Wholesale Fishmerchant', an elderly man who had no rugby background was wondering if he should make the trip to Limerick. He was being encouraged by the man whose name was over the door, a much younger fellow who was wearing a white coat.

'Come on, Dan,' said Bill Walsh, 'we'll get two tickets and the two of us will leave here on Tuesday morning.'

But Dan Canniffe wasn't sure. He was still recovering from an operation earlier in the year for prostate cancer. He was afraid the excitement of the match might be too much for him. But he was also torn, for the Munster team was to be captained by his youngest son, Donal.

Walsh could see there was no point in pushing it, so he left his office manager to decide in his own time. The two men had worked side by side for twelve years and for all but the previous twelve months or so they had called each other 'Mr Walsh' and 'Mr Canniffe', the employee out of deference, the boss through respect for a man he considered one of the finest he had ever known.

Lately, their friendship had grown stronger and Walsh had been moved by the older man's generous response when he had come to him for advice on matters of a personal nature. Thus did they become 'Bill' and 'Dan'.

They had met in 1966 when Walsh's business was getting off the ground and he needed someone to help him with his book-keeping, a good man he could trust to keep an eye on things when he was buying fish in Baltimore or Schull or even as far away as Dingle.

Dan Canniffe had just retired as a garda sergeant after thirty years in the force. The major events of his life had come

144

in fourteen-year cycles. He was married at twenty-eight and widowed at forty-two. At fifty-six he had married again and handed in his badge. He had moved to a house on the outskirts of Cork city with his new wife Kay, a nurse.

He was an impressive looking man, six feet one and imposingly built. Many years before he had hurled for both Cork and Dublin, marking the great Mick Mackey of Limerick in the All-Ireland hurling final of 1934. As he neared his sixty-ninth birthday his hair was still dark, his appearance immaculate; fingernails carefully clipped, always the starched shirt and the silk tie. There was still something of the matinée idol about him, the quality that caused a commotion in London one day in 1938 when Dan and his wife Maisie were on their honeymoon and a crowd surrounded him as they left a shop, convinced he was the Hollywood film star Robert Taylor, who was known as 'the man with the perfect profile'.

His life had changed utterly around 2 a.m. on 4 August 1951. Maisie had gone to a meeting of the local Irish Countrywomen's Association on a bicycle purchased in Longford the week before and a source of pride to her, for it was seldom she bought anything for herself. A sergeant's salary didn't go far when you had seven young children.

She called on a friend when the meeting finished and by the time she got up to leave it was 1.30 a.m. 'I'll be killed!' she told her friend, thinking of Dan and how he'd be wondering what was keeping her.

When she was thrown from the bike, her forehead struck the stone edging of the footpath. Later they found a loose nut in the front wheel, animal hair between the spokes and a twenty-yard trail of blood leading to Maisie Canniffe's body. A garage man called Tom Diffley and the local priest knocked on the front door of the garda station and when

Dan was given the news his legs collapsed from under-neath him and Diffley had to move sharply to break his fall. When the two men left he sat awake for the rest of the night, waiting for morning, wondering what he would say to his children.

They left Dromod soon after and went south. Jack Lynch, the minister in charge of the gardai, fixed it for him. Anything he could do for a fellow Cork hurler in distress he was going to do. Dan had no choice but to break up the family. Three of the children moved to the heart of Cork city, where his married sister Bridget was childless at fifty-three. The other four went with him, first to Killenaule in County Tipperary, and later to Rathcormac, twenty miles from Cork city.

These were the circumstances which led to Kieran Canniffe, the eldest child, entering Presentation Brothers College the following September, where his classmates included a feisty boy named Tom Kiernan. Nine years later the youngest son, Donal, followed the same path.

Donal was reared at 60 McCurtain's Villas, a redbrick terraced house overlooked by the three spires of St Finbarr's Cathedral. His father took the bus into Cork once a week to see the rest of his family. The boy's first memories of his father would be of the stranger in a policeman's uniform who came to visit and then disappeared into the night.

When Donal began to show rich promise as a rugby player Dan's pride was evident in the scrapbook he kept, charting his boy's progress. The pain caused by the shattering of his former life he kept to himself, along with the angina with which he had been diagnosed later in life. This affliction was, most likely, the reason he wasn't sure about attending the match. He told Walsh he would wait until the weekend and make a decision then.

He got on with his work. It was the busiest day of the week, for tomorrow would be Friday and people needed their fish. It was his responsibility to make sure they got it.

Flight BE835 to Shannon was almost empty. On board, Dinah Maxwell-Muller wondered if she was wasting her time and her boss's money. At first, part of her had imagined, fancifully, that the tape might be some kind of secret weapon, but she took an interest in rugby and she began to think better of that now. She spotted her man immediately when she walked into the arrivals hall at Shannon a little before one o'clock. She handed over the tape with a smile and he thanked her and directed her to the airport hotel, a short stroll away.

It was a beautiful day and with time to kill she took a walk in the afternoon. In the evening she went to the bar for a drink before dinner. Unbidden, a man with an Irish accent joined her.

'How much?' he asked quietly.

'I beg your pardon?'

'How much do you, ah, charge?'

Using language that could not have been described as ladylike, Dinah Maxwell-Muller told him to go away.

She had barely heard of Munster rugby that morning and now, after doing it some service, she had been taken for a prostitute. She hoped Mr Kiernan would be happy with his videotape. She hoped it might somehow help his team against the All Blacks. But she doubted it.

Chapter Fifteen

Be a Thinker

In the second match of their tour the All Blacks had defeated Cardiff, destroyers of Munster the previous year, and the fourth fixture was seen by some in Munster as another indicator of how Kiernan's team might fare against them. The London Counties selection that lined up on a fine day at Twickenham on Saturday 28 October included six players from Middlesex, four of whom had taken part in the demolition of Munster five weeks before. Theoretically, the full London team should have been even stronger than Middlesex, but the New Zealander shouting from the sideline as the All Blacks ran riot disputed this point with vehemence.

For Earle Kirton, the Middlesex coach, London Counties were a shambles lacking the soul of a true team like his own. The All Blacks did not have to play very well to batter them 37–12, but for Jack Gleeson there was the pleasing sight of a lineout that had finally clicked. The first-choice pairing of Andy Haden and Frank Oliver was utterly superior. They were leaving for Ireland, where they would play three matches, in excellent shape.

The All Blacks dined like kings alongside the vanquished men of London, drinking fine port from the ceremonial Loving Cup at the Guildhall, where royalty and the great leaders of state had been entertained since 1411. As a string orchestra serenaded them from the Minstrels' Gallery at the west end of the magnificent Great Hall, the All Blacks were given to believe that Munster would be another pushover.

'God help them,' the Middlesex players said on being told that Munster was next on the New Zealanders' itinerary. 'You'll murder them.'

For most of the tourists, the Munster match was just another provincial fixture. They were vaguely aware that Munster had a decent record in pushing touring sides close, but with the first Test now seven days away their minds were drifting towards Lansdowne Road. The game at Thomond Park was one to get out of the way before Ireland provided the first serious examination of their tour, and so the Middlesex players were telling them what they wanted to hear.

'We stuffed them – you wouldn't believe how bad they were.'

'You mean London Counties stuffed them?'

'No, Middlesex did.'

'Who're Middlesex?'

'One of the London Counties.'

'And you guys today – you were all of them?'

'Correct.'

'Maybe they've improved since then. Bound to have.'

'Well, put it this way, they couldn't be any worse.'

Only three of the thirty-man party – Haden, Bryan Williams and Bruce Robertson – had been in Cork five years before, when the Munster team captained by Kiernan had drawn 3–3. If they had any expectations of another close contest, the Middlesex contingent had done an excellent job in disabusing them.

It was agreed among the All Blacks that a wonderful time

was bound to be had by all in Ireland. Those who had been there before were unanimous: it was a bloody great place to visit.

Shortly before one o'clock the following afternoon they boarded a flight for Shannon. They had not yet announced the team to face Munster but with the Ireland match coming four days later the expectation was for a second-string XV, or at least a line-up shorn of many of the marquee names.

Two men on the plane thought differently, and when it came to team selection they were the only two who counted. Gleeson and Mourie had decided Munster were to be treated with due respect. They had an unbeaten record to protect and the prospect of finishing the tour with a perfect record was looking increasingly real. They regarded the evidence of the Middlesex match as largely irrelevant. The results they considered relevant were not recent, but drawn from the history books:

1954: Munster 3 All Blacks 6
1963: Munster 3 All Blacks 6
1973: Munster 3 All Blacks 3

Rarely, if ever, had an All Blacks coach and his captain been so close. They were perfect for each other, quiet but determined men who regarded rugby as a game that demanded intellect above all, a game that exposed character and the lack of it. They had come to know one another two years before, when a New Zealand B team coached by Gleeson and captained by Mourie toured Argentina. The tour was a success and its legacy was clear: Gleeson and Mourie were the coming men of New Zealand rugby. When Gleeson got off the plane and was met at the airport by the men from the New Zealand Rugby Union, he cut to the chase and told them: 'Mourie will be the greatest New Zealand captain of all time.' It was only a question of when Mourie would lead the full All Blacks team and he did not have long to wait. When Gleeson was handed the reins as coach the following year there was only ever going to be one candidate to succeed the retiring Tane Norton as skipper. The Mourie era had begun.

But who exactly was this quiet young farmer from the North Island's west coast? What kind of rugby player could recite Shakespeare word for word, as Mourie had one night in the small Argentine town of Carlos Paz back in 1976? Gleeson understood him, for he was not unlike him, but to the rest of the Eighth All Blacks Mourie could be an enigmatic figure. People said he used silence as a weapon, that he knowingly cultivated a mystique around himself, that he was distant and aloof. He didn't chase women. He barely touched alcohol. When he closed the door of his hotel bedroom at night he was alone, by tradition the only player not required to share, and the book he was reading set him apart, too. It was *Zen and the Art of Motorcycle Maintenance*, a four-hundred-page 'literary chautauqua' that, among other things, argues 'the cycle you're working on is a cycle called yourself'. Nobody asked to borrow it when he'd finished.

Physically he was in magnificent shape and his slim frame gave him the appearance of a man taller than his six feet. He was fitter than any other All Black, perhaps any rugby player in the world. He drove himself punishingly hard, because he never wanted his body to be the master of his mind. When a crisis came, as it surely would, Graham Mourie wanted to be ready for it. His philosophy was that leaders needed a clear head when things were not going their way. 'It is important in the playing of the game,' he would later say, 'to be completely involved in the physical action and yet to have another part of me standing back and taking a quiet look and computing the whys of what is happening all around.' That was the thing about Mourie the flanker: he was everywhere. You could find him on the shoulder of an All Black centre who was about to get buried, or in the way of an opposing wing who could see the line beckoning up ahead; wherever you needed him, Mourie turned up.

The New Zealand journalists covering the tour found him courteous and sincere but ultimately elusive. 'He did not put up barriers,' wrote the doyen, Terry McLean. 'They were there.' But for Ron Palenski, one of only two press men to follow the Argentina tour and the reporter who knew him best, Mourie was not the man of mystery others perceived him to be. 'He wasn't aloof,' Palenski reflected years later. 'He was just shy.' There was something else. He kept his distance from the other players because he was the one who would have to drop them if they did not perform. He and Gleeson were the men who made the hard calls.

The rugby people of Munster knew that their team had come close to beating the All Blacks on three successive tours, but what few tended to mention was that their task had been made easier by the weakened nature of the All Black XVs sent out against them. In 1973 there had been no Ian Kirkpatrick or Grant Batty, no Sid Going or Joe Karam, and the great battle of 1963 had taken place without such irreplaceables as Colin Meads, Wilson Whineray and Kel Tremain.

When the team picked to play at Thomond Park was announced later that Sunday, every one of the All Blacks' acknowledged stars was in it, from the Test locks Haden and Oliver to the first-choice wings, Wilson and Williams, and the preferred props, Johnstone and Knight, with Mourie leading them out. Only McGregor and the coltish Graham had not played a full Test. Munster could scarcely have been paid a more meaningful compliment.

		Age	Height	Weight
15	Brian McKechnie (Southland)	24	5.8	12.4
14	Stu Wilson (Wellington)	23	6.0	13.7
13	Bruce Robertson (Counties)	26	6.1	13.0
12	Lyn Jaffray (Otago)	28	5.10	13.0
11	Bryan Williams (Auckland)	28	5.10	14.0
10	Doug Bruce (Canterbury)	31	5.10	11.10
9	Mark Donaldson (Manawatu)	22	5.9	11.10
1	Brad Johnstone (Auckland)	28	6.2	16.2
2	John Black (Canterbury)	27	6.0	14.8
3	Gary Knight (Manawatu)	27	6.2	17.3
4	Andy Haden (Auckland)	28	6.6	17.2
5	Frank Oliver (Southland)	29	6.3	16.11
6	Graham Mourie (c, Taranaki)	26	6.0	14.2
7	Wayne Graham (Otago)	21	6.2	15.0
8	Ash McGregor (Southland)	25	6.1	14.12

Back home New Zealand's prime minister Robert Muldoon was launching his re-election campaign in Hamilton by promising 'more of the same', and that also summed up what Gleeson wanted from his players in Limerick. They had to keep winning – and preferably with style. To the great delight of Russ Thomas, the tour manager, the British press was by now falling over itself to proclaim these All Blacks as a class apart, on the pitch as well as off it.

Not everyone was convinced, however. For Terry McLean, unanimously voted 'champion shit-stirrer of the tour' by the players, they had beaten nothing but a rabble at Twickenham, 'a shameful group of nondescripts', and if these represented the best London could muster, 'then God help London: and God help, too, the game itself'.

'I gave them socks!' he railed over dinner in Limerick the

night after the Twickenham match. 'No All Black side should ever play that badly. I said so in my report!' When he heard the team selected to play against Munster he saw in it confirmation of his suspicions that Gleeson was rattled. Readers of the *New Zealand Herald* were left in little doubt that their man on tour was not in the least impressed.

ALL BLACK CHOICE IS DISTURBING

From T. P. McLean, Limerick

Amid the rave notices the All Blacks are receiving it is significant from the choice of the team to play against Munster tomorrow (4 a.m. New Zealand time) that they are worried about possible weaknesses.

While it is true that one All Black team after another have found Munster to be incredibly heroic and implacably unyielding, it is still strange that the touring selectors have decided to cast into the match as many as ten or eleven certainties for the match with Ireland at Dublin on Saturday.

The implication is not that they are determined to keep on winning. Rather, some of the choices suggest that the management is quite seriously concerned about players and positions.

Munster play hard. Like Ireland they take no prisoners. Is it therefore not a risk to play so many established stars? If for the sake of victory over Munster players of the quality of Graham Mourie, Stuart Wilson, Frank Oliver and Andy Haden were to be hurt . . . the possibility of defeat in the Test could be increased.

The All Blacks should win tomorrow. But will they win on Saturday?

Joe Kennedy, a fifty-five-year-old Limerickman who worked in the stores department at Pan Am, was waiting at Shannon airport when the All Blacks' plane touched down. For years he had been the Munster branch's liaison man to the touring teams. Night and day he was at their beck and call. He fixed up their golf games. He took them down to Ballydoyle to gaze upon the racehorses trained by the great Vincent O'Brien – and it wasn't everyone who got past the gates there. Above all he accompanied them to Bunratty Castle for a medieval banquet which culminated in one of the touring party being thrown in the dungeon, to the hilarity of everyone else.

Everyone apart from Joe. He hated the damned banquet.

He had run the gauntlet with the Springboks in 1970, ridden the bus with them from the Shelbourne hotel in Dublin to Connolly Station while anti-apartheid protesters rioted alongside. The South Africans had wanted to jump the Limerick-bound train at Nenagh and then head for their hotel by bus under police escort, but the gardai insisted they stay on board and take what was coming to them. When the train pulled into Limerick they could see the station was overflowing with people. Then they stepped on to the chessboard platform and Joe Kennedy heard a noise that would stay with him for the rest of his life. Cheering. Even though he abhorred apartheid as much as the next man, he felt a tingle of pride, for the Springboks were in Young Munster territory, among *his* people, and as rugby men they were welcome.

For four days and nights he was holed up at their hotel while a mass protest was planned for outside Thomond Park. The Springbok bus was to be escorted to the ground by twenty-four motorcycle outriders; eight hundred gardai would form a human shield against the protesters; bomb-disposal experts awaited a summons; sniffer dogs were led into the ground.

The day before the match he took a phone call from a man he vaguely knew, the leader of the local Dockers' Union.

'Joe, we're closing the docks tomorrow,' the man said.

'Why's that?'

'Because we're going to the fucking match.'

'Well if you're going to the match, I don't have to worry about the protesters, do I?'

'No, Joe. You don't have to worry about them.'

'Listen,' he told the officers of the Munster branch, 'for Christ's sake will ye deliver three hundred free tickets to Limerick docks. Nobody will want to stop this crowd seeing the match. Suicide would be a mild way to get rid of yourself, compared with confronting them.'

The dockers got their tickets. The protest was peaceful.

Now, for the third time, Joe was among All Blacks and he had always thought them a fine body of men. The latest tourists seemed to him a somewhat restrained bunch, and the man introduced to him as Jack Gleeson cut a subdued figure. Perhaps the entertainment planned for that evening might enliven him, Joe considered. They were bound for Bunratty. He winced at the prospect.

Jack Gleeson had talked up West Wales before the game, but he knew well that the international at Lansdowne Road was likely to represent a far greater test. He felt the Munster match would provide him with the final pieces of information he needed before deciding on his best XV. As he sat at the front of the bus with Mourie and Russ Thomas, and was driven towards the Royal George hotel in Limerick city, Gleeson did not know that the match that would threaten to wreck his tour was just forty-eight hours away. He did not know that Kiernan, his opposite number, had spent weeks plotting the All Blacks' downfall. Nor did he know that his days as New Zealand coach were numbered, that cancerous growths which would soon become half the size of tennis balls were already forming in his liver. Within twelve months and four days Jack Gleeson would be dead, but not before he had spoken the words that would forever serve as his epitaph: 'Rugby is a game of thought. Play the game at strength and be a thinker.'

Gleeson was not the only thinker in town that day. Heavy morning rain had drenched Kiernan and his players when they assembled for a training session on a saturated pitch overlooked by the Clare hills, at St Munchin's College, the school where Larry Moloney and Colm Tucker had learned their rugby.

It was a Bank Holiday weekend and most of the boarders had gone home, so only a handful of die-hards were there to watch the Munster forwards drive a scrummaging machine up and down the pitch, and listen to Gerry McLoughlin complain loudly that the contraption had no pads. In his college days Kiernan had believed rugby was all about running the ball and he had been slow to appreciate that nothing was more likely to cost you a match than a front row that lost more battles than it won, even if the margin did not seem significant.

Standing there, in his boots and shorts, commanding the players by their surnames ('Ward! Put it down there!' 'Barrett – go across! Cover!') he could have named a dozen fundamentals that Munster had to get right on the big day, but the one at the top of the list would have been the scrum. If that went backwards, they could forget about it. And so he worked the pack hard that morning, both in the set scrum and the loose. He tossed the ball towards one of the forwards and told him to go down on it, until the rest of them rucked it back to Donal Canniffe. The scrum-half was six feet tall and he regarded himself as a ninth forward. As captain, he did not want a pack leader. He wanted to call the shots himself and the forwards were there to protect him. He told them: 'I want clean ball and tidy ball. Under control. That's what I want.'

And once Canniffe shipped a spinning ball to Ward, with his trademark torpedo pass that meant Ward could stand forever away from him, he wanted the Number 10 to kick it behind the opposition, to have them turning, scurrying backwards while Munster charged in pursuit. That was the plan. But then, that was usually the plan.

That night Kiernan took the players to an industrial unit on the Dock Road, one of the few places in Limerick where a video recorder could be found. They crowded into a small room and gathered around a television screen, and the tape hand-delivered by Dinah Maxwell-Muller was loaded into the machine. On it was the previous week's *Rugby Special*, featuring forty minutes of highlights from the second match of the tour, the game against Cardiff.

Almost all of those present were seeing it for the first time, because only homes on Ireland's east coast could pick up the BBC's signal. In Munster, the number of channels was about to be doubled to two: RTE2 would be launched in four days' time, an event considered so momentous that the national broadcaster decided against sending its solitary outside broadcast unit to Thomond Park. When the rugby commentator and head of sport Fred Cogley protested that the match should be covered properly, he was told it simply wasn't possible. Besides, what was the big deal? The outside broadcast unit would be back in Dublin by Saturday, in time for the real match – the international at Lansdowne Road.

The first image Kiernan's players saw was of the Welsh players emerging from the Arms Park tunnel, their faces set in grim determination, and then came the All Blacks, zigzagging across the famous turf, all swagger and measured passes, as if they were in Cardiff not only to beat the Welsh but to educate them in the finer points.

Once the match started they struggled, for a while, to impose themselves, but with twenty-eight minutes on the clock Stu Wilson struck, and you could see the life being sucked out of the home players there and then. Cardiff were readying themselves for their own throw at a lineout when, near the top right-hand corner of the screen, the All Blacks centre Bill Osborne could be seen gesticulating to Wilson on the opposite wing. Cardiff took the ball cleanly at the back of the line and worked it sweetly inside, when suddenly Wilson appeared from nowhere and took off, the intercepted ball tucked under his right arm, the line seventy metres ahead, the try a certainty. Even though there was no one near him, Wilson did not shorten his stride until the ball was grounded, one-handed and with an emphatic downward sweep, under the posts. In full flight, he was a magnificent sight.

'Heartbreak for Cardiff!' said the commentator Nigel Starmer-Smith. 'Stu Wilson needed no second invitation!'

Kiernan made observations as the tape rolled, but for him the exercise was not about serious analysis of the opposition's strengths and weaknesses; it was more a matter of letting his players see what the All Blacks looked like, to show them they were not supermen, not without frailties, even if you had to look hard to find them.

Ten of the players selected for Thomond Park had played against Cardiff, including all of the big names, and Seamus Dennison was taking a good look at the tourists' midfield. This was his patch. Dennison could see he was going to be busy, because not only was Wilson coming into the line off the right wing, but Bryan Williams was intruding from the left. When Wilson scored his second try, the Cardiff defence had been caught out by the extra man in their midst, this time Williams.

'What a try by Stu Wilson!' cried Starmer-Smith. 'Well, it was orthodox and superbly executed, the extra man in the outside centre position made by Bryan Williams, who covered across to join them from the left wing to set up Stu Wilson.'

Dennison was a thinker, and he could see he had a problem. Years later, he described the thoughts going through his mind as he sat and watched the All Blacks that night on the video machine, a contraption he had never before laid eyes on.

'I'd played on the wing myself, so I knew the position. You ran up and down your track and that was it – you rarely ventured anywhere else. That was someone else's problem. But these guys were coming into the line and causing havoc. I was asking myself, "What am I going to do if one of them comes in? Do I stay on my own man or do I go in and take him?" For me, it was a straightforward decision. I was going to take him. If I didn't, he'd have a field in front of him. He'd be off like a greyhound, with the rest of them alongside him. There'd be no stopping him. So subconsciously, I knew that if he came in, he was going to be my problem. He would be mine.'

Not everyone found the tape helpful. At the back of the room, unseen by Kiernan and most of the others, Tony Ward crept out. The man upon whom Munster were depending more than any other had been unnerved.

He had arrived in Limerick four years before, as a student down from Dublin. Before long Garryowen got to hear about him. That was the thing with Garryowen: they didn't mind where they got their players, just so long as they were good. They put him in at out-half and after a couple of matches strange things started happening. Road-sweepers and bus conductors and all manner of passers-by started talking to him out of the blue, people he'd never seen before, stopping him in the street and calling him by his name.

'Well Tony, what about Saturday?'

'Aboy Tony, will we beat Shannon?'

'Jesus, Tony, great drop goal, in fairness to you.'

And he thought, '*Tony?* How could these guys know who I am? I'm just a student down from Dublin! This can't happen – fellas sweeping the road don't follow rugby.'

After a handful of appearances in Garryowen's light-blue jersey he found himself named in the team for a Munster Senior Cup final in which his opposite number was Barry McGann, the Cork Constititution, Munster and Ireland out-half. Garryowen were already on the pitch when McGann ran out and saw the man who would soon take his Munster place standing there with his hands on his hips and his socks around his ankles.

'That's all I need,' he said to a fellow Con man. 'A soccer player.'

Tony Ward announced himself that day and won a medal that, at the time, meant nothing to him. He didn't know that all over Limerick city could be found men like Gerry McLoughlin, who would tear down brick walls for a Munster Cup medal. He became a marked man, a trophy for Garryowen's most bitter rivals.

'Kick the film star!' they would roar at Young Munster and Shannon.

He registered also on the radar of the rugby establishment, the die-hard conservatives in the Munster branch. They didn't like him much. He was too flashy, too different, too much of a bloody soccer player. And because his game was based on instinct, there were others who didn't trust him, who threw their hands up in exasperation when some of the spontaneous things he tried didn't come off and he gifted points to the opposition.

Kiernan knew he had an out-half with all the skills necessary to put the All Blacks on the back foot and to take whatever chances might arise. But he also knew that if Ward was caught in possession even once, or if he did something crazy and it backfired, the consequences might be terminal for Munster.

Chapter Sixteen

Tony Ward's Story

Jesus, I was petrified. That night when Kiernan showed us the video, the question running through my mind was: 'Do we have the right to be on the same pitch as these guys?' I was thinking about the haka and how frightening that would be. I was thinking about their rucking. If you got caught on the wrong side of a ruck, you got massacred. Just looking at them on a television screen, all in black, was enough to unnerve me. Everyone said they were invincible, that they would go through their tour unbeaten – and you weren't going to get an argument out of me. I sneaked out of the room. The video might have been helping some of them. It was intimidating me. They looked brilliant, flashing the ball around. It was awesome, total rugby. I was anxious enough as it was. I didn't need that.

I'm a pessimist by nature. I've always been a worrier. Before a big game back then, I would think of all the worst things that could possibly happen. It was like living the pressure before it had happened. In my head, I would take kicks at goal and I would miss. The pressure would mount. How would I deal with it? I'd visualise the match coming down to the last kick, a penalty in front of the posts. Come the hour, come the man. I'd step up to take it. It might sound strange, but it helped me. To bring out the best in me I needed to imagine the worst.

Back in 1978 I believed I was the best out-half in the world. I didn't say it to anybody. I just believed it myself. Once I got out on the pitch, once I'd got the worrying out of my system, I would experience a powerful feeling of inner confidence. The nerves would disappear. I'd feel great about myself. There was no player who worried me, no one I didn't think I could outperform. I don't know where that confidence came from. It was just the way things were then. It made me the player I was – intuitive and instinctive and infuriating all at once. I needed that surge of self-belief, I thrived on it, so when it was taken away from me I was never the same again. It happened the following year, in Australia, but that's another story.

For as long as I can remember, sensitivity has been part of my make-up. I know when I'm wanted and I know when I'm not. There are certain players that you handle with kid gloves, with tender loving care, and I was one of them. When I put on the red Munster shirt I was aware that there were people who idolised me and that made me play better. Later on I played for a Welsh coach who didn't understand the way I was. He used to treat me like he'd treat a Willie Duggan. If you said to Duggan, 'Willie, you're a fucking load of shite', he'd go and play out of his skin. If you said it to me, I would play like every word you'd said was true.

When I was twelve or thirteen I was playing out-half for my school, St Mary's College in Dublin. One day, for some reason, our coach Fr D'Arcy decided to put me on the wing. We were playing Willow Park and I was marking a boy called Joe Rekab. Physically, he was much bigger than me and he was black into the bargain. Back in the sixties, you just didn't see black people in Ireland. I was terrified of him. He scored try after try and I never laid a hand on him. At half-time, Fr D'Arcy rounded on me in the dressing room. 'Ward,' he said, 'where's your party dress?' That hurt.

I was a working-class boy in a middle-class, fee-paying school.

Where I lived, on Priory Road in Harold's Cross, it was soccer, soccer and more soccer. None of my friends had the slightest interest in rugby. I lived in a Corporation house with five women. There was my mother, June, her mother, Elizabeth Donnelly, and three aunts – Renee, Bernie and Ann. My father had died when I was five. I never knew him at all. My mother did two jobs to put me through school, one during the day at the Irish Hospitals' Sweepstakes Trust and the second one four nights a week at the local greyhound tracks. I was very aware that she was working hard to send me to this school, whereas for others it was a lot easier to do it. Did that affect the way I grew up? I suppose it did. Certainly, not having a father affected me. I've only seen the odd photograph of him with me as a baby. My mother was the breadwinner, so she couldn't come to matches at school to watch me. But I realised at the time how fortunate I was to be having the education I was getting.

I didn't know anything about Limerick when I went there as a PE student. I knew practically nothing about Munster rugby, just that Cork Con were from Cork and Garryowen were from Limerick. The first time I played for Munster, Tom Kiernan was coach and we were playing Australia. It was 1976 and Musgrave Park was packed. I was doing well, feeling great. When my hero, Shay Deering, scored a try in injury time, the crowd poured on to the pitch and I had a conversion to level the match.

Standing over that ball, midway out on the right-hand side, I didn't know that Munster had a long history of gallant failure against the touring teams. I did know that for a right-footed player it was the hardest kick in the game. You're expected to get it and it looks easier than it is. The colour writers in the Sunday papers will tell you that all kinds of things go through a player's mind at a moment like this. These days, I'm a journalist myself but colour writing isn't my thing. I can tell you what was going through my head right then, though: nothing. In the heat of the moment, you don't think. You just get on with it. Sometimes it goes over and sometimes it doesn't. That one didn't. Munster lost, but all I can remember is a feeling of a job well done. We had given it a rattle, gone down with all guns blazing. For most people, that was enough.

Kiernan told us that to beat the All Blacks we would have to take every chance that came our way. I was the kicker, so that meant me more than anyone. He got inside me, he knew what I was like. I was always going to worry about the All Blacks before the match, but deep down I felt I would deliver once the whistle blew. All I can tell you is, I felt good about myself at that time. I knew the Munster supporters were with me. I felt I belonged. I was representing them and everything they stood for. They loved me for that and I loved it myself. I'll tell you what hit me when I ran out on to that field. I felt that I was them. We were one and the same.

I knew Tommy Kiernan wanted me in his team. I didn't need to know any more than that. Thomond Park was made for me that day.

Chapter Seventeen

The Killaloe Kids

It was a week for history. To their astonishment, the wives of the Munster branch members were invited to the Bunratty Castle banquet on the night Kiernan showed the video. Bill O'Brien, though, had not lost the run of himself: the tab was being picked up by the De Beers diamond company. Still, it was another bold step down the revolutionary road. They'd be giving the players a free match ticket for their wives next.

Regaled by pretty girls in velvet dresses, the All Blacks enjoyed their night without ever being in danger of a hangover from too much of the house speciality, Bunratty mead. Joe Kennedy enjoyed the company, if not the pageantry. The following morning, Bank Holiday Monday, they made for their training ground, the same school where Don Clarke and Colin Meads had attracted huge crowds fifteen years before. Their box-office appeal had not waned: Crescent College was thronged again as they went through their paces, moving the ball sweetly into the hands of Wilson and Williams and crashing into the tackle bags.

On the other side of town a handful of New Zealand journalists turned up at St Munchin's College to watch the latest opposition train. Kiernan conducted the session in boots and shorts, his voice carrying into the countryside, his face a study in deadly seriousness. At such times he could have, as Moss Keane put it, 'a puss on him that would stop a fucking clock'.

'Move up! Move up now! Go!'

'Jog to the twenty-two, build to the halfway and piss in!'

It was a slick session and after it one of the reporters complimented the coach.

'You've a damned fine team here, Tommy.'

Kiernan shook his head dismissively.

'They're no more than a decent bunch of lads,' he said.

For weeks every rugby follower in the province had been talking down Munster, fearful of what the All Blacks might do to them. Now, on the eve of the game, the last thing Kiernan was going to do was talk them back up, especially in front of a bunch of newspapermen. Instead, he gave them something different for the following day's paper, a seemingly heartfelt tribute to the excellence of the Eighth All Blacks and an endorsement of the theory that they could win every one of their matches.

'I think we would all stand up and cheer if the All Blacks carry on through their tour as impressively as they have started,' he said.

It wasn't for nothing that people said Kiernan was a great politician.

In the afternoon, resplendent in their black blazers, most of the All Blacks went horseracing. Munster fetched up at Killaloe, where four pleasure cruisers took them up Lough Derg. A few were thinking it was a pleasant way to pass an afternoon when they were hit full in the chest by a blast of water that came from nowhere. They looked up and saw that the players in the boat alongside them were shaking with laughter. They looked again and noticed that in between

Tony Ward and Les White someone was holding an empty bucket. It was Kiernan.

All hell broke loose. Buckets, hoses, anything that could be used to propel water from one boat to another was seized upon. Many years later the team secretary Jim Turnbull remembered looking at Kiernan as they stepped off the boats that afternoon and seeing a satisfied man. In his mind's eye Turnbull could still see the happy faces of the players he once served. And he recalled thinking to himself, 'These fellas would die for one another.'

That night at the Royal George hotel Jack Gleeson and Graham Mourie held a team meeting and reminded their players that Munster had a great tradition against the big touring teams and deserved respect. The others wondered when tradition had last decided a rugby match.

There had been one enforced change, with the Number 10 Doug Bruce crying off and being replaced by Eddie Dunn, eight years his junior and his rival for the Test position. The implications for Munster appeared not to amount to much. Both were gifted players, Bruce the more durable, Dunn blessed with the capacity for unexpected brilliance. The late replacement, it seemed, was the coming man of the Blacks' backline. 'I shall remember him for a long time,' Carwyn James had said of him the previous week after the Cardiff match. 'That little chip over the top, that grub kick, that offer of a feint pass, that foray on the blindside – it was all thinking stuff, very fine, the mark of a good player.' To this tribute, no less a judge than Barry John had added: 'He has hands, rhythm, a head. He is a beautiful player.'

No one in the Square Bar could find optimism at the bottom of a pint glass. Sean Healy, the younger of the brothers who had been brought up in a tenement flat around the corner, would often argue that anything could happen with a crooked ball. ''Tis the day that's in it, nothing else,' he would say. 'The eighty minutes that's there.' But he thought better of making a case for Munster. Sean was fifty-two now, his brother Stephen fifty-four. Between them they had put down seventy years plastering the walls of Limerick. Stephen had bow legs from years of carrying bags of plaster up ladders and even now the blurring speed at which he and Sean went about their work intimidated lesser men who made their living with a hawk and darby.

Fifteen years after they had seen Munster go so close against the Fifth All Blacks, the cut and thrust of the front row still informed most of their rugby conversation. They had never stopped fighting the cause of Limerick props, of damning the kind of injustice that cost men like their old friend Ter Casey an armful of caps. The latest victim of anti-Limerick bias, they strongly believed, was Gerry McLoughlin. In Stephen's view, it was a disgrace that Ireland had over-looked him for the All Blacks Test the following Saturday. A disgrace, but hardly a surprise.

'You'd want to go away to a monastery for a month to try and figure out the Irish selectors,' Sean would say.

Neither brother expected to see the All Blacks beaten on Irish soil in their lifetime. The 1963 team had given their all and come up short. They were some of the finest men ever sent out by Munster and people still talked about the day Mac Herewini saved the All Blacks' bacon. But this team? Based on the evidence of their London tour, they'd be lucky to keep the margin of defeat down to twenty points.

'Isn't that right, Stephen?'

'That's right, Sean.'

In Cork, Dan Canniffe was watching *The Joe Louis Story* on television when his daughter Deirdre rang. She asked if he had made up his mind about travelling to see Donal lead out

Munster and volunteered to take him. But Dan said he wouldn't bother. It wasn't that he feared for his son and Munster; he just didn't feel up to it. It was a pity, but Donal would not want for support.

Thanks to a little manoeuvring by Kiernan, Gerry McLoughlin lay down in a hotel room that night, the only Limerick-based player afforded the privilege. With an eighteen-month-old baby at home he needed his night's sleep, Locky had protested. He had to be ready for everything Gary Knight could throw at him. He wasn't to know that Knight had been taken by Gleeson to a doctor's surgery earlier in the day, where Morgan Costelloe had examined blistering below the ear on the right side of his face and said it looked suspiciously like the early onset of facial herpes, otherwise know as scrum-pox.

Better to give it time to clear up, the doctor said, but with his other tighthead prop Billy Bush less than right Gleeson felt he didn't have that luxury. They agreed that if Knight's face was no worse the following day he should play, with his face protected by bandages.

Locky liked to know as much about the man facing him as possible. If the newspaper had it right, Knight had some serious credentials:

Name: Gary Knight
Born: 1951 (same as himself)
Birthplace: Wellington
Province: Manawatu
Height: 6ft 2in (three inches taller)
Weight: 17st 3lb (two stone heavier)
Occupation: Salesman
Nickname: Axle
Other: Champion wrestler of New Zealand, 1973.

Competed in 1974 Commonwealth Games. Won bronze medal (over 100kg class).

But could he scrummage, really scrummage? That's what Locky was thinking when the lights went out on the night before the big match.

Chapter Eighteen

The First Half

Brendan Foley: I was up early on the morning of the match. I had work to do, selling cases of minerals to pubs and shops. They gave me a half-day so I could play against the All Blacks, so I put my gear in the back of the car and drove from place to place, taking orders. People stopped me to talk about the match; fellas on their morning break, women out doing their shopping, asking if Munster had any chance. I said, 'Yeah, we'll give it a go, give it our best shot, see what happens.' They expected that much from us. If we were going down, we had to go down fighting. That was our tradition.

Johnny Cole, touch judge: My boots were finely polished from the night before. Shorts were snow-white, creases would cut the finger off you. I always made sure I looked the part. There was no free gear then. I drove down the town. I could see the crowds gathering, people drinking outside Flannery's pub, people making their way over the bridge. Sammy Benson's marching band was playing behind me, fifty or sixty kids in green cloaks and yellow monkey hats, blowing trumpets and banging drums, spread out across the road, stopping the traffic. The potholes were full of rainwater. It lashed down that morning, but now the sun was coming out, right on cue for the match. Just as I got to the ground, the All Blacks' bus pulled in. The driver reversed and parked in front of the Shannon clubhouse, getting a good spot. The All Blacks got off the bus. I could see these guys. Awesome people. Frightening.

Susan Healy, Munster supporter: My father's name was Stephen Healy. He lived for two things – rugby and us, his family. My brothers didn't play rugby. I used to feel sorry for my dad over that. I'd say, 'If I was a boy I'd be playing for you.' I had a very close bond with him. I hung out of him, hung on his every word. I was only a girl when Munster played the All Blacks but I knew he'd take me with him. He took me everywhere. Even when he was going off to a match in Cork, and the car was full of his friends, he'd say, 'Don't worry, I'll squeeze you in.'

Afterwards we'd go to the pub, along with my Uncle Sean and the rest of the gang – Donal Brock, Sean Mac, Joker Plunkett, Dollars Mulcahy, Willie Ahern, Sky Kenyon, Phonsie O'Donnell. Lots of them and one of me, but they didn't mind and I loved being there with them. They were the real people. We'll never see their like again.

I'd sit alongside my father and listen to the stories and the banter, just taking it all in. I was learning about the game. Sometimes I might be afraid that I'd read something wrong. I'd say to him, 'What did you think of that, Dad?' And if my father said something about a match, that was gospel for me. I wouldn't care what anybody else thought.

That day we set off on foot after lunch along with my mother, Kitty. It was pure excitement. Uncle Sean was long gone. It was too big a day; he was in the pub early. Half cut when he got to Thomond Park. The plan was that we'd meet on the popular side, on the halfway line, but there were so many people there we were pushed down further, squeezed in like sardines.

Paul Cochrane, All Blacks supporter: We arrived at the ground in our transit van. We called her The Grey Mare. We'd bought her in London, especially for the tour. We travelled all over Britain and Ireland in her – four of us, all from New Zealand, all rugby mad. We were young and we didn't have much money, but we knew we were going to have a great time. Munster was the first of three matches in Ireland. Not in a million years did we think there was even the slightest chance that the All Blacks might lose. We were there to have a good time and to see another All Blacks victory.

The night before the match, we were drinking in this bar in Limerick when Dave Leggoe pointed over and said, 'Look, it's Stu Wilson!' He'd come into the bar with another All Black, can't remember who now. He told us they'd escaped from the hotel. He was in great form, buzzing. We asked him about the Munster match . . .

'What do you reckon, Stu? Pretty straightforward, right?'

'Yeah, shouldn't be a problem, guys.'

I don't remember him staying out on the town very late, but I do remember that he was confident, very confident. He'd been scoring a lot of tries, plus he knew the All Blacks had never lost in Ireland before. He was like the rest of us, thinking ahead to the Test match against Ireland on the Saturday.

At Thomond Park we stood on the side opposite the stand, between the ten-metre line and the twenty-two. There weren't that many All Blacks supporters there, partly because the tour had been put together late, partly because some of the New Zealanders who lived in London had planned to go to Wales, not Ireland. Nobody expected anything much to happen in Ireland – and certainly not in Limerick.

Gerry McLoughlin: The first time to do anything is hard. First Cup medal. First time to play for your country. First Irish team to beat the All Blacks. It's only human to have doubts. You don't know if you can do it or not. Outside of Munster, people made you feel you weren't good enough. But Kiernan put the belief into us. He convinced us we could do it.

He went through the whole thing, but Kiernan was a back. I knew that when it came to surviving in the front row that day, I was going to be on my own. You only get an opportunity like that once in a lifetime. I was thinking, 'This is it, Gerry. This is it. You've got to do the business.' I thought I was good enough to take anybody on, but I had to prove it. Not to myself, but to other people.

There'd be fellas only waiting to have a go off me if I didn't stand up. Things were different then. They'd support Munster on the big days, but once the match was over they'd be Garryowen again, or Young Munsters. They were the kind of people who lived and breathed rugby, people who knew what they were talking about. They'd have loved it. They'd have said, 'You went backwards on the big day.'

Colm Tucker: The warm-up was like a war zone. Steel studs hopping off concrete ground. People were smoking fags. Somebody said, 'Open the fucking window, we're going to die in here.' The old dressing rooms were long and narrow, about ten feet across by twenty feet long, everybody in on top of everybody. Donal Canniffe wanted a bit of treatment from Vincent O'Connor, our masseur.

'What's the problem?' Vincent says.

'It's my ribs, they're a bit sore,' Canniffe says.

176

'Put your arms up, so.'

Vincent could put a rib cartilage back into place with his hands. He was gifted, but sometimes what he did hurt you. Next thing Canniffe did a lineout jump in the dressing room.

'Go way from me for fuck's sake!'

I always made sure my gear bag was perfect. I'd take out my boots, my gumshield, everything. Just to make sure it was all there. Then I'd check it again.

Locky never checked anything. He'd drive you mad, looking for his stuff.

'Boots!'

'They're there in front of you.'

'Bandage!'

'In your bag. Sit over there will you, Locky? Jesus Christ!'

Gerry McLoughlin: Pa Whelan was our hooker. He always wanted me to do things his way, but you should never give in to your hookers. They can be a selfish breed. Ninety per cent of them are more interested in personal duels than the result of the match. I wouldn't say myself and Pa were ever that close. We respected each other, though – in our own way. You have to be slightly mad to be a hooker. And Whelan was slightly mad. You let him worry about himself. He didn't worry about the props.

I didn't want anyone telling me what I had to do – not Whelan, not Kiernan, nobody. There's nothing anyone can do for you when you're getting kicked in the head. You're the one who has to take the punishment. In the end, it comes down to determination. Do you or don't you want to survive?

I knew better than anyone, I didn't need to be told. At half-time in a match once, Noel Murphy sent the physio out to me with a note. Written on this piece of paper was: 'McLOUGHLIN, KEEP THE SCRUM UP'. I nearly gave the fucking physio a kick up the arse. How dare anyone tell me what to do?

Whelan knew I was a destructive type of animal. He knew he could rely on me, didn't put any extra pressure on me, let me do my own thing. In the front row, you either know it or you don't. He allowed me the latitude to bring out what was in me.

I was on my home ground. I was ready. And I was bitter. Tucker was the same. We were bitter because we'd never been capped, never got any recognition. We had been through Munster Cup campaigns every bit as difficult as international campaigns, the way we saw it. This was a chance for the elite in Dublin 4 to come down and see what could be done by the boys who weren't recognised. Normally, wild horses wouldn't drag them down to Limerick.

In the changing room I stuck my head under the bench and started driving against the wall. What if Gary Knight caught me in a bad position? I had to be ready for the worst-case scenario. If the pressure was coming down on me, the last thing I wanted to do was give away penalties.

Brendan Foley: Tommy always had a theory that two guys wouldn't play well on the day. Which two was it going to be? I was sitting there thinking, 'Please God I won't be one of them.'

Colm Tucker: Then Donal Canniffe told us, 'Today, in this red jersey, we are representing the people of Munster.'

I went out on that field feeling like a giant.

Johnny Cole: Munster ran out after the All Blacks and the people in the stand banged their feet on the floor. Because it was a wooden stand, the noise was so loud it felt like their feet were going to come through the floor on top of me. We went out ourselves then. The gateman held the gate for us, and we ran on to the pitch. Inside my stomach the butterflies were dancing around with hobnail boots.

Gerry McLoughlin: Just before the kick-off they took a team photograph, for posterity, but I don't remember that. The All Blacks did the haka – I don't remember much about that either. All I was thinking of was the first scrum. I loved to scrummage against a tall prop and Gary Knight was tall. He had a scrum cap on and his face was covered in bandages, but I wasn't bothered about that. It was the last thing on my mind. The only thing I was thinking was, 'I've got to hold him. I've got to show him I'm going to be able to handle him.'

Most people haven't got a clue what happens in a scrum, but I'll tell you. Back then, I never passed on any knowledge to anyone, not even my own brother, in case they might get the better of me.

Every scrum I ever went into, I set the agenda. I had to make sure the rest of them were as focused as me, especially the back-row forwards. I mean, *somebody* had to make sure that the importance of the scrum was fully understood. As props, our heads were on the block. Nobody blames the back row if the scrum goes back.

It's a war, right? You're trying to break people in two and stop them from breathing. You're trying to put his head in his chest so he's thinking about other things. A man is only as strong as his weakest point. So you take him at his weakest point – the top of his head, the pole. That takes experience, a lot of technique and a lot of trickery. You've got to make sure you fool the referee, distract his attention.

You're thinking, thinking, thinking position. It's not about speed into the scrum, it's about picking your spot. And the best position hurts you. The blood is rushing to your head. You're in a pain zone. But you know the other guy is suffering more. He can't breathe. He can't support his neck. You know he's going to crack, you can feel the weakness coming. And then he gives. Half an inch is all you need. You know you have him, there's no way back for him. He splits out from his second row. He's got no one behind him and you drive through him.

Donal Canniffe: Tommy had told us that any ball that we got, we had to put it back behind their forwards, so that their momentum was reversed. If they're going back, you've got them moving in the right direction. We had to stop them before they crossed the gain line. We knew going out that we were going to spend our afternoon tackling. We expected them to be stronger and fitter, and able to last the pace better than us if it came down to the wire. So we had to put them out of their stride, make them go backwards to retrieve the ball, so that they couldn't get enough momentum to hurt us. That was the theory, anyway. That was the plan.

Colm Tucker: At the kick-off, I went straight in and hit some fella and this guy turned around and looked at my number. 'You're number seven,' he said. As if to say, 'Your card is marked, I have your number, you're in for some special treatment.' 'And you're number five,' I said. 'We'll be meeting each other during the game. Have a nice game now.'

If I hadn't stood up, I'd have been gone. From then on it was all commitment to the cause, absolutely ferocious commitment. If you got a slap, you just got up and gave one back. I can remember getting a kick on the back of the head and the crowd going, 'It's number five!'

Gerry McLoughlin: Usually they go low, the Fran Cottons of this world, they try to get under you. And if you come up against a prop who's an almighty scrummager – fierce and dynamic and low to the ground, with a big second-row behind him, or an eight-man shove – all of a sudden you know you're going to have a torrid time. You're going to spend the whole eighty minutes just trying to hold him. And then where's your energy going to come from for the rest of the match?

Gary Knight: I used to be a wrestler. It's a sport that sets you up well for playing in the front row, that one-on-one element. I liked to keep low to the ground, that's the way I scrummaged. You've got to keep the other guy low, but never let him go to the ground. If he does that, you've failed. It's all about keeping him low and sustaining that pressure until he reaches breaking point.

Gerry McLoughlin: The first scrum happened in the first minute, over on the far side of the pitch. It was our ball. That meant more pressure. It meant we were expected to win it. You'd prefer their ball first off, because it gives you a chance to get into it. You've got eight guys pushing against seven. There was twelve thousand people looking at that scrum. Practically everyone I knew in Limerick was there, scattered all over the ground, or sitting on the wall on the far side, looking down on that scrum, waiting to see what was going to happen.

That was the moment of truth for me – the All Black Test prop pushing against me on our ball. In the front row, it's easy to be confident if you know you're good enough. But when you scrummage a guy for the first time, especially somebody with Gary Knight's reputation, you never know what you're up against until you feel the pressure and you find out what he's got, what his technique is. After a few seconds, you can tell and so can he. You know if you're going to do a job on him, or if he's going to do a job on you.

We went down and straight away I knew I was going to be able to scrummage as I wanted. I knew I wasn't going to have a problem with Gary Knight. Jesus Christ, it was a huge boost to get in the first minute of the match. I'm not saying he was a bad scrummager. All I'm saying is I could handle him.

Les [White] was doing a job for us. He was a decent player and I had a good bond with him. So I'm thinking, 'We're going to be fine here', when next thing the pressure comes through on the tighthead side, they start driving forward and Les gets shoved backwards. That came as a shock to me. The angle was right getting in. We were set. The wheel was ready, but it was a slow heel. You could have said Pa Whelan didn't hook the ball fast enough. But then again, far be it for me to blame the hooker. Because you wouldn't know what hookers would be up to.

Tom Kiernan: First we missed the catch from the kick-off, then we lost the first scrum badly. I was sitting in the stand, alongside the selectors. And I'm a bad man to watch a match, always was. I can't help myself. I'll say, 'Why did he do that? Why didn't he do the other thing?'

Stu Wilson: Five minutes in, we were fine and I was feeling great. I was thinking, 'Let's put some points on the board here.' So we pulled one of our favourite moves, which involved me coming in from the blindside wing. And it looked good. The links in the chain were all there. The ball came to half-back from the forwards, it went through the inside backs, Lyn Jaffray popped up to me and just as I came on to the ball I could see it, that hole, the same hole that had opened up in the earlier matches on the tour. I thought, 'This is great!' I could see everything unfolding. It was perfect.

Seamus Dennison: Some people think tackling is about bravery and fearlessness, putting your body on the line and dying for the jersey. They're wrong. Any pigeon can throw himself at somebody. What matters is whether you make it count. More than anything, tackling is about timing. And if your timing is right, it doesn't matter how small you are. For years I worked at getting it down to a fine art. I was so small, I had to. If you're eleven stone and the guy coming at you weighs fifteen or sixteen, you're not going to take him down with brute force. But that doesn't mean you can't take him down.

It's all about when the contact is made – and who is deciding when it's made. If I'm running up to tackle a guy and he's carrying the ball, he has all the advantage and I'm going to get milled. But if I can create a situation where I hit him before he's expecting contact, then the advantage is mine. If I come up at a certain pace, and then in the last two or three strides I go quicker, I'm going to hit him before he's expecting to be hit. It might only be a foot, but every inch is going to hurt him. It's a mind thing. It's not how fast you are or how big or how strong you are. It's all about getting yourself into the position you need to be in.

I saw Wilson hovering. As soon as he came in, it was going to be up to me to go and take him. I wasn't focused on him, because I had Bruce Robertson to worry about. But I was conscious of him being there. Hovering. Then he made his move, and I made mine.

Stu Wilson: I got the ball and then I got the spot tackle with it. The hole just closed on me and this little fella absolutely blew me back. He just propelled straight into my ribcage. It was a great tackle. That's the worst thing you can get, man and ball together, especially when you're not expecting it. I was thinking, 'Why's he here? He shouldn't be here! There should be a nice little hole there for me to run through.'

Seamus Dennison: I poleaxed him. It was just dandy. His body direction was facing me and I hit him straight on with my shoulder, a right good thump. I buried him and that was it. He went down and I went down. I knew I had him. I knew by the contact. And I knew he wasn't expecting me to make the contact that I made. I was fairly handy at the old tackling. My shoulder was sore, but I knew I was all right. I was up before he was, anyway.

Corris Thomas, referee: It was the most incredible tackle I ever saw in seventeen years as a referee. Stuart Wilson came through at a hundred miles an hour on a switch ball and it was literally as if he had run into a brick wall and just slid down it. He collapsed in a heap. He didn't go backwards. He just crumpled. I looked around and every Munster player had grown twelve inches. You could sense it, you really could. I'm not being romantically reflective; it was a hard-nosed observation I made at the time. I thought, 'These guys are bigger than they were when they ran on a few minutes ago.' It happened in the middle of the park and of course the crowd reacted, but it wasn't a wild cheer. It was like, 'Phwooah!' Gasps, really.

With a collision like that you expect both players to go off. You stand nearby and try to avert your gaze if there's blood. But they got up and carried on. I thought, 'Oh my God! We're in for a game here today.' In that one tackle, Seamus Dennison confirmed the reality to the Munster team. The reality that they could win.

Greg Barrett: It was a big psychological moment. It proved to us that what Tommy had been saying all along was actually true. They were the same as everyone else. They were only ordinary guys.

Larry Moloney: End of the day, it's fifteen guys against fifteen guys. End of the day.

Stu Wilson: So then I was thinking, 'Oh well, that didn't work. They obviously saw that move, or else they heard about it. But, typical All Blacks, we thought, 'If this doesn't work once we're not going to just throw it out the window.' So we had another crack at it ten minutes later. We shifted the same move out one further. Instead of running in around the inside centre, the hole we were trying to create for me went inside the outside centre. Next thing I know, I'm on the floor again. Same guy, same tackle, same result. I got smashed. With this one, I think it might have hurt him just as much. It was a gang tackle, that one. A few other guys came in after him, just to make sure I wasn't getting up.

Seamus Dennison: Mossie Finn came over and said, 'He's still down! You're all right, get up!'

Moss Finn: Wilson was disgusted. You could see it in his eyes. It was, 'The cheek of that little fucker to tackle me, with my level of ability'. There was a stare in his eye after it was over. It was a real condescending leer.

Stu Wilson: So I was going, 'Heck, I've been brought in twice, on one of my favourite moves, and the hole has been created but somehow the hole closed on me and I got beaten up by two big tackles. If this keeps up I'm going to be fodder.'

I wasn't that keen to get smashed like that. I was expecting holes.

Seamus Dennison: Shortly after that second tackle, we were back in much the same situation and I told Moss Finn and Greg that they were going to do the same thing again, and that this time they were going to skip Wilson. This was their other move. They would bring him in there, commit me to taking him and then they'd miss him and give it to Robertson. I said to Greg, 'Make sure you come in and make sure Moss is ready to come in again.' We couldn't have him standing outside on his own, leaving gaps open. There was no way they were coming through. Our discipline was unreal. Nobody was going to let the team down, or let Tommy down. Just wasn't going to happen. Whatever it took, that's what we were going to give. Because we were all in it together. It was shit or bust.

Graham Mourie: As a touring team you expect to be put under pressure by good sides in the early part of the game. But you expect to come back. You know you're fitter than them. You've got to soak it up and then play.

Susan Healy: My father was taking it all in. At first, he was quiet, thinking away to himself. People who didn't know him might have thought he wasn't even reacting, but he was. You just had to look at his face. He loved watching the scrums. He'd tell me what was going on in the front row. He'd say, 'In there, you'll do anything to survive.'

Gerry McLoughlin: Second scrum, we had to hold them. We had to set out our stall. We had learned our lesson from the first one. I knew I had the measure of my man – I wasn't going to be driven around the place. That meant I could be more accommodating to Les on the other side of the scrum. I could be a team player. I'd played tighthead all my life so I knew what it was like for him. I was thinking, 'Now, Gerry, now's your chance to show that selfishness mustn't enter your play. You must give Les the advantage that you've always demanded.'

Les White: I was thirty-four and I'd never been an international, so this was it for me, the biggest match of my life. That's the way I was looking at it. I wasn't six feet tall and six feet wide with no neck, so I had to have technique. And playing in that Munster front row was hard. Whelan would have us driving a scrummaging machine up against a brick wall in training. He was aggressive then, but when he came up against real opposition – when the first contact was about to be made – he would go mad. I can't recall his exact words. Let's just say he was a great exponent of the F-word.

Gerry McLoughlin: The push came on and they couldn't budge us. Some people were surprised by that, but they shouldn't have been. I was the guy doing two hundred scrums a night at Shannon, not Gary Knight. Why should he be the one to budge me? Just because he was wearing a black jersey? It didn't work like that.

Brendan Foley: Locky never lacked faith in his own scrummaging ability. He was a fair prop, no doubt about it. He didn't care who the other guy was – the contest was only going one way as far as he was concerned. It didn't matter if he was playing for Shannon, for Ireland or the Lions. He nearly got us killed in South Africa once. He gave an interview to the paper the day before a Test match. We were short four or five of our best players and they had a massive pack. He told the newspaper reporter that he reckoned we'd take the Springboks up front, that they were weak in the scrum.

When it came to being a team player, Locky would mean well. It was just that he couldn't help himself. He had his own theories on scrummaging, which didn't tally with ours.

He wanted to come in on the prop and hooker to stop them striking for the ball. When he was caught up in the excitement of it, when he could feel that he was grinding the other guy down, he'd often drift. He wouldn't look any worse for that, which was important to Locky, but it wasn't much use for the tightness of the scrum. If you haven't the eight tight, you're going to be blown apart. We didn't want him drifting, we wanted to shove.

I was behind him that day, so it was up to me to control him, and the only way to make him tighten up was to grab him by the balls. He did whatever you wanted then. Once you had him by the balls, the rest of him followed. I stretched out my right hand to him once. I said, 'See that hand, Gerry? That hand was the making of you. You'd be nothing without me.'

Donal Canniffe: The first ball I got, I put up what I thought was going to be a good garryowen. That's what you did at Thomond Park against the touring teams, because you knew the crowd were going to give their full-back hell. This time, it went too far. It was an easy ball for a quality full-back, but [Brian] McKechnie made a mess of it, dropped it in the middle of the park. A huge roar went up.

Donal Spring: I was chasing Canniffe's up-and-under when McKechnie dropped it and the whistle blew. I heard it, but I kept running anyway, because I was nearly at McKechnie by then. I walked up to him and said, 'You're finished! You'll never catch anything today!'

Gerry McLoughlin: Kiernan told us we had to get to the lineouts faster than them. He said we couldn't allow them to get any psychological advantage, because they can be intimidating if they get there fast. If they're all in place, waiting, and you arrive in dribs and drabs, you're in trouble before the ball is thrown in.

They had Andy Haden and Frank Oliver, two of the best jumpers in the world, so we didn't think we were going to win a lot of ball. We were trying to disrupt their lineouts. Everything was illegal, that's the way it was. Rugby was all about how well you could bend the laws. My game was barging. I liked to be number three in the line because you could disrupt more there. I considered myself an expert at pulling guys down and stopping them from doing things. You had to do it, because usually they'd have some prima donna jumping. When that guy went for a ball, he was jumping against a prop and another jumper, which isn't easy. You're there and you've got a job to do and the first thing you do is play the referee. With Corris Thomas, I felt that you could get away with things. And once you feel like that, you use it to your advantage. I'm not sure if I should be telling you all this. When this comes out, I'll have to leave the country.

Brendan Foley: After about ten minutes we got a lineout over the far side. We used three code words for our signals – 'scrum' for the front of the line, 'half' for the middle and 'wing' for the back. Canniffe would call the throw. He'd shout out three letters, but only the middle one would count. If he said 'R-U-G', the U in the middle would mean the ball would be going to the front. That's where I was standing. The ball was called to me. I took it and drove up a couple of yards and the next time I saw it, Wardy had it in his hands and he was running right to left across the pitch.

Moss Finn: Wardy was far and away the best player in the world at that stage, there's no doubt about that. But there was a weakness in his game which they didn't pick up on. He came off his left leg all the time because he could jink off it.

Tony Ward: When the scrum-half's hands were on the ball, and I knew it was coming my way, I usually had a Plan A in my mind. But that went out the window once I took the ball. I just reacted. I never knew what I was going to do, which could be infuriating for the people playing with me. But equally, a gap might open out of nothing. Canniffe found me and I did the first thing that came into my head. It was just a chip; it could have gone either way. But it was placed deliberately as an attacking ploy. I just hoped it was going to work in our favour.

Donal Canniffe: Wardy sent it almost flat across the field. It was one of the worst cross-kicks of his life. It was far too shallow.

Jimmy Bowen: These days you'd shoot Wardy for that kick. Who would ever chip it in their own half? I thought he was going to kick it long, which a normal out-half would have done – put it down into the far corner. Then all of a sudden it was chipped over, so I followed through.

Stu Wilson: Tony Ward was a class player. They had absolutely no intention of moving the ball through to their wing-threequarters: it was never going to go further than Ward. He banged one down towards me and it just jagged badly, typical of a rugby ball. One minute I thought it was coming my way, the next I was on the floor and the ball was gone.

Jimmy Bowen: I didn't have to break my stride. The ball bounced perfectly, waist high, and it came into my arms. I was gone past Wilson before he knew what was happening. It all opened up in front of me. I just seemed to go away and I was gathering momentum. By the time the full-back came up to me, I was flying.

Brian McKechnie: The ball landed in between me and our backline. I was too far back to get near it. It was one of those ones where you think, 'There's no way I'm going to get to this on the full.' So I just stopped and waited to see what was going to happen. It bounced straight up in the air and straight into this guy's hands. I mean, it couldn't have bounced any better for him. He came flying upfield and I was the last man back. I was standing flat-footed and he was running full tilt. He just shot round me. I never got anywhere near him.

Susan Healy: I felt my arm being grabbed, so tightly that it hurt me. It was my father. I looked up at him and his face was purple. He just erupted. There was a string of words; I can't remember what they were. He was roaring. He'd seen that something was about to happen. He was good like that. Nearly every time he got excited, there would be a score. You didn't know where the excitement had come from – it seemed to come out of nowhere – but really it had been building and building. It happened so fast, I thought he was going to explode.

Jimmy Bowen: I kept running. I thought I could make it all the way. Somebody dived and got a hand on my ankle but he couldn't hold me. I was only ten yards left of the posts. Then I saw Bryan Williams, coming across from their left wing and I thought, 'He's going to get me. I'm not going to make it.' So I changed direction, checked back inside. Somebody launched himself at me but I stayed on my feet. I turned around and there was more Munster fellas than All Blacks. Greg Barrett had come on my outside, Christy Cantillon had come on the inside. Christy had made up huge ground.

Gerry McLoughlin: It just shows you how hard Christy Cantillon was scrummaging.

Christy Cantillon: The ball hit me in the chest and I caught it on the rebound. Then I remember looking to see the line and thinking, 'I'll never get there.' Next thing, I'd hit the line. We all just jumped up in the air. Unbelievable.

Brendan Foley: The crowd behind the goal were dancing around the place when Jimmy was running towards the line. There was so many of them, they spilled on to the grass behind the posts. Then Christy dived over the line and there was total bedlam. Kids jumping up and down, older fellas going wild with the excitement of it. Just as I was turning to run back to our half, this coat went up in the air, in between the posts. I can still see that coat clearly, it's one of my abiding memories of the day.

Gerry McLoughlin: My father was under the stand. He'd taken my brother Pat with him. Pat was about fourteen then and my father had lost him. Next thing he saw him behind the goal when Christy Cantillon scored the try. There was about twelve of them playing rugby behind the posts. Nobody had expected the All Blacks to be defending their own line, so that was their field. Nobody had noticed them.

Johnny Cole: I was the only Munster man in the ground who couldn't cheer. That's because I had a job to do, running the line. The other touch judge was a Dubliner, Martin Walsh. It's true there wasn't that much responsibility on us, but there we are in the photograph with the Munster team. Part of history now, you could say.

I was on the stand side and Jimmy Bowen passed me like an express train. There's a try then so I run around by the posts. The crowd are going delirious and Martin says, 'Jaysus, a great score.' I was gasping. Tony Ward takes the ball for the conversion and Martin says, 'I'll go back, you go forward.' We'd always look at one another before we put up the flags but by then the crowd had everybody told and Munster were 6–0 up against the All Blacks.

Joe McCarthy, cameraman: I was the cameraman who shot the Munster try. The film of it that they're still showing today – that was mine, I know it was mine. After the match people started cribbing, saying the pictures weren't up to scratch, that the players were too far away, but they didn't know what they were talking about. In actual fact, I did well to get what I got.

I was a freelance cameraman, living in Cork. RTE called me up and said they had a job for me – Munster and the All Blacks. I had my own camera – an Arriflex sixteen millimetre, fixed on a tripod. I loved sport and I understood it. That's a big advantage if you're a cameraman at a match. Before the match a builder arrived in a truck to put up a temporary scaffold in front of the stand, twelve feet off the ground, with two ladders leading up to it. We were a bit low down but you had to take what they gave you – there was no room in the stand for cameras. We told them we wanted to put the scaffold up near the halfway line but somebody said, 'No, I don't want you going too near, the crowd will be too big there.'

They sent us down near the twenty-five-yard line. I mean, it wasn't exactly the best position. Afterwards people came out of every corner, giving out like hell about all sorts of things. They said RTE should have sent the outside broadcast unit, but that wasn't the way things worked then. Outside broadcasts were rare.

Even though it was single-camera coverage, we had two cameras. The idea was not to miss a score. The other cameraman was Pat Kavanagh, down from Dublin. When my magazine ran out after ten minutes he'd take over while I loaded more film. Then I'd take over from him. Of course, Christy Cantillon's try was on the wrong side of the pitch for us. I followed the ball all the way to the line. Afterwards, Nigel Starmer-Smith of the BBC said we'd done very well. He knew what he was talking about. The other fellas didn't.

I was delighted when they scored the try, but it didn't mean they were going to hold on to the lead. I was thinking, 'The All Blacks might come back and score six tries.'

Bruce Robertson: After their guy went over for the try I looked down at my leg and there was blood coming out of it. Just as I'd tried to tackle him his boot had caught me and cut it open. I knew that was it for me, the gash was too deep. But then it wasn't as if I'd been playing very well. Every time I ran at them I was hitting a red brick wall.

I limped off the pitch and the doctor said I'd need stitches. He said, 'I hope you don't mind, but would it be okay if I stitched your leg up after the game?' He said he didn't want to miss anything. I said, 'Okay doc, that's fine.' I went up and sat alongside Jack Gleeson and the rest of the guys. I was thinking, 'Things can only get better.'

Seamus Dennison: Robertson went off and they brought this big hoor called Bill Osborne into the centre, alongside Jaffray. They should have had him there in the first place. Jaffray was the weak link.

Graham Mourie: Sometimes it's easier to defend, if that's all you're focused on doing. Once they got ahead they became fanatical. You can use all the clichés and superlatives you want to describe their tackling, but the facts are the facts. They were just not going to let us get over the advantage line.

Colm Tucker: They came back like a shot, hit us for fucking ten, threw the whole kitchen sink at us. If you went down on the ball, God be with you. You were taken away with the ball and all. The All Blacks shoed a lot that day – but that's the game they played. If you're on the wrong side of a ruck you must accept the consequences. And the consequences were that you were going to get shoed off the ball.

Tom Kiernan: For the next fifteen minutes they pounded us. The pressure was savage.

Colm Tucker: I remember one ball bobbling on our line. Wardy took it and they were expecting him to kick for touch. He put a grubber kick through from outside, Dennison came on to the ball and we ended up back down on their line.

Next thing there was a kick ahead and the full-back, McKechnie, caught the ball and he was shaping to pass. As he got it away I came in on top of him and I hit him in the midriff. And a split-second after I hit him, Greg Barrett came in and gave him another pasting. We cut him in two. 'Jesus,' I said, 'this fella's fucking dead.' It was a double-impact tackle. But he just got up off the field.

Donal Canniffe: You could see McKechnie was shaky. About five minutes after the try we got a penalty over on the stand side. Wardy took a kick at goal, but he didn't make great contact with it. It started drifting left of the posts. McKechnie was there waiting for it, under no pressure.

Brian McKechnie: The previous one had bounced straight up in the air and this time it was one of those kicks where he didn't strike it that well. My first reaction was to let it go, to let it bounce over the dead-ball line. Then I thought, 'What if it bounces back infield or something like that? If that happens, we're in trouble.' So I went to catch it and I missed.

Gerry McLoughlin: Stupid knock-on, scrum to us virtually on their line. And for the front-row forwards, this was a big scrum, the biggest of the match. If they were any good – if they were as good as people said they were – they were going to drive us off that ball. People watching a match see a scrum on the line and they think, 'They're putting everything into this, everything they've got in the tank.' But it doesn't work like that, not with me anyway. I could never lift the tempo on my own line or on their line – it would be the same through-out the whole field. Every single scrum was important and that meant you got the feel then. If you're being honest throughout the whole field, you know exactly what's happening. You can't hold yourself back, take a rest and put the emphasis on the big scrums. You just can't do it.

He should have been down trying to drive me back in that scrum, but he didn't do it. I was able to get under him. I was comfortable and I wasn't going back one inch.

Gary Knight: We couldn't budge them. We were just totally cleaned out. Their tails were up. That's all there was to it.

Gerry McLoughlin: We knew after that. We just knew. We thought, 'If they can't do it there, they're not going to do it anywhere.'

Gary Knight: When you're a touring team, when you're the All Blacks, wherever you go to play it's a big deal. You know that for a lot of those players it's the most important game of the year. Sometimes it means more. Sometimes it's the biggest game of their lifetime. And, to me, it felt like that's what we were up against. They threw everything at us. They just kept coming.

Tony Ward: Our pack were doing their job, holding the scrum. I stood back in the pocket, waiting for the ball to come to me.

Fred Cogley, TV commentary: Munster right on the All Black line, Canniffe puts in, Ward waits. That's Ward. A drop at goal . . . it's over!

Tom Kiernan: God, he could do that in his sleep, Wardy. He was an instinctive player and people didn't know him.

Ron Palenski, New Zealand journalist: A few of us had walked around the ground before the game. We had sensed from the atmosphere that the day was going to be something special. You do sense these things, sometimes, in sport. Even before the score was 6–0 or 9–0, we didn't think the All Blacks would win. It was the level of commitment from Munster, the atmosphere in the ground, the body language of the All Blacks.

Stu Wilson: At 9–0 down we weren't panicking. We thought, 'We're getting pinged a bit, but the opportunities will come.' We had three-quarters of the match to come back. But Mourie was a little bit frustrated because we were going backwards all the time. Munster were winning the war on the advantage line. For people who don't know rugby, there's a line where someone gets tackled and it goes right across the field from where the tackle takes place. If four All Blacks arrive and they drive over that line – and all they've got is two Munster jerseys to compete with – then it's like a tank going forward through the troops. The problem for us was that Munster were getting there first. We were always behind the advantage line, so they kept going forward.

Corris Thomas: I heard what some people said afterwards. They said Munster were first to the breakdowns because they were living offside. That didn't surprise me, not one little bit. I expected people to say, 'God, weren't they offside?' Because from where they were sitting they were only looking at it one-dimensionally. Whereas I was looking all around to see if it had an influence, and, if it did, then that's when I would penalise.

Tommy Kiernan is a bright guy and he'd probably done his homework on me. He knew as well as I did that when the ball is being touched by the scrum-half, at the scrum or at the breakdown, it's open play and everybody can sprint forward. It looks bad. By the time the ball gets to the centres, they're all over them. They look offside, but if they time it right, it's not illegal. Munster did time it right. They knew exactly when to move up.

Martin Walsh, touch judge: Corris Thomas gave seven penalties in the entire game. It was unbelievable. He gave an unbelievable display that day. What happens is this: a referee will go out on the field of play and within the first five or ten minutes he will lay down how he is going to referee the game. Players of that quality instinctively know what he's going to do. And then they go on the gamble. They live on the margins. Everything depends on the interpretation that the referee on the day has. And Corris Thomas decided, 'I'm going to live with it.'

Seamus Dennison called the bluff on the gamble with a crash tackle. That settled it. The lines were drawn then. Everyone knew there was going to be fearsome tackling in the middle of the field and if the All Blacks didn't want to come up, that was their fault. The next day Jack Gleeson was cribbing about them sort of things, but they could have done the same.

Stu Wilson: It was borderline, what they were doing. But then it's a bit much for us to complain about them just maybe bending the rules a little bit. I was saying to our guys, 'Well, look, if he's allowing it for them, why don't we start cheating a bit? If they can get away with that, we can too.' I've seen a few All Blacks cheat in their time, don't you worry about that. But I knew what Gleeson and Mourie would think – that it would be lowering our discipline. They felt that if you don't have self-discipline in an All Black team then you've got nothing. You've got anarchy.

Donal Canniffe: There's no such thing as an illegal position as long as the referee is applying the law as he sees it. If the referee says you're not offside, you ain't offside and that's the end of it. You can talk about it forever and a day but the referee is law. You play the referee.

Les White: We weren't winning much lineout ball. We weren't winning any, actually. Moss Keane said to me, 'You've got to stop that fucker Haden jumping.' So I started standing on his foot and grabbing hold of his arm. He wasn't too happy about it. Next thing this haymaker came across – bang, hit me right smack on the nose. I knew straight away he'd broken it. Haden looked at me and said, 'That'll fucking stop you.' I must admit, I didn't do it again. I told Moss, 'You'll just have to fucking jump higher.' I was dazed for a while. My nose was swollen, a big bump in front of my eyes. For the rest of the match it felt like I was looking over the brow of a hill.

Donal Canniffe: As the game went on they were dominating the lineouts. They had far more possession, enough to win any match. It's usually a straightforward game when you're on the offensive. Mistakes come and you kick your penalties. But we weren't giving away any penalties and they couldn't control the ball they were getting.

We were able to get at Donaldson and disrupt their ball. It was getting to the stage where I was almost saying, 'I don't want the ball. When they have the ball, we're making hay.' Not having it wasn't hurting us and the more the game went on the more it was hurting them.

You could see the doubt on their faces. You could see them thinking, 'Are we going to turn this around?'

Stu Wilson: They wanted to try this move again just before half-time and I said no, cancel it, I'd rather have something else. I knew where it would end up – with me getting buried by another big tackle. It doesn't matter how good you are or what sort of reputation you've got as an All Black side. If you put pressure on an opposition side, they will crack like everyone else. That's the beast of the game, that's what makes it great. It still happens, no matter who you are. Everyone reacts under pressure. You start to get a little bit anxious. 'When is this game going to turn for us?'

Donal Spring: The All Blacks had 90 per cent of the ball. After a while, we didn't even contest their lineouts. We got more mileage out of their ball. It was a sieve, porous beyond belief. Mossie Keane was competing with Haden and making sure he didn't catch it. Haden was slapping everything down to Donaldson. Donaldson spent the day being swallowed up by Whelan from the front and myself, Christy and Tucker from the back.

Mark Donaldson: We got too much ball, far too much ball. People can say we should have changed our tactics, but when you've been dominating teams up to then, and when everyone says you can't win matches unless you've got the ball, then an absolute reverse of your normal game is not easy.

They kept knocking us over. It was a fifteen-man defence, totally watertight. They had this bald bloke with a beard [Seamus Dennison] playing second five-eighth and he was knocking the hell out of us. There wasn't much of him but, Christ, he could hit. Their fire was up; that's what legends are bloody made of.

The crowd played a huge part as well, but that wasn't

exactly a surprise. I was in the crowd in Cork in 1976 when Munster nearly beat Australia. I was nineteen then, having a bit of an OE, an overseas experience. Munster should have won that day. I don't think too many of us had first-hand experience of the Munster passion, but I didn't really think to mention it. I was a junior member of the team. There were far wiser heads than me.

Stu Wilson: Half-time came and we knew we had a fight on our hands but we were still in it. We just hadn't got going. We hadn't even started the bloody car. I thought we should get a bit of mongrel dog going, outmuscle them up front. People were saying different things, trying to keep positive . . .

'Look, we're better players than they are, we've just got to lift our game.'

'They can't keep this intensity up for the eighty minutes. This team cannot play with us for eighty minutes.'

'Once we get some points on the board, we'll wear them down in the last twenty minutes.'

But, at the same time, we had our doubts. Or at least, I did. I was telling them, 'There's not a lot of holes in there, guys. Not a lot of gaps.'

Tony Ward: Donal was giving the team talk in front of the stand, telling us we had to stay focused, that we had a chance to make history. We were 9–0 up against the All Blacks and the only thing I can remember is the silence. It was eerie. There was no crescendo of noise. People must have been talking, but we couldn't hear anything. It was just a stunned silence, as if people were finding it hard to believe what they were seeing.

Tom Kiernan: In the first half, things had gone as well as you could humanly get. But it still didn't mean we were going to bloody well do it. There's a factor involved – you can call it luck at the end of the day – and if you don't have it you won't win. Doesn't matter who you are. I knew the worst was going to come at the start of the second half. They were going to try and go through us.

Chapter Nineteen

The Second Half

Bill Walsh, fish merchant, Cork: We knew the match was on, but we weren't listening to it in the office. We had a radio but we only listened to news; we never listened to sport. Anyway, I thought it might have been too much for Dan, with Donal being the Munster captain. He was very proud of Donal.

We had one office between us, a big one. He had a switch-board – three lines with four extensions. People wanted to know what type of fish was coming in.

He was a very quiet man, a very mannerly man, and a very respectful man. I never heard him saying a bad word against anyone, never. His hours were flexible. He came in in the morning when it suited him and he went away in the afternoon. Around half-three I said, 'Ah Dan, can't you go away home now?' His plan was to listen to the second half of the match on the radio at home.

His wife Kay would telephone him every day, maybe a few times a day. At ten to four he said to me, 'Kay's outside St Patrick's Church, I'm going up.' She had told him that Munster were doing well, that they were leading.

The church was only around the corner from us, on the Lower Glanmire Road.

'Off you go, Dan,' I said.

Christy Cantillon: It felt unreal. Half an hour before the game I'd been thinking to myself, 'What the fuck am I doing here?' I had big doubts. I didn't want to make a fool of myself. We didn't want to let ourselves down, be beaten by twenty or thirty points. Seamus Dennison was sitting down directly across from me, saying nothing. And his eyes were revolving in their sockets. I looked at him and I thought, 'Jesus, if he's like that, I can't be too bad.' And now here we were, 9–0 up against the All Blacks.

Paul Cochrane: It didn't seem real to us. We were looking at each other, just shaking our heads, not really believing what we were watching. At half-time we went down to the toilets and people realised who we were, because we had our London New Zealand sweaters on. So we started getting it from everyone . . .

'Nine-nil, guys. *Nine-nil!*'

'What's wrong with your All Blacks?'

'Come on Munster!'

But I don't think they really believed it either. Their boys had forty minutes to hold out and everyone knew the All Blacks were capable of turning the match around in five. We were worried, no doubt about it, but we still thought we'd come back. We thought we'd see a different team in the second half.

Donal Canniffe: Coaches weren't allowed to talk to their teams at half-time then. We huddled together in the middle of the field. I told them, 'Keep doing what you're doing. Keep making the tackles. Keep concentrating because we're forty minutes away from immortality.' As soon as I said it, I was aware that it was an unusual thing to say. But then, I knew what had happened to Munster teams in the past, how close they'd come without doing it. I'd been there myself in '73. One mistake, no matter how small, and they'd come back to us.

Bill Walsh: My lad Gary Crowley came running into the office. He was very upset. He said, 'Mr Canniffe is after collapsing.' He said he was on the pavement outside Barry's Timbers. I said, 'Dial 999.' I dashed over then.

Just as I got there the ambulance was arriving. Somebody else had called them. He was on the ground, dressed in a suit. He was always dressed in a suit, always groomed. You'd never see him unshaven. Even his nails were always perfect. And he looked very well when he was dressed up. He looked immaculate. I opened his collar. He would always, always have a tie on. I'm the same myself. I can't go out without a collar, I'm not dressed.

I stepped aside then and the ambulance man took over. They asked me if I knew him. I said, 'He works for me. I'll go with him in the ambulance.' The second man was working on him with oxygen and various things. I said, 'Dan, you'll be fine. We're on our way to the North Infirmary.' I thought I saw a flicker in his eye.

Gerry McLoughlin: The most important part of the match was just after half-time. They were coming at us a hundred miles an hour in the first twenty minutes of the second half. They came through the middle, middle, middle. I was making tackles I shouldn't have been there to make. They didn't move the ball wide, they just came straight at us, thinking we'd wilt. They had total belief in themselves. Our centres were making unbelievable tackles. Practically the whole team was. There was no way we were letting them through. We kept holding our own in the scrum, but there were times when our three back-row players would be gone, and all eight of their pack would be scrummaging. I had to try and push them on my fucking own.

Paul Cochrane: Straight after half-time the All Blacks went on the attack. They were giving it everything, really getting stuck in now. They hit this ruck right in front of where we were standing and we started jumping up. Next thing Gary Knight rucked somebody out of it, really ripped into them, and all the frustration we'd had over the first half came to the surface. We just started roaring.

'That's more like it!'

'Get into them!'

'That's the way, Blacks! Let's go!'

For the rest of my life I'll remember what happened then. The linesman turned around and glared at us. Then he brought back his arm, the one holding his flag, and he moved towards us. We could have sworn he was going to attack us with the flag. He had this look in his eyes. But then he turned back towards the play. We couldn't believe it. The linesman!

Graham Mourie: One of the things I tried to have in my bag when I went on the field as captain was a fallback position. Before the match started we went out there as a team, knowing what we wanted to do. But you can never assume that it's going to happen, so what do you do if it doesn't?

I was still a relatively young captain but I had a reasonable understanding of the tactical implications of the game. At that stage my mind was saying, 'We're getting knocked over, we're not making any progress up front. We're probably not going to be able to bash our way through them. We're not making any progress in the midfield so we're not going to be able to run our way through them. So what's left? We've got to put the ball behind them.'

Jim Turnbull, Munster team secretary: Everyone else was up in the stand, but I was on the touchline. You had to be, with the togs. If a fella needed a new pair of knicks, I had to be there to hand them over. Even though we were nine points up, I didn't think we were going to do it. I couldn't see us holding out against the All Blacks. Tommy came down from the stand. He was agitated, you could see it was getting to him. I asked him what he thought. I said, 'We won't win this really, will we?' He didn't think so either. Our feeling was, this is too good to be true. But then the minutes were ticking away and the All Blacks hadn't scored yet. People around me were holding their breaths. Maybe, maybe, maybe . . . just maybe.

Bruce Robertson: Jack Gleeson was a controlled person. He never got emotional, or at least he never let us see him that way. But it was obvious he was unhappy with the way things were going. And he just had to sit there and take it. We all had to.

Bryan Williams: It was depressing. I could feel I didn't have the legs. My hamstrings were tight. I knew it wasn't going to be me that was going to run a hundred metres to score the try that pulled us out of it. But you don't like to walk off in a game like that. We were in trouble. You're going to do what you can. All Blacks don't give in like that. They don't surrender.

Graham Mourie: We tried to change our game and put the ball in behind them but we ended up giving the ball back to

Munster rather than putting them under pressure. Our kicking wasn't accurate enough. We had a fly-half on that day who was a runner. He wasn't comfortable playing a kicking game. Eddie Dunn was a fantastic attacking player, but Doug Bruce was more of a tactician. Had he been on the field we might have controlled the game better. The reality is that when you start with a plan which is not succeeding you have to have the players to make Plan B work. What we tried to fall back on didn't work.

Stu Wilson: No matter who we played in the Number 10 jersey, it would have made no difference. Doug Bruce would have had the same pressure on him. I'm telling you, we could have played all fifteen Test players and it would probably have been the same story.

Donal Spring: Doug Bruce kicked everything. He played a tighter game. Eddie Dunn was a runner. He suited us down to the ground. The more he ran, the happier we were.

Eddie Dunn: They called me 'Hands' Dunn. I was an individualist. Being part Maori, I had natural flair. It was my heritage. I wanted to play the expansive, fifteen-man game, the kind of game Jack Gleeson liked. I wanted to keep the ball in play, to keep possession. If I got the ball in my hands I'd usually run with it. Then I'd be thinking, 'Will I do a cut pass? Will I make it a scissors pass? Or a cut-back? What about a dummy?' Kicking wasn't my game. That made me different from most first five-eighths. For me it was all about peripheral vision. If the first move wasn't there, I could carry on to the next. I had three or four options in my mind. When things were going my way, I had the game to make things happen.

I wasn't supposed to play that day. I'm not making excuses, but I wasn't mentally prepared. The afternoon before, I'd played golf, badly. Got off the course, went back to the hotel and they told me my good friend Doug Bruce had pulled out. I was in.

We were taken by surprise. Badly caught. We weren't expecting that kind of onslaught. Our backline was under unbelievable pressure. We tried to change things and it got worse. I didn't kick well. I was thinking, 'What the hell's happening here? Nothing's going right for me.'

Paul Cochrane: Midway through the second half a strange feeling came over the ground. It's hard to put it into words; you had to be there. We'd spent the whole game waiting for the revival and the All Blacks still had plenty of time to turn it around, but for some reason we just knew it wasn't going to happen. I've never, ever seen a team as committed as Munster. There were a couple of very inexperienced All Black forwards out there – Ash McGregor and Wayne Graham – and when the going got tough they weren't able to cope. But it wasn't just them. I was looking at great players like Bryan Williams and Stu Wilson and I could see they didn't have it in them.

Stu Wilson: In the second half I tried to get through a couple of times, but again I just got smashed up and belted. When you've got guys trying to do things on their own, trying to do superhuman things, then you know you're desperate. The team isn't working. Twenty minutes into the second half I just thought, 'Nope, we've just got no chance.' We were being beaten right across the park, all positions and all players.

Colm Tucker: They were starting to lose it. They called a lineout under the stand and Andy Haden started bollocking the hooker, John Black. 'Are you fucking stupid?' he said. 'It's a tap off the top!' Jesus, he was a huge man, Haden.

Andy Haden: Maybe we had an embarrassment of possession, but nobody told us to stop winning lineout ball.

Eddie Dunn: I should have changed my position, played deeper, stood off them more. But I was expecting the players around me to make things happen. There was no continuity between forwards and backs. They didn't know what our game plan was. We didn't know what theirs was.

Olann Kelleher, unused Munster substitute: We were all sitting in the stand. There was no bench in those days. All the time we thought we were going to be beaten. It just didn't seem real to us. We were looking at one another, thinking it just couldn't last. All they needed was two tries and we kept expecting them to come back and take over. Until the second drop goal.

Peter West, match report, **The Times:** *So came the last quarter and the drop goal that put the icing on Munster's cake. Ward's long diagonal kick had Wilson rushing back desperately to retrieve the ball before it rolled over the goal line. He could not quite manage it, so it was a scrummage five. Munster heeled untidily and Canniffe was dispossessed.*

Colm Tucker: Canniffe was harried and hottled. Next thing the ball came out to me. I looked up and I saw the posts. Then I saw Haden, coming at me. You make a decision. Somebody asked Jimmy Greaves once: 'How did you score that goal?' He said: 'I haven't a clue, I just scored it.'

Tom Kiernan: He had the sense to pass it. Normally forwards would tuck it under their hands and fucking run. He passed it to Ward, who saw there were no other options, so had a pop.

Fred Cogley, TV commentary: Now to Ward. The drop at goal. It's over! Tony Ward has done it!

Tony Ward: I thought, 'We're within touching distance now. We're going to make it.'

Graham Mourie: That was it. That was the big nail. Suddenly we had to get twelve points. We'd tried Plan A – it hadn't worked. We'd moved on to Plan B. That didn't happen either. We were getting bashed and we didn't have what it took to get out of it.

John Mason, match report, the Daily Telegraph: The machine-gun staccato blasts of 'MUN-STER! MUN-STER!' fuelled sore, weary bodies. In the final minutes it was the All Blacks who were stumbling, grey and tired, from one spot to another.

Bill Walsh: In the ambulance, on the way to the North Infirmary, I spoke to him.
  'You'll be okay, Dan.
  'Hang on, Dan. We'll be there in a minute.'
  He never spoke, but I really felt he heard me. I'm convinced he heard me.
  Traffic was light. We were up there in a few minutes. There was a special entrance, we were whipped in and everything

was ready. They asked me who I was and I told them. They said, 'Wait there so, then.' They brought me out a glass of water. They seemed to think I was his son.

I said to myself, 'In the name of God, what am I going to do?' I was thinking of Mrs Canniffe, sitting in her car outside St Patrick's Church. The ambulance had driven up the Lower Glanmire Road, where her car was parked.

It came into my mind that I had to get the responsibility off me. I had to work quickly and do the right thing. I made a phone call to Kieran, Dan's son. When Dan came to work for me, I gave all my insurance to Kieran. I was hoping against hope that he wasn't gone to the match. I knew it was still going on. But they said sorry, he wasn't in the office, he wouldn't be back. They put me through to his partner, Ken Stanton. I said, 'Ken, I have some bad news. Would you try to help me out? Mr Canniffe is after collapsing.'

Tom Kiernan: I was sitting alongside the selectors, doing all sorts of scoring permutations in my mind. It just was tense and worrying. I knew they'd have to score three times to win. I was sort of cutting my cloth and saying, 'Fine now, that's another score they have to get.'

Donal Spring: We talked and talked and talked, keeping each other going. If a guy is not talking he's probably not even thinking. Whelan never shut up. Ginger never shut up. Foley and Mossie were at it all the time.

With about ten minutes to go, there was a scrum over in front of the stand between the twenty-five and the ten-yard line. It was their put-in. We wheeled the scrum and pushed them over the touchline and kept going until they were up against the wall. The looks on their faces. 'What the hell is this?' The pushing didn't stop until they were nearly in the crowd.

Tom Kiernan: With five minutes to go I was saying, 'Well, it takes a minute and a quarter to score a try and convert it. They're running out of time now.' But even then it was worrying. We'd seen it go wrong too often. I couldn't relax.

Martin Walsh: With about three minutes left, there was a lineout exactly on the halfway line, outside the gate. I could hear someone behind me.

'Martin, Martin . . .'

I turned around and it was Tommy Kiernan. He'd come down from the stand. He says to me: 'If he asks you what time is left, tell him it's all up.'

'As if I wouldn't,' says I.

I'll never forget that as long as I live.

Johnny Cole: I was over on the warm side of the pitch, the Sixpenny side, opposite the stand. I remember the warmth, the sun in my face, blinding me when I looked across the field. On the other side you could feel the chill.

The place was going mental. There was still a few minutes left but everyone knew it was all over, even the All Blacks. They'd stopped talking. That's when you know. Even if they'd had another twenty minutes it wouldn't have made any difference. Being so close, I could see into their eyes. There was nothing there. They just wanted to get off the field.

I had to be careful not to trip up. There were young lads running around my legs, ready to charge on to the pitch; hundreds of people camped all the way up the touchline, waiting.

Corris Thomas: Moss Keane came over to me and said, 'How long to go, ref?' I looked at my watch. We had ninety seconds left, so they needed to score three times to win. Two converted tries and something else. I said, 'Let's put it like this, they can't beat you now.' He jumped up in the air.

Johnny Cole: I knew the time was up, so I had one eye on Corris Thomas and the other on the ball. It was about ten yards from where I was standing, just inside the All Blacks' twenty-two. It came into my head that I had to get the ball, that it would be a great souvenir. I was thinking, 'Blow it up. Go on, blow it up while I have my chance.'

Gerry McLoughlin: The whistle went. People started running on to the pitch, making for the Munster players they knew. Pat O'Donnell jumped on top of me. We were staunch enemies but firm friends. We grew up together. My cousins came down off the wall and made for me. My father was there. My brothers were there. My whole family was there. I was surrounded by people I knew. We were playing for Munster, but at the same time it was a Limerick thing. We were after beating the All Blacks and they could die happy. It was a huge thing for my father. He was proud as punch. For a bus driver's son to be on a team that beat the All Blacks . . . He died of a haemorrhage the following year and I was just so happy that he was around to see that day.

As soon as it was over I was thinking, 'They can't keep me off the Irish team now. They'll have to pick me.'

Jimmy Bowen: At a moment like that you want to be with your own people. My father was there, I went looking for him. I thought he'd be near the tunnel. I was making my way through the crowds when I saw him. His name was Seamus Bowen. He's dead now. I went over to him. He was standing there with rosary beads in his hand. He never knew anything about rugby but he was always there for me, went to all my matches. He showed me the rosary beads. It's hard to describe what it felt like.

John Mason, the Daily Telegraph: *Large, craggy Irishmen – and small ones, too – were crying at Thomond Park. Not in their most extravagant of dreams did they seriously believe that Munster would succeed where every other Irish side since 1905 had failed. Yesterday at 4.34 p.m., those fond, hazy notions had become legendary truth.*

Stu Wilson: When he blew the whistle I'm sure there was more of them there. They must have jumped the fence because it was on the radio and they said, 'Heck, I'd better get down to see this, this is history.' They were just in a frenzy.

Paul Cochrane: The New Zealanders in the crowd were dumbstruck. I mean, we take our rugby very seriously. When the whistle went, some of the people around us were saying, 'Bugger this, let's get out of here now.' But we stayed.

I ran on to the pitch. It was absolute delirium. The atmosphere – in thirty years of watching rugby all over the world I've never experienced anything quite like it. I've been to Eden Park, the Arms Park, Parc des Princes – you name it – but nothing has ever matched that little ground in Limerick. I was just trying to take it in, still in shock really. I found myself right next to Moss Keane. People were trying to chair him off the pitch and slap him on the back. Something came over me. I reached out and touched Moss Keane.

Johnny Cole: Hundreds of people were rushing past me, roaring and shouting. I ran on to the pitch trying to catch sight of the ball, but the sun was in my eyes and the players were getting swallowed up by the supporters. I got up close to Corris but he didn't have the ball, so I doubled back into the crowd and then I saw it out of the corner of my eye. Bryan Williams was holding it.

'I'll take that,' I said.

Gentleman that he was, he handed it over. It was one of the old brown Gilbert balls, a laced one. The day being dry, it finished up nearly as good as new. I stuck it under my jersey. The crowd was funnelling towards the wicket gate leading to the dressing rooms.

Martin Walsh came across from the other side of the pitch. He could see the bulge under my jersey.

'I have the ball,' I said.

'Jaysus,' he said, in his Dublin accent. 'Moind it.'

Olann Kelleher: We went into the dressing room. Seamus Dennison was crying. He was my hero because he was so hard and so small. There were these little windows into the dressing room and kids were being lifted up to them. You could see these little hands coming down with autograph books. I'd never signed an autograph in my life. It was unheard of for a non-international. So I signed most of them. They kept coming down for more and more. I was becoming aware of what it meant. I turned to Mossie Finn and I said, 'Moss, you'll be a hero forever.'

'A hero?' he said. 'Shur I didn't even touch the fucking ball.'

Johnny Cole: I got the ball into the referee's changing room. It was a tiny room with a concrete floor and wood-panelled walls, painted blue. There were no hangers, just three chairs in the centre of the room and we had our clothes draped over the back of them. I took the ball from underneath my jersey and had a good look at it. Then I stuck it inside my bag and zipped it back up.

People started coming into the room, other referees and alickadoos, smoking cigarettes and congratulating Corris on a job well done and saying would you credit it, Munster after beating the bloody All Blacks, and not just beating them, holding them scoreless. Martin said the All Blacks were a decimated and disgruntled crowd of men.

The door opened again and a fella called Jimmy Sparling, the assistant treasurer of the Munster branch, stuck his head inside.

'That's three pounds and four shillings you owe for the ball,' he says.

'For what ball?' says I.

'For the ball you stuck under your jersey.'

I had no intention of handing over a bob. That ball was mine by right. I told Martin I was going, that I'd be back for my shower later.

'What d'ya mean going?' he says.

'I have to get the ball out of here. I can't leave it out of my sight.'

'Are ya serious?'

'Martin, don't you realise?' I says. 'That ball is part of history. Munster are after beatin' the All Blacks with that ball.'

I opened the door and I saw the Munster players walking back out, still in their red jerseys. Even then the noise was unbelievable.

'Mun-ster! Mun-ster! Mun-ster!'

Susan Healy: My father was beside himself, just elated. He was losing his breath because he wanted to talk about it so much. There was so much he wanted to say. I'll always remember him telling me, 'This'll go down in history! This'll go down in history! We'll never forget this day! We showed them what we're made of!' It wasn't often he expressed himself that way. He wanted to make sure I realised how important it was, that I'd seen something special. I didn't really understand then that he'd waited all his life to see something like that. Of course I knew what rugby meant to him, but I didn't appreciate the significance of what was after happening. At the time I thought, 'Yeah, next year it'll be something else, a better match.' But as good as Munster are now, people will always go back to that game. He talked about it for the rest of his life.

Donal Canniffe: There was people coming out of the walls from all sides. A few minutes after we came back in the second time, somebody came over and said, 'You're wanted on the phone'. I presumed it was a reporter, or somebody to congratulate me. I walked out of the dressing room. I was still in my togs.

Ken Stanton, Canniffe family friend: I called Thomond Park. I was expecting it to be difficult to get hold of anybody, but I got straight through. Someone went to get Donal and after a few minutes he came on the phone. I told him his father had been taken ill, that he'd had a heart attack and he was in the emergency ward of the North Infirmary. I told him he should get back to Cork as quickly as he could.

Bill Walsh: The surgeon and the nurse came out. They still thought I was his son. I said, 'No, he's working with me. What's the position?'

They said they were very sorry to say, he's dead.

So then my mind was going a million miles an hour. I

called Ken Stanton again and told him. Then I rang my office.

'How's Mr Canniffe?' they said.

'Look, I'll tell you when I come back. He'll be okay, he's here now in the North Infirmary.'

He was dead, but I couldn't tell them. I said, 'Would one of you go over and see if Mrs Canniffe is there? And if she is, would you bring her into my office?'

I knew very well she'd ask to know why. I said, 'Tell her he got a bad turn.' I told them to not to say he was shifted by ambulance. I told them to make a cup of tea for her. I told them to make sure to tell her to lock her car.

Donal Canniffe: I came back into the dressing room. It hadn't sunk in. All I knew was I had to shower quickly and get down to Cork. I was only back a minute when I got another message. There was another phone call for me. It was Ken again. How he got through so quickly I'll never know. It was a public phone. I don't know how he even got the number. He said, 'Donal, I'm sorry to have to tell you that your father has died.'

I said, 'Look, okay, thanks very much.' I put the phone down and came back. I told Tommy I had to go. Told him the reason. I disappeared as quickly as I could. I had to go home. That was it.

Bill Walsh: I had no transport then. I asked the girl in the North Infirmary would she hire a taxi for me. It came straight away. I got back and the lads were all anxious. I was the name over the door, but they were the boss. That's the type of relationship we had.

'How's Mr Canniffe?'

'He's up in the North Infirmary and they're working on him.'

Then I saw Mrs Canniffe.

'He's collapsed,' I said. 'He's up in the North Infirmary. I'll bring you up there now . . .'

I couldn't tell the woman he was dead. I could not. I could not. I couldn't be . . . I wasn't . . . how will I put it? I felt I could not tell the woman, 'Your husband's dead.' I knew Kay very well too, like. I had got to know her. I just could not do it. I thought it would be a shock to her.

I knew she was a nurse. I mean, that was one thing in my mind, at least. I knew she was medical and that she probably would handle it much better than me. So I said, 'I'll bring you up now and we'll see how he is.' She was very upset. At that time she thought he was only after collapsing. I said, 'I'll drive you up to the North Infirmary straight away.'

My car was in Alfred Street, a blue Ford Escort. We drove away. She had started calling me 'Bill'. She used to call me 'Mr Walsh' until a week or ten days before, but she was calling me 'Bill' then.

'How is he, Bill?'

'He has all the care in the world. The ambulance was very good, they put oxygen on him.'

But she'd know all that, you see? I told her I loosened his tie and the ambulance men took over. I said, 'We'll go up now.'

We got to the hospital and I handed her over to the matron. She brought her to the doctor. She came out then. She was in tears. I mean, they were very united. Very close.

I may have broken down, I don't think I did, but I cried a bitter tear on my own.

Wayne Graham: We got into this little changing room at the back of the stand and sat there for a very long time. It was only my second time wearing the jersey. I was sitting beside Bryan

Williams. In 1970, when I was thirteen years old, I watched him playing for the All Blacks in South Africa. He was an unbelievable player. He was a god to me. All of a sudden I'm sitting next to him in the changing room and tears are running down his cheeks. It brought it home to me what it really meant to be an All Black. Jesus, it was a wake-up call.

Gary Knight: I shouldn't have played. I was crook straight after, all my glands were swollen. They took me to the hospital and kept me there for six days. It was probably the best place to be.

Eddie Dunn: They made me the scapegoat. Dougie Bruce came into the team and he stayed there for the Tests. They closed up shop. They didn't want my kind of game any more. Not after Munster. After the tour was over, we packed our stuff into individual boxes, mementoes of the trip that we'd picked up along the way. They put the boxes on to a ship and sent them back to New Zealand. When the ship docked, I went down to the port to pick up my box. My wife was with me. The box had 'EDDIE DUNN, ALL BLACKS' printed on it, in big letters. I went over to get it and straight away I could see there was something else written on it, in even bigger letters, red ink. I turned to my wife.

'God, would you look at that.'

Someone had scrawled 'WHAT ABOUT MUNSTER?' across it. It was just my box they wrote on. Nobody else's.

I've never been allowed to forget it. Even to this day, the kids I teach remind me. They read about it in books. They say, 'What the hell happened in Munster?'

Joe McCarthy: We had the whole match on film, nine magazines of it. The people who said it should have been done on outside broadcast, with a lot of cameras around the ground, came out of the woodwork then. Everyone knew after the event that Munster were going to win. Had they been beaten, nobody would have said anything.

We handed over the magazines to a courier and that was the last I saw of them. He took them off to Dublin to be processed. They showed about ten minutes of it the following evening. I don't know what happened to the rest of the film we shot. They said it was mislaid. Nobody ever saw it again.

Donal Spring: The fact that there was no proper TV coverage was the best thing that ever happened. Every time I watch the few minutes of the video I have, I wonder if I should destroy it. Even though it was a great match, it's better that it lives on in people's imaginations.

Gerry Healy, son of Stephen Healy: Straight after the final whistle I came across my Uncle Sean. He was roaring. I still have a picture of him in my head, standing at the railing on the popular side. He was saying, 'Eff the *Irish Independent*! Eff the *Irish Press*! Eff them all! We showed them!' For Sean, and for my father, it was all about showing the people in Dublin – the Irish selectors and the newspapers and the snobs in Dublin 4 – that we had the best rugby players in Munster. For years they had ignored great Munster players and then they'd patronised us, making out we weren't as good as them. Now we were after beating the All Blacks and it meant the world to them. Sean was the real Harry Secombe that day, tipping the glasses up and down on his nose. He was well steamed.

Paul Cochrane: The significance of it was dawning on me. I was wandering around trying to get hold of a programme, but it was impossible. Just as we were leaving the ground we saw the All Blacks on the bus. They were all sitting there with their heads down, looking out the window, staring into space. We were calling out, trying to tell them to keep their chins up, but I don't think they were even aware of us being there. In the back seat, playing a guitar, was Bryan Williams. He was trying to cheer them up but he was getting no response.

I said to the guys, 'Right, this is what we're going to do. The first Munster man you see, buy him a beer and congratulate him. After that, you won't be able to pay for another one for the rest of the night.' And that's exactly what happened. The first bar we went to, we saw these guys and shouted them a Guinness. That was the last drink we paid for all night. I swear we had as good a time as any Munster supporter. Well, nearly. Even though we got beaten, it's still my favourite rugby memory. I spent years trying to get the programme. One of the guys I was with managed to buy one on the day and I pestered him non-stop. He lives in Melbourne now and two years ago I went to visit him. When I got there he said, 'I've got something for you.' He handed me the programme for Munster and the All Blacks.

Tom Kiernan: At the final whistle, the only feeling I had was relief. Nothing else. I knew it could have gone the other way so easily. How many times had we gone out and been beaten by a fraction? Had the All Blacks scored first, it would have been very difficult for us to come back at them. We just didn't have the possession. The fact that Munster scored first meant the All Blacks had to come at us. A lot of things had to happen for the try. It could have gone wrong on a number of occasions. You could do that in practice a hundred times and not score. But the anticipation Bowen showed when he picked up Ward's kick ahead pleased me. It showed he was alert. It was evidence of sharpness.

The way it all washed out, that was Ward's perfect match. You only have those once in a blue moon anyway, once in a career maybe. He did all the things I wanted him to do – I couldn't have asked for a more disciplined game. I don't think he was caught in possession once.

I've said a million billion times, there were a couple of stages where we could have cracked. All it was going to take was one bad bounce of the ball. After everything, it was just relief. Thank God. It's over and we've won. In the middle of it all then, we heard about Donal's father dying.

Bill Walsh: My children loved Dan Canniffe. They saw him as a grandfather. He'd do their homework with them in the office. There was nothing he wouldn't do for them. Any problem I had, I confided in him. He helped me more than I can tell you, more than I can tell anyone. He was a father figure to me.

I felt the loss of Dan Canniffe as much as the loss of my own brother. Back at work, my lads were devastated. We couldn't speak. One of them had to go away that evening for fish. I sent two of them, on account of the night that was in it. I felt one man on his own might be upset.

Donal Canniffe: I went away with Mary, my wife. Somebody offered to drive us back to Cork but I said no, I'd be okay. All I remember about the journey was that it was mostly a silent one. Neither of us really knew what to say. The shock was setting in as I drove. I was just thinking about getting home. The match was gone. We had to prepare for a funeral.

Kieran Canniffe, brother of Donal: That night I went up to the North Infirmary. He was laid out in the death house. I collected the few bits and pieces he had on him. One of the things he had in his pocket was a memorial card for my mother. She died in 1951 so he must have had it on him for nearly thirty years. I broke down at the funeral when my Aunt Nora was going away. She was my mother's sister. I said to her, 'Both of them died at the side of the road.'

Gerry Healy: After the match I went away with my own friends. That night was all about getting langered – I think that would be a fair description. Being a drinking man, like my father and my Uncle Sean, I hit all the pubs.

That day for me was the ultimate in sport. It was almighty. You can't surpass it. It can't happen no more. What those fellas did will be talked about in this town forever more. It'll be passed on from generation to generation. In a hundred years' time they'll still be talking about it, because it can never be taken away from us.

Stephen and Sean met up after the match and went drinking along with their old cronies. They were all there, just enjoying their pints and talking about the match, then having the singsong.

My father's party piece was 'Put More Turf On the Fire, Mary Ann'. Sean would sing 'Stand Up And Fight'. He'd be clenching his fists when he belted it out.

> *Stand up and fight until you hear the bell*
> *Stand toe to toe, trade blow for blow . . .*
> *Stand up and fight like hell!*

Chapter Twenty

The Immortals

The All Blacks were late for dinner. Just as it seemed to some they might not show at all, their bus pulled up outside the Limerick Inn hotel and they alighted in their number ones, each of them gripping the tail of the next man's dress suit as they danced into the hotel and up and down the winding staircase singing, 'Hi-ho, hi-ho, it's off to work we go!' The post-mortem could wait. They weren't going to rain on Munster's parade.

The Munster branch stretched to one glass of wine per man. After that, the players had to buy their own, for £1.50 a bottle. They dug into their pockets to toast the greatest win in the history of Munster rugby. It would be another three days before Les White finally made it back to England, during which time he saw the inside of what seemed to him like every pub in Limerick, in the company of his fellow prop and tour guide, Gerry McLoughlin. But for many of the other Munster players, duty called all too quickly. They were back at work the following day.

Tom Kiernan left the dinner early, left his players to it. He wanted to go home. The following day was 1 November, the start of the shooting season. In the morning he pulled out of his house at eight o'clock and drove to the same stretch of land his father had first taken him to thirty years before.

Driving, he felt a weight lifting from his shoulders. He had been ashen-faced at the final whistle, so tensed up he could not even bring himself to smile. Slowly, he had allowed himself to savour the moment, privately and without fuss. Now he thought to himself, 'What a change in twenty-four hours.' Already people were hailing his achievement, saying he had outfoxed Jack Gleeson, pulled off a miracle. Few knew how much he had put into the preparation of his team, how he had overcome the conservative elements within the Munster branch and fought for unprecedented time with his players. Some looked at the result and wondered if Kiernan could do the same for Ireland as he'd done for Munster. But that was for the future. Alongside him in the car now was his eleven-year-old son Cameron, the latest in the line of shooting Kiernans.

It was a successful morning: father and son brought home four pheasant, a haul that would have pleased even Michael Kiernan. For a second day running, Tom Kiernan was left to reflect that things didn't get much better.

As the Munster coach was shooting, Jack Gleeson was holding court at the All Blacks' hotel in Limerick, giving his first considered reaction to the team's defeat. Later, it would be claimed on his behalf that he was misinterpreted, but in truth his comments left little room for ambiguity. He was indignant, angered by what he described as Munster's 'kamikaze tackling'. He knew full well that, back home, the result was being regarded as an unmitigated disaster and, cornered by a handful of press men, he lashed out.

'If we are going to strike teams who are just going to stop us playing then the public is going to miss our fifteen-man style of rugby,' Gleeson complained. 'You cannot ask our players to play against kamikaze tacklers all the time. You cannot ask them to keep getting knocked over. All that style does is to beat rugby.'

It appeared that Gleeson, still visibly stunned by what had happened the previous afternoon, was suggesting it simply wasn't fair for others to launch themselves at his players. Instead, they should be allowed free rein to express themselves.

Terry McLean, the most trenchant reporter on the tour, answered Gleeson with withering scorn the following day in the *New Zealand Herald*:

What Munster intended and achieved was exactly what Waikato set out to do in the first game of the 1956 Springboks' tour of New Zealand. The ball was set bouncing behind the Bok scrum-half, with the Waikato forwards tearing hell for leather after it. Should they [Munster] have conceded defeat and sold their souls, or make the most of what they appear to have, basing it all on enormous courage, sublime team spirit and a willing-ness to die for the cause? The All Blacks could have had, as Mr Kiernan himself readily admitted, the winning of the game if they had used the ball scientifically. They did not. They were beaten. Was this enough to justify wholesale condemnation of the Munster/Waikato techniques?

It was the tour manager, Russ Thomas, who let slip that Munster's tactics had already led to a drastic reassessment of priorities. Sitting on the hotel staircase, Thomas admitted: 'The tactics may have to be altered. We may take a look at a different style.'

There was no 'may' about it. The die had already been cast by the time Thomas briefed the media. Among the leaders of the Eighth All Blacks, Munster's victory proved so traumatic that the entire tour was transformed because of it. Set against the national need for a successful team, Gleeson's attack-minded principles counted for nothing. Neither he, Thomas nor Mourie was prepared to run the risk of other teams aping Munster's methods. And so the fifteen-man game was immediately ditched. Instead of entertaining, the All Blacks were now hellbent on winning. Instead of making new friends, they looked after number one: the New Zealand public back home. There would not – could not – be any more defeats.

'The main lesson from the match for us is quite simple,' Thomas went on. 'We must never miss a tackle. We missed one yesterday and it cost us six points and the match.'

Amazed by the result, the wider world of rugby soon learned that no proper television pictures of the match existed. If you weren't there, if you didn't see it with your own eyes, you pretty much had to rely on the testimony of those who were. It would become, as the playwright John Breen put it, 'the last folk memory', and those who were in the ground will never tire of telling the tale, or embellishing it.

Many could not bear to confess they had not been there, so they pretended they were. Some had no choice but to own up. 'I wish I was there,' telegrammed Limerick's rugby-loving film star Richard Harris, on location in Johannesburg. The news, gleefully reported in every South African paper Harris could lay his hands on, brought an end to his ten-month stint on the dry: 'I can't think of a better occasion or excuse to reacquaint my liver with the drowning sensation of a drop.'

Among those closer to home who were honest enough to admit they had missed it, there was frustration. When it became clear that they would never have the chance to see the match on television, frustration turned to outrage. Three days later, the match was still the lead story on the front page of the *Limerick Leader*.

Limerick rugby fans are irate at the failure of RTE to provide live coverage on either radio or television of Tuesday's historic rugby match at Thomond Park. The station put out approximately ten minutes of film on Wednesday night at 6.30 but as there had been little announcement of this, most of those interested never saw it. Those who did see the film were disgusted with the quality. 'They were like midgets out there,' said one disgruntled follower. 'You could hardly pick out a single player.'

Mr Tony Lyons, RTE Information Officer, said it would have taken a staff of fifty to send an outside broadcasting unit to Limerick. Instead, the majority of staff were in Cork for the launch of the second TV channel, RTE 2. When it was pointed out that it was a momentous occasion for Munster rugby, he replied: 'RTE 2's launching is even more momentous.'

The lameness of RTE's excuse was self-evident. The match and the launch of the new station were two days apart. But, more than anything, it was the failure of the national broadcaster to cover the game properly that ensured its mythology in Munster and beyond. For it is not as if the All Blacks had never been humbled by so-called no-hopers before.

Six years earlier, in the steel town of Workington, north-west England, a team captained by the great Ian Kirkpatrick had gone down 16–14 to North-West Counties. Study the photographs of the scenes that followed the final whistle then and the similarities with Thomond Park at 4.34 p.m. on

31 October 1978 are striking. In front of a ramshackle stand, defeated All Blacks trudge past the supporters who have poured on to the pitch. Behind them, the heroes of the hour are being mobbed, backslapped, chaired off. On people's faces there is utter joy. Surrounded by scribbling press men, the winning coach says: 'We beat them with heart and with courage. We outthought them, confused them and mesmerised them to prove that England has the players to shatter the myth of this invincible New Zealand power. They came here for a soft touch. We showed them that English rugby isn't a soft touch any more.'

But who talks now about the first English provincial side ever to beat the All Blacks? Their great victory is forgotten. Look again at those old photographs and perhaps you can see why. High above the North-West supporters celebrating on the far side of the pitch is a vast television gantry, equipped with the latest technology of the age, there to capture every detail of the triumph, to be pored over by those who could not truthfully say, 'I was there.' Against the certainties of filmed evidence, folklore has no chance.

The All Blacks took Russ Thomas at his word. They did not concede another try on tour until the dying minutes of their sixteenth match, the international against Scotland – a total of 876 minutes without their line being breached, or nearly eleven consecutive games, four of them Tests.

Such parsimony did not come without a price. Wilson, who had scored four tries in his first two matches, managed only three more in the ten games he played thereafter. After starting the tour as the main strike weapon, he ended it like a muzzled dog, always chasing but seldom threatening. He had Munster to thank for that, specifically Seamus Dennison.

Four days after the Munster match the All Blacks needed a

try two minutes from time to beat Ireland, and a bitterly disputed penalty with one minute on the clock to get past Wales. England, though, were easily brushed aside and a nine-point victory over the Scots at Murrayfield gave them the distinction that had eluded all of their predecessors. Their place in the history books was secure: they were the Grand Slam All Blacks.

On Saturday 16 December they ran out at the Arms Park in Cardiff for the eighteenth and final match of their tour, against the Barbarians. Five years before, on the same ground, the same fixture had produced one of the greatest occasions in rugby history and, for Gareth Edwards, arguably the finest try. It was in expectation of seeing a similar brand of champagne rugby that a capacity crowd of 47,500 turned up, though most of them also wanted to see these All Blacks finally beaten on Welsh soil. Three days earlier there had been bloodshed at Bridgend. The Welsh captain JPR Williams had been vigorously raked by John Ashworth, who said in his own defence that he could not distinguish JPR's head from the ball. Now Welsh blood was up. The Arms Park craved a Baa-Baas victory.

Of those cheering for the All Blacks that afternoon – the expats in the ground, the Kiwis watching live TV coverage at four in the morning back home – none were as desperate for a New Zealand win as the group of men gathered in front of a television at the Shelbourne hotel in Dublin. After their triumph at Thomond Park the Munster team had watched with escalating glee as the New Zealanders beat all before them. Now there were only eighty minutes between the Munster boys and a claim to fame that would guarantee them immortality: *the only team to beat the Grand Slam All Blacks.*

They were in Dublin because they were one match away from a Grand Slam of their own. The following day they were playing Leinster at Lansdowne Road. Gerry McLoughlin, struck down with scrum-pox after the All Blacks match, the legacy of his battle with Gary Knight, was fighting fit again. The next day, in front of the Ireland selectors, he would stake an irrefutable claim to the position of tighthead prop against France in four weeks' time.

But for now, nobody in the small hotel room wanted an All Blacks victory more than Locky. He was in dread that the burden of expectation on them to produce exciting rugby might cost them the match. For a start, they had recalled Eddie 'Hands' Dunn at Number 10 and everyone knew the kind of game he played. Wilson and Williams were on the wings – and this time they were expecting some proper ball and some holes to run through. In all, eleven of the team beaten by Munster were playing. Even Gary Knight was back in harness.

Amid all the partisanship, Kiernan was staying silent. Was he, too, hoping for a Barbarians win? It was impossible to tell. As Mourie led the All Blacks into the cauldron, Locky turned to his coach.

'Who'd you want to win, Tommy?' he asked.

'Put it this way,' Kiernan replied. 'You'll never hear me cheering for a team from the southern hemisphere.'

'You mean you want the Barbarians to win?'

'I hope it's a draw,' Kiernan said, the flicker of a smile crossing his face. He knew as well as anyone that Munster's victory would better stand the test of time if it proved to be a singular triumph.

The Barbarians had nine Lions in their line-up, among them the Welshmen Phil Bennett, Brynmor Williams, Elgan Rees and Derek Quinnell, the Scotland full-back Andy Irvine, the England hooker Peter Wheeler and the Ireland prop Phil Orr. Added to these were two brilliant Frenchmen from

Go, Jimmy, go: Bowen leaves them for dead, with the try line beckoning

(*Facing page*) The Tackle: Seamus Dennison is a blur as he moves in for the kill. 'It was as if Stu Wilson had run into a brick wall and just slid down it,' recalled referee Corris Thomas

(*Above and below*) Going to war: the packs collide in the lineout

Donal Canniffe: 'We're forty minutes from immortality'

Touchdown:
Christy Cantillon hits the line and Thomond Park erupts

Stand-off: all eyes on the ball that would soon become part of the story

Gerry McLoughlin: 'I was making tackles
I shouldn't have been there to make'

Tom Kiernan: 'We'd seen it go
wrong too often. I couldn't relax'

(*Overleaf*) Euphoria

(*Below*) Best foot forward:
Christy Cantillon gets one away

Triumphant threesome:
Brendan Foley, Gerry McLoughlin and Colm Tucker, with admirers

History men: twenty years on, the Munster team celebrate their achievement,
lining up as they did back in 1978

Toulouse, Jean-Claude Skrela and Jean-Pierre Rives. They were truly formidable.

In the BBC commentary box, Gareth Edwards and Bill McLaren were expecting the All Blacks to cut loose and put on a show. Word had reached McLaren that the All Blacks were considering doing a haka in the middle of the match, a PR stunt designed to win back some of the goodwill lost by the furore that followed the Bridgend episode. Edwards set the scene:

'I'm sure the crowd here today will really enjoy the All Blacks expressing their ability. We've seen a tendency to play a rather tighter game but the opportunity here has really arisen and with the Barbarians meeting the challenge I'm sure we're going to see a lot of open rugby, Bill.'

Locky was appalled. Open rugby? He didn't want to see open rugby – he wanted winning rugby, grinding rugby, anything that got the job done.

The All Blacks, though, wanted to end their tour in the same way they had started it – with a charm offensive. Two of their supporters, one of them a Maori, ran around the perimeter of the pitch with a banner that read: 'RUGBY – A WAY OF MAKING FRIENDS'. Russ Thomas, no doubt, had put them up to it. In the committee box, he and Gleeson waved regally to the Welsh faithful. The Bridgend episode, they told all who would listen, was a mere hiccup, an unfortunate accident. The friendly All Blacks were now ready to bid farewell by leaving a good taste in Welsh mouths.

Awarded three penalties in the opening minutes, they elected to run all three, each time to a burst of applause around the ground and howls of protest in the Shelbourne hotel. Every time Dunn made a darting break or flashed an ambitious pass, Locky roared at the television screen. It was as if he was back berating the Sexton Street schoolboys for trying to play the pretty stuff.

'Stop leavin' out the fucking ball!'

'Stop chucking it around! Don't do that!'

But with the Grand Slam in their back pockets, nothing was going to stop the All Blacks from playing the game they had left New Zealand to play, the one they had left behind at Thomond Park.

Up in the commentary box, Bill McLaren was purring with pleasure at what he was watching. Again and again the All Blacks attacked with speed and verve.

'That was a marvellous piece of play and the crowd appreciated it to the full, Gareth!'

It was exhilarating and for most of the match it was also effective. With fifteen minutes left the game looked safe for Mourie's men, who led 15–7. Then, calamity. A looping pass from Skrela found Mike Slemen unmarked and on the burst and nobody got near the Englishman as he scored in the corner. Faced with a difficult conversion from just inside the left touchline to make it 15–13, Bennett started it miles right but then the ball began to curl around. When the flags went up, McLaren had to shout to make himself heard.

'Every Welshman in the crowd was blowing like blazes to make that ball turn inside the posts!'

At the Shelbourne they held their heads in their hands and feared the worst. The All Blacks should have had the match sewn up long ago; now they were in danger of losing it. It was at this moment that they chose – to a torrent of abuse from the Munster team – to perform their haka at a tap penalty, a sight never before seen. It backfired almost immediately: the Barbarians were awarded a penalty for offside, a long kick which would make it 16–15. McLaren sensed an upset.

'My goodness, the All Blacks may be regretting this because

Andy Irvine here is going to have a pot for goal. That's the halfway line – you can see it's got to be a mammoth kick. It's high enough! Is it straight enough? It hit the middle of the bar!'

The Munster players punched the air with relief, but it proved short-lived. Soon after, Bennett slotted another penalty and the Baa-Baas were ahead. Just when it looked all up for the All Blacks, with little more than a minute left on the clock, they were awarded a penalty twenty-seven metres out and marginally left of the posts.

Up, after several deep breaths, stepped Brian McKechnie, the accountant from Southland who had suffered ritual humiliation at Thomond Park. The Munster players groaned when he picked up the ball.

Number of kicks at goal already attempted by McKechnie: 8
Number of times McKechnie successful: 1
Feelings for McKechnie at Shelbourne hotel: contempt, bordering on hatred
Look on McKechnie's face as he placed the ball: terror

The full-back took four steps backwards and then stood bolt upright, his arms fully extended by his side. He barely glanced at the posts. His eyes were fixed on the ball just ahead of him. His kicking technique was to step forward and flail at it with his right toe. What he was doing there, with his success rate so far, was anyone's guess. But there he stood. McLaren, for one, seemed sceptical.

'The world waits breathless for Brian McKechnie. He really has had one of his worst days for kicking. McKechnie then . . . has he got the legs? No! he's pushed it outside!'

The Munster players, spitting with rage, did not spare McKechnie.

'Useless bastard!'

'Fucking clown!'

'He's cost us, lads! He's after costin' us!'

The Arms Park broke into a deafening chorus of 'Land Of Our Fathers', but it wasn't quite over. In the final seconds, with the All Blacks laying siege, Irvine carried the ball over his own line.

'Scrum five. We've played a minute of injury time and the Barbarians are leading by sixteen-fifteen. They've beaten the All Blacks only once before. Loveridge . . . the drop goal by Eddie Dunn . . . a lot of room . . .'

In Cardiff, Dublin and all points of New Zealand, time stood still as 'Hands' Dunn gathered the ball at chest height, seventeen metres out, left of the posts. So sweet was the diving pass from his scrum-half that Dunn had a split second to settle himself before striking the ball with his right foot. Rives broke from the scrum and launched himself at it. He got so close to a charge-down that the ball seemed to brush against his fingertips, but the contact made by Dunn was too good, his timing too perfect, his target too close. Bullseye.

'It's there! He's done it!'

Dunn, emotionless, had swivelled on his heels before the ball had even reached the posts. He just jogged back to his own half, like it was nothing. But inside he felt good about himself. He felt like he'd paid his dues. Some said he had cost them the Munster match; now he had saved his team at the very death.

Back at the hotel there was pandemonium. At the sight of the ball sailing through the posts the Munster players had erupted. Now, as the final whistle blew, they began hugging one another and dancing around the room. If anything, the euphoria was even greater than the feeling they had experienced when Corris Thomas blew for full-time six weeks before. Back then, overwhelmed by relief and

238

tiredness, they had been swallowed up by the crowd before they knew what they had achieved, or what it meant.

They knew it now. Canniffe, their captain, had called it right at half-time in Thomond Park. They were the Munster immortals.

Epilogue

Three Stories

Limerick, twenty-five years later

Peter Clarke is my name. I was a bus conductor all my life. I was there when Munster beat the All Blacks. Course I was there. It was the best day of my life.

I wound up with two tickets on the morning of the match. I gave the other one to Butch Donovan, Lord have mercy on him, a great rugby man, an Old Crescent man, a gentleman of all times. Some people are making out they were there when they weren't. I can think of a certain fella but I can't tell you his name because it could be taken for libel.

About one o'clock the day after, myself, Tony Clohessy and Minih Griffin were above in Tony's pub, the Tanyard. Your man was telling everyone about the match. We knew he was bull-shitting.

Minih said, 'Jaysus, wouldn't it have been a great match only for the shower of rain?'

'Oh Jaysus, 'twould,' he says. 'That's right. That killed it for a small bit.'

Not a drop of rain fell that afternoon. We knew how to set up these guys.

Tony produced a duck then. His daughter brought it down in tinfoil, opened it and the oil ran out of it. I'll tell you one thing now – it was the sweetest duck I ever ate. They all came over, looking for a bit of it. We told them, 'No. No way. This is for us. We're still celebrating.'

Johnny Brennan has the ball from that match in his museum. He loves showin' it to fellas. He's only up the road. I'm not sure of the number, but they'd know him in McGrath's pub on the corner.

McGrath's, Carey's Road

Johnny Brennan? Are you going to see his fucking museum, are you? I'll take you up there. You know he has the ball from the All Blacks match? Must be worth a few bob, I'd say.

I'm more of a soccer man myself, but I played rugby with Young Munsters. Scrum-half for the junior team. In the senior team there was a fella by the name of Dickinson. He was a better scrum-half than me. Was it Tony Dickinson or his brother? There was two Dickinsons. I played all the way up to the final of the Transfield Cup and got dropped, right?

They made out he was better than me. They said he had more experience. And I said to them, 'How has he more experience than me? I played all the fucking matches up to the final.' They lost the match the same day and I was delighted. But I'm Young Munsters all my life. I wouldn't play with nobody else.

That All Blacks match, it's like the time Kennedy got shot. Everyone remembers where they were when they heard the news. Will I tell you why, will I? It's because every fucker in town says he was actually at the match.

I wasn't at it, though. I don't mind admitting it. I'll tell you where I was – down in Patsy Nicholas's pub in Gerald Griffin Street. The place was full. Everyone in the pub thought the All Blacks would beat the arse off of them.

I was drinking away and one of the lads came in after and said, 'Pa, I met your wife outside in the match.'

I said, 'How do you mean you met my wife outside in the

241

match? She doesn't follow sports and anyway she's in Dublin with her fucking boyfriend.'

He was my best mate. She ran off with the fucker. They used to get me drunk. She was working above in the Spotted Dog and I was gullible enough to be with him. They took my car off to Cork and I hadn't a clue. She dropped me off at work and they went away driving. The whole lot. I'd fucking choke her.

I heard about the match in a pub and she could come the whole way down from Dublin, herself and himself, and get tickets for it. As far as I was concerned she had no interest in rugby. She never watched a match once with me.

She owed me money. My house went on fire when my daughter made her First Communion. She got three and a half thousand from the insurance and took it all on me. Fucked off and left me there with my youngest daughter.

They came up to the house the day after the match to see my daughter. Well, her daughter as well. This one was like me, mad about sport. She had a motor car hired out. Well, he had. I let the air out of the four wheels, to get her arrested, and I phoned up the cops.

The cops came and said, 'You're after interferin' with that man's car there.'

I said, 'What d'you mean? I didn't interfere with his car at all. The tyres were punctured. And there's an arrest warrant out for her, for three and a half fucking thousand pound.' Which back then was good money. I said, 'Give me back the money and ye can fuck off.' I was going to hit him. The cop pulled me back.

About two years after the All Blacks match Limerick were playing Galway in the All-Ireland final above in fucking Croke Park. There were sixty or seventy thousand people inside in the field and who did I bump into? Her, him, his mother-in-law and his fucking brother. I'm not telling lies. She took my daughter on me that day. My niece from England was minding her. I didn't come home at all that Sunday. Or Monday. I came home Tuesday and my daughter was gone. She knew I wouldn't be home, so she took the child then. And my mother told me, 'Don't follow her.' Because if I did, I would have done something. I haven't talked to her since. Since that rugby match.

C'mon. I'll take you up to your man. It's straight up the road here. I built his museum for him, you know. Well, I helped him. Reporter or something, are you? I worked for a newspaper myself actually. The Limerick Leader. Here in town. I got sacked from that. Sacked by a Shannon supporter. D'you know why he sacked me? For drinking above in the Desmond Arms. Of a Sunday. They were bringing in a new printing press and I was supposed to be helping them take out the old one. A Shannon man sacked me. Here's Johnny's. I'll knock on the door for you. Now.

Johnny Brennan's museum

Some people say I'm the biggest rugby supporter in town but I'd say that was my mother. She used to go to all the matches in Thomond Park. She was Josie Brennan and she'd never miss a Young Munster match. She was eight decades following rugby – 20s, 30s, 40s, 50s, 60s, 70s, 80s and 90s. Two months before she died she was at a Munster Senior Cup final in Thomond Park. Garryowen beat us. She wore black and amber, the hat and all, the whole lot. She was eighty-five when she died. She was only sick for a few weeks. Got a stroke a week after I came back from the Lions in South Africa.

What happened was, I used to collect a few rugby photographs and keep them in this room here. But when my mother got a bit old she couldn't go up the stairs so I said I'd build on a small room for my photographs. Somebody said, 'Johnny, are you buildin' a museum?' You know the way fellas would be passin'. But I had no intention of buildin' a museum. It just happened off the cuff.

I took out a mortgage on my house and I'm still payin' for it. I

243

got a penny off nobody. There's three new rooms. There was only a garage there before. Peter Clohessy gave me a hand with the first room. He gave me the mixer and he took the levels with Micky Hehir. I built the first room when she was here. She said: 'Johnny, what are you doing? The house will fall down.' I couldn't build the second room or the third room with her here because she didn't understand. But she would go up to Dublin every year and stay with my brother for a couple of weeks and I'd build then. I'd lash into it until she came back and she wouldn't know really.

I was the bagman when Munsters won the Cup in '80. That's me there, at the back. And that's the ball from that match. That's my aunt there, jumping up when Mick Sheehan scored our try. That's a bit of grass from Lansdowne Road in 1993 when we won the All Ireland League. I went out on to the field and dug it up. You couldn't water it because if you did it would take the authentic out of it, you know? They're Aidan O'Halloran's boots. He kicked the penalty that day.

That's my mother with the Bateman Cup there. It's on display in Weir's jewellers of Grafton Street in Dublin, it's there thirty or forty years. And there's no names or nothing on it, showing who won it. We got it down for my mother's eightieth birthday and we had to insure it. I had it going around the road, inside in a plastic bag. My mother was saying, 'Where's he gone with the cup?' Young Munsters are the only Limerick team to win it, the only Limerick team now. Thank God no one will ever win it again. They can't equal what Young Munsters done.

There's a lot of work involved in being bagman. Young Munsters only had one set of jerseys. Before I took over, they'd dry 'em in a chipper, Patsy Naughton's in Parnell Street, and the junior team would wear them the following day then. You couldn't get 'em washed because you probably wouldn't have them until seven o'clock at night after the match. The heat from the fisher would dry 'em, but they'd be all mud. My mother said to me that

I hadn't a dinner for ten years. I'd be gone from ten in the morning to twelve at night. I'd have to make sure the jerseys were laundered. My mother used to dry them here in front of the fire, twenty jerseys all around the front room.

In '81 she went off to Lourdes. My brother Michael picked her up off the train in Dublin and she had two big bags. Michael said to her, 'Mam, what's inside in the bags?' She said, 'They're the Young Munster jerseys.' She put them into the bath over in Lourdes and had 'em blessed. We were playing in the final of the League after she got back. But Shannon beat us.

Her brother – my uncle – played scrum-half for Ireland. He was M. D. Sheahan, Michael Danaher Sheahan. The great Ter Casey played the same day, against England. The talk that time was rugby, rugby, rugby. To be capped that time, you had to be either a doctor or a Protestant. My uncle was a labourer. To get on that time, you had to be good. He worked below in CIE and he'd come up here for his dinner.

Richard Harris was up here once. He'd have known my uncle. Well, he heard of him that time, you know? He was very interested in all the old photographs. There was no bullshit about him. He was sound. He sat down with all the kids in the front for an hour, signing autographs, and took 'em off in the limo up around Weston. It's all rugby, the Hyde Road area. It's a working-class area. They call Young Munster 'the boys from the Yellow Road'. The Yellow Road is the one by the park. I don't know where they got the name. My mother used to say to me that years and years ago, when they were buildin' the road, the clay was yellow. And the furze bushes used to be shinin' and they were yellow. That mightn't be true.

There was three footballs used the day Munster beat the All Blacks. Johnny Cole had one and Gerry McLoughlin had one I think and that's the other one. But my one is the only one that's signed, see?

Come up to the light here, I'll show you something. Watch the marks . . . that's where it went into the trees in Thomond Park. And it is authentic – I could tell you how I got it.

De Beers sponsored the match and the chauffeur for De Beers was a fella by the name of Cyril Kiely, who played with Young Munster. He drove the boss to the match that day and after the match he drove him back to the plane, probably a private jet. And the boss, as we'll call him, had that ball signed by all the players and Cyril got it off him. Cyril's a personal friend of mine. He said: 'What's the use of me having it at home? You can have it above.'

There's no signature opposite number nine. That was Donal Canniffe. His father died, so he didn't sign anything. But I met him later and he signed it for me. See? And Graham Mourie. I met him too. See?

Now there's a ball down the town hall, in the mayor's office. I went down to have a look at it. They had it stuck on top of a plinth and they were showin' it an' all. They had the date of the match engraved under it. But . . . there was a nozzle in it! This one is a laced ball, see? There was no nozzles that time. I mean, it wasn't even the right colour! I knew straight away but I didn't say anything to anybody. I wouldn't say nothin' like that.

I'm closing down the museum on 31 October, the twenty-fifth anniversary of the match. We're goin' buildin' another museum in the lane opposite Charlie St George's pub.

The tourism crowd will send out brochures sayin', 'When you come to Limerick, go to the Limerick Rugby Museum'. It'll be included in the walks of Limerick, like Frank McCourt's walk.

I'll be the curator. I'm goin' addin' to it, I'll still be collecting. We'll have all the stuff in the house here on display. It'll stay there forever. Everything except the ball from the All Blacks match. I'm taking that into the grave with me.

Afterword

Forty Years Later

1. Locky's Story, Part 2

What happened next? I got capped.

Five of the Munster team were picked against France a few months later. They called out the Irish team above in the Shelbourne Hotel and myself and Colm Tucker were on it. Two Shannon men. About time, wasn't it?

I was the tighthead prop, up against Gerard Cholley – a huge man. I had Pa Whelan alongside me as hooker. Straight away he told me to bring down the scrum, but I didn't take instructions from hookers, especially Garryowen hookers. Anyway, I was used to Pa's antics – I'd been playing against him since 1973. I was well able to handle Cholley that day. He got dropped after it.

My father died later that same year. He never said much to me about my rugby – we weren't a talking kind of family. Even to this day, I'm like that with my own sons. Leave them off and see how they get on. My father only expressed his emotions in the pub at night-time – the Tanyard Inn, a Young Munster pub. It was a big thing to walk in there when your son was playing for Ireland. A bit of pride, like, you know?

I played for Ireland until 1984, but I never felt that success took me over. I wanted to be the same person I was before I was ever capped.

I had a lot of kicks in the teeth between 1981 and 1987. First off, I lost my teaching job over going to South Africa with Ireland. I had great respect for the Christian Brothers, so I don't think I could ever blame them. I made my decision and I learned a lot on that tour – things that stuck with me, like the poverty we saw in Soweto.

Back then, Ireland was going through a recession and things weren't too rosy in the garden, with four children to feed. I opened a pub, but business is never easy. So it was difficult to make ends meet.

It was a matter of necessity that I left the country – I had to find something to support my family. They stayed in Limerick until I got fixed up with work across the water. I took off for London, on my own, with a duffel bag on my back. I came back fifteen years later with the same duffel bag.

I was never afraid to back myself. I worked three or four jobs in London and then I got a chance to buy a pub in Wales – the Richard Llewellyn, in Gilfach Goch.

I was happy that the kids were brought up in Britain, where they had very little. They were grounded in that village. It's a quiet mining valley and there was rugby everywhere. My family have had a lot of change in their lives, but if you can adapt to change it makes you a more rounded person.

Getting your life in order is ongoing – you have to keep working at it and appreciating every day for what it is. I'm sixty-seven now and I've gone through soul-searching times, but I've never been so happy as I am today. I have peace of mind. I've never had much money, which is a blessing. Over the years I've had just enough to survive. If someone had handed me a couple of hundred thousand, I'd be frightened.

I've always felt alive as a human being. I've always had spirit. All my kids have spirit. My wife has it too, even though we're separated more than fifteen years. If you have that inside you, it makes you a better human being, it makes you alive. The minute your spirit goes, you're fucked. So you have to get up off the chair. You have to keep going, for as long as you can.

I've had the variety of everything – good health and bad health, marriage and divorce. I've had the kids with me and now the kids away from me. Heartbreak is the worst pain you can have. Heartbreak and loneliness. I didn't want to leave Wales – I'd gotten to like it – but I had to leave. It was like moving away from Ireland in the 1980s – sometimes you just have to get up and go.

I didn't like Limerick when I came back. For a few years I hated the place – it wasn't the city I had left in 1987. It was the peak of the Celtic Tiger, my friends were all doing well and I felt like a failure. I often asked myself, 'Why did I come back here?' For a long time I was too proud to talk to people about those feelings, so I just put up with it.

It took time, but gradually I started falling back in love with Limerick. I suppose I really came back because I wanted to be in a place where I could just be myself – and I got there in the end. Anyone who knows Limerick will tell you that you can't fool anybody here. Even if you're well known, you have to be down to earth, with the same principles, the same values and the same way of living that you had before you got a bit of fame.

I went into politics and I tried to do my best for disadvantaged areas in the city, so that people living there would get opportunities. To be honest, though, I'm not sure you can get much done as a politician. You have to fall in line with the system. And the system can change you completely, if you let it.

When I lost my seat on the council, I was disappointed for two or three hours. The following day, I felt it was the best thing that could ever have happened. I'd never go into politics again – it's an invasion of your life. All I want to be now is an ordinary person, getting on with life. You can be anonymous and just tip away on your own. And if you pass on, not many will miss you. Which is great, it doesn't bother me.

Not too long ago I went through a two-year depression, but I've come out of it without any medication. I know there are times when I have to get out of the city and away from everything. Every couple of weeks I go away somewhere, on my own, in silence. And I find it's not one bit lonely. You make a choice, and there's a great feeling of, 'Well, I'm doing this now because I want to do it.'

To be able to let go of the kids was massive for me. My three sons live across the water and my daughter is here. For years I was spending every day on the rugby field with the boys. And then, all of a sudden, there comes a time when you can't be part of their daily lives. You realise that you're clinging on to something that can't continue in the same way. So I stopped – as subtly as I could, without them knowing it. They'll probably read about that now, but it won't bother them. And while I wouldn't have a lot of contact with them, there's a presence there. And once you feel the presence of somebody, you can connect with that person any time.

I find now that I know myself better, after all these years. Even in the worst of times, I always saw a little bit of hope at the end of every day. I felt suicidal, I was close to suicide, but I managed to hold on to some hope. There was always something that gave me a lift and made me feel alive. In the end, it was dancing that lifted me out of it. Dancing and meditation. I danced for seven hours a day in Lisdoonvarna for two weeks.

I've been very lucky in that the sports career I had has helped me in other ways. I think it goes back to the discipline I had as a rugby player – going out in the muck on the dark nights in the back field at Thomond Park. It gave me the discipline to practise every day – whether it's learning Irish, or ballroom dancing, or something else. I'm good at practising little things in life. Everything is practice.

In 1987, the year I emigrated, I was asked to play a match for the Wolfhounds against Llanelli. Before the game, someone handed me a brown envelope. I said, 'I don't want it.' They said, 'You've a pub to run. You've a family to feed.' So I took it. It was the first time in my life someone had given me anything to play. I'll never forget that moment. Taking money for rugby.

People sometimes ask, 'Would you like to have been a professional rugby player?' I would have hated it. I wouldn't have been able to do it. Why not? Because sport to me was nothing to do with money. You did it because you loved it.

These days I look upon life as a gift. If I croaked in the morning, if I lay down, I'd still have had a great life. There isn't anything that bothers me now. The world gave me everything and it owes me nothing.

2. All's Changed

There's a total disconnect between the modern game and the rugby that we had. The whole thing has changed remarkably from our time. In terms of an emotional loss in my life from not having an involvement in the game since I retired, I would say I'm not missing what isn't there any more.
Moss Finn, 2018

The legend of Munster's achievement in 1978 has grown with each passing year, perhaps because the idea of an almost full-strength All Blacks team being held scoreless by a provincial side seems even more miraculous and unrepeatable now. Thirty-nine years later, in an RTE television poll, it was voted by viewers as one of Ireland's top three sporting moments of all time,[1] finishing ahead of anything achieved by Irish rugby teams in the amateur or professional eras, and even seeing off every highlight produced by the national games of hurling and Gaelic football.

---

[1] Ireland's 1990 World Cup victory against Romania, after penalties, was voted no. 1, ahead of Padraig Harrington's first golf major, the 2007 British Open Championship at Carnoustie.

Thirty years passed before the All Blacks set foot in Limerick again. And by 2008, almost everything had changed, even Thomond Park. There were two hakas performed on the night the gleaming new stadium was officially opened. The one that will live forever in the memory of all who witnessed it came from four New Zealanders wearing Munster jerseys, men drawn to the province by the professional game.

The Munster haka has taken its own place in local sporting folklore, immortalised in a photograph that was soon framed and mounted in many a local pub. Galvanised by a proud tradition, Munster almost won again that night, but they left the field after writing another page in the chapter of glorious failures against the mighty All Blacks, joining the teams that came up just short in 1954, 1963 and 1973. And so the achievement of the 1978 team stood alone, still.

On that November night in 2008, thirteen years after the dawn of professionalism, the modern Munster team were champions of Europe for the second time in three years. Their first title had come two years before amid tumultuous scenes at the Millennium Stadium in Cardiff, which was thronged with 65,000 of their supporters. By then, the tournament had become the holy grail for Munster and their vast support base.

Another 15,000 watched the 2006 final on a big screen in O'Connell Street, Limerick. Not many of them would have known that one of the key driving forces behind the creation of the European Cup in 1995 was a Munster man who had already done his province some service: Tom Kiernan.

The rugby played on the night the All Blacks returned to Thomond Park – and, increasingly, in the professional game in the years since – often resembles a different sport, played by men bigger and more powerful than those on the team sheets of 1978.

There would be no place in today's game for a centre as slight as Seamus Dennison, because bravery in the tackle doesn't count for enough when your opposite number has a weight advantage of seven or eight stone. Dennison was down for eleven stone and twelve pounds on the official team sheet, but he was never asked to step on a weighing scale in all his time with Munster and reckons he was a stone off that on the big day. 'Everybody put their weight down for more than what it was. I was finished playing rugby for years before I got to twelve stone, for Christ's sake.'

The fifteen Munster men who beat the All Blacks never lined out together on a rugby field again.

They hammered Connacht with the same backline eighteen days later, but two of the pack were injured. A week before Christmas, they were another man down in beating Leinster – a victory that gave them the 1978 interprovincial championship, and with it a mini Grand Slam of their own.

At the time, Kiernan was asked to compare that interpro title with the All Blacks win and he declared it 'equally pleasing', but history has not been kind to the domestic fixtures from autumns past. Forty years on, the Munster–Leinster rivalry is almost exclusively defined by battles fought in the professional era and the 'Historic Results' section in the Munster Rugby website starts with the 1995–96 season.

By 1981, when Australia were beaten 15–6 in Cork, only McLoughlin, Tucker, Foley, Cantillon and Ward made the starting Munster line-up. And by the time New Zealand next ran onto a Munster pitch, for a match played in Cork two days after the fall of the Berlin Wall in November 1989, even the youngest member of the 1978 team, Moss Finn, had played his last game in a red jersey.

Among Finn and his team-mates, there is nothing but admiration for their modern-day successors, but there is also a shared dismay that the rise of Ireland's four professional provinces has come at the expense of the club game that nurtured their own playing careers.

Finn has been running the family sports store in the heart of Cork city for decades. He doesn't sell any Munster jerseys these days – a rival chain bought up the merchandising rights – but Finn's Corner has been a good vantage point from which to observe the transformation of the Irish rugby landscape. He has cheered for the Munster of Paul O'Connell, Ronan O'Gara and Peter O'Mahony as much as the next man, but he dislikes the way the past and present are sometimes joined by marketers selling a version of history that jars with him.

'I don't like the way they eulogise the tradition of Munster and use it for commercial gain in the modern world,' he says. 'They pay lip service to the old regime. They take the history – Mick O'Callaghan's bandaged head in 1963 against the All Blacks, Tommy Kiernan standing alone against Australia in 1967 – and they use those guys to make the Munster brand of today more commercial. As if they're one and the same thing, which they're not. But it comes down to the Yankee dollar, you know?

'That's not being chippy, because I think Munster today are wonderful. But I don't buy into that eulogising, not when the clubs that produced those great players from the past are falling asunder.'

Johnny Brennan, the former Young Munster bagman who built a museum at his home in the heart of working-class Limerick, no longer shows visitors around his triple extension on the Hyde Road, a space that once seemed bigger than the original house. The three new rooms that were mostly a shrine to club rugby are empty now and the space feels abandoned; Johnny lives alone and has no need for it. After lying in storage for more than ten years, part of his huge collection was put on display in an exhibition space alongside Charlie St George's pub down the road, but Johnny finds there isn't much interest these days in the black-and-white photographs, match programmes, newspaper cuttings, jerseys, club ties and other memorabilia he collected lovingly for more than forty years.

A different kind of rugby museum has been planned for the middle of town, in a towering space billed as 'a digital interactive visitor centre' and made possible by 'an initial investment' of €10 million by the Limerick billionaire J. P. McManus. The Limerick Rugby Experience, with its '4D interactive galleries', will recreate some famous moments from the history of the game in a way Johnny Brennan couldn't have imagined on Young Munster's greatest day back in 1993, when he dug a piece of turf out of the Lansdowne Road pitch and framed it for posterity.

'Times have changed an awful lot,' he says. He lists off some of his close friends – all lifelong supporters of the club game in Limerick – who are no longer alive: Frank 'Dollars' Mulcahy, Mogwah Lysaght, Tom Clancy, Didi Sheahan, Mickey Cross, Sam Browne – all gone to God. 'Back when they were around, it was all rugby, rugby, rugby, rugby. But now the clubs aren't getting the gates and they're finding it very hard to survive.

'I go to the odd Munster match in Thomond Park and there's a great atmosphere there, but I think a lot has been lost. It's all about money now. You don't have the friendships you had in our time. There's different people following rugby and the young fellas now wouldn't know anything about the history and the rivalries.'

You'll still find him at Tom Clifford Park on Saturday afternoons, with his fellow Young Munster diehards, cheering on the black and amber. They marvel at the brand of rugby their team plays in the All Ireland League – a competition that used to mean everything, back in the nineties before everything changed.

There is a handsome tankard on display in the exhibition alongside Charlie St George's, and a note from the man who donated it reads: *To Johnny, a great Young Munster man in good times and bad. All the best always — Tom Kiernan.*

From one devotee of the game to another.

As he flips pancakes at his kitchen hob in the heart of Limerick city on a sweltering summer afternoon, Gerry McLoughlin remembers the day when he found out that the fierce rugby rivalry he grew up with had become something different.

It was January 2000 and Munster were in Wales for a Heineken Cup pool game against Pontypridd. Six thousand of the faithful had turned up for the Ponty game at Thomond Park two months before, but there was no more than a scattering with them at Sardis Road that day.

Nobody saw it coming, but the Munster rugby phenomenon was about to take off in an extraordinary way. Within four months they would bring 40,000 supporters with them to the final at Twickenham. And even then, the Red Army was only getting started.

But back to Pontypridd and a phone call that left Locky in a state of confusion.

'I got the biggest shock of my life. Brian O'Brien rang me – he was the Munster manager at that stage. He knew Ponty was a rugby-mad town and he said, "Can you give me a pub where Galwey and Claw can have a quiet drink together?"

'I couldn't get my head around that. It was a huge shock to me. I thought: Why would Mick Galwey, a Shannon man, be drinking with Peter Clohessy, a Young Munster man?

'I had never seen that happen. I mean, I just couldn't see how you could do it. When we played, there was a huge divide. Okay, Tommy Kiernan brought us together for the All Blacks match – but that was more or less a one-off. The normal situation was that you'd go drinking with your own mates in your own part of town. That was bred into us at Shannon. It went back to the fifties when we were a junior club. Some people in Limerick didn't want us to be given senior status and we felt we'd been hard done by.

'Even when we got success as a senior club, we never changed our thinking. So I genuinely couldn't walk in the door of a Garryowen pub or a Young Munster pub. Even now, I've never been in Charlie St George's.

'I'd been in Wales for thirteen years at that stage and I really hadn't been keeping up with what was going on back home. So that day I was thinking to myself, "What's going on? Where has this come from?"'

By the time he moved back to Limerick, a couple of years later, the Munster team of Galwey, Clohessy and a legion of other household names were one of the biggest stories in Irish sport.

'And when I looked around at what was happening, I felt like I'd moved back to a place I didn't recognise any more.'

3. Absent Friends

Colm Tucker was a modern rugby player long before the game went professional. Among the many tributes paid following his death at the age of fifty-nine, there was a recurring theme: he was an athlete far ahead of his time who would have thrived as a wing forward in today's faster and more physical game.

Obituary, Irish Times, January 2012

The first reunion of the history men was at Abbeyfeale Rugby Club, to mark the opening of a new clubhouse. 'I was thrilled that they all turned up,' recalled Seamus Dennison, by then one of the town's most famous sons. 'It brought it on a long way from the days of Abbeyfeale rugby fellas changing in the local cinema.'

More recently, after most of the team were feted with a standing ovation at a black-tie function in Dublin's Mansion House, Donal Spring shook his head in wonderment at 'guys in their thirties taking photographs on their iPhones of a bunch of old fellas who won a rugby match forty years ago'.

Applauding from a table close to the stage that night were the two daughters of Moss Keane, Sarah and Anne Marie. Their father's death from cancer at sixty-two, in October 2010, was the first loss suffered among the thirty-one players who took the field at Thomond Park in 1978.

Colm Tucker was only fifty-nine when he died barely four months later, of lung disease. 'Colm had the kind of power I never saw in anyone else,' said his fellow Shannon soldier, Gerry McLoughlin. 'Because of that, it was a shock for me to see him so sick.'

Amid the obituaries and tributes to Moss Keane, the word 'indestructible' appeared often. He was larger than life, they said, and it made no sense that the colossus could be taken so soon.

'Dad loved his team-mates,' said Sarah Keane, when recalling the Mansion House reunion of 2017. 'When they stood on stage accepting their award, Anne Marie and I were deeply moved. Then they sang together and you couldn't help but shed a tear. For us it was joy and sadness all at once – bittersweet.'

Jimmy Bowen: It's extraordinary – the two biggest and strongest guys on our team were Colm Tucker and Moss Keane. And they're both dead.

Seamus Dennison: Tucker was like Mr Universe, a specimen of a man. For that to happen to him, to be hammered like that, was an awful shock. And Moss was the other powerhouse in our pack. You just couldn't believe it.

Larry Moloney: We've lost three of the fellas who were togged off that day. Micky O'Sullivan hit us first. He was the replacement full-back, he'd have come on for me. Micky died young, very young. There's part of it missing now, no matter what. We'll have a reunion this year for the fortieth anniversary of the match. In ten years' time, if we meet again, there might be another few gone. That's the sad part about the whole thing.

Jimmy Bowen: Micky O'Sullivan was one of my best friends. I knew him from the age of seven or eight. We soldiered together at Pres in school and at Cork Con. He was a smashing guy, very competitive. He should have done a bit better than he did, but there was a lot of competition. Larry Moloney was a great full-back – and there was no shifting him in that Munster team.

Gerry McLoughlin: Moss Keane was the most loyal second-row you'd ever find in your whole life. I'm sure he was often asked: 'What was wrong with McLoughlin today?' Moss would turn the other ear to the selectors.

Pat Whelan: Moss was the most intelligent, brilliant guy you will ever come across. There was this image of a different kind of man, one that he created about himself. It was a caricature. It was totally … untrue, basically.

Sarah Keane: The real man gets lost in the public perception of who he was. Dad cared what people thought of him – that was his vulnerability. I think it was something he concealed. When he was writing his book, I was joking with him. I'd say, 'Jesus, Dad – it's so bloody clean! Would you not throw in more of the boldness?' And he would just look at me and say, 'It's a fucking book I'm writing, Sarah – not a confession.'

When he was out and about, he only cared about making people laugh. He could make small men feel ten feet tall, while always shrinking himself. But that was only part of who he was. He was this big, gregarious character in public, but at home he was quiet, gentle, spiritual – and very religious. When we were kids, there was never a car journey we made without prayers. People joked about him flicking holy water at the Ulster players in the Ireland dressing room, but I think he may have concealed the sincerity behind that as well.

Greg Barrett: When I think back to the type of people who came to play in the red Munster jersey, there was all sorts, every type. You needed someone who could bring everyone together – and Moss was always fantastic when anybody new came in. He knocked down any barriers, immediately.

Brendan Foley: Before he was ever sick, Moss had given up the drink and the cigarettes. I often wonder if he suspected there might be something wrong, because Moss was very intelligent and he had great instincts.

Sarah Keane: After he stopped drinking he really went deep into himself. He meditated a lot. Every morning he would bring me into the sitting room and we'd say this Celtic prayer. He'd make me read it out, so that he could get into the actions. It was all about bringing gratitude into our hearts. Later in his life, the part of him that cared about how people saw him lessened – and his spiritual side grew. But he combined that with a kindness and a sense of fun that we saw every day.

I think every one of us has greatness in us – Dad just learned how to tap into his. I remember watching him, one day, through a new glass front in our local supermarket. I saw him lighting up the people he came in contact with – the other shoppers, the girl at the checkout. Then he turned to come back out to the car, looking like he didn't have a care in the world. Less than two weeks after that, he got his diagnosis.

Christy Cantillon: Mossie had cancer of the oesophagus. Once you have it, it's a tough battle.

Sarah Keane: We evolved so much as a family over the eighteen months of his illness – I mean spiritually. He fought his cancer like he was taking on the All Blacks – head-on. He imported a healing crystal bed from John of God in Brazil and he'd lie on that twice a day. We had a game plan, if you could call it that, in the spare bedroom. It listed all the supplements he was taking – and when. It stretched from the ceiling to the floor.

We would sing together – we'd sing 'Stand Up and Fight', the Munster song. Even through the chemotherapy, he never lost his hair – it used to confound the oncologists. People said it was like one of those Paul O'Connell jokes – his hair was afraid to fall out.

I remember the day we knew he wasn't going to make it. There was a look between us. We'd been importing a nutritional supplement called Genista from Canada. It was a herbal cocktail – Dad was always into his herbs. I was taking some detox patches off his feet and he said, 'Should we order more Genista?' I just looked up at him – and he knew, as he said it. There was a look on his face that said, 'We've given it everything here.'

Up until that moment, there wasn't even a question of him dying. I'd say to him, 'You're going to beat it. No fucking way is it going to be any other way.' We were fierce close. Really close. Yeah. Yeah.

Brendan Foley: Three or four days before he died, I went up to see him. We shook hands when it was time to leave. I knew, from the handshake, that I wasn't going to see him again. I remember Anne, his wife, telling us that the night before he died, or the night he died, he had to face east so that the rising sun was at his feet. It was one of these traditions. I don't know if it was religious, or something from Kerry. But Moss was larger than life. He spread himself around, as the man says.

Sarah Keane: He died during the night, half three or four. We were all around him and his final words were, 'I'm off.'

I spoke at his funeral. I talked about the spiritual journey we'd all been on throughout his illness. He cultivated this inner strength and resilience – and it was contagious. He took us by the hand through it all and he prepared us. So Anne Marie and I found that when he died, there was this resource within us – something we didn't have eighteen months before.

Moss Finn: He was the greatest human being I ever met. Because he could talk turkey, you know? If you walked into the Western Star after a match, or the Con bar or the Lansdowne bar, there would be a crowd around Moss Keane, waiting for the spontaneity of what he might say.

Donal Spring: Mossie was one of my best friends. I'm godfather to one of his daughters, Anne Marie. I met Mossie when I was thirteen at the Ardfert GAA pitch. He had one uncle and no aunts, on his father's side. His uncle was a priest called Fr Matty, who married my parents in 1944 – and buried both of them.

I couldn't lift Mossie's coffin – my back wasn't up to it. To be asked by the family to give the graveside oration was an honour. I spoke about how unique he was. There was only one Moss Keane. In some ways, part of Moss's difficulty was that he was so selfless – he gave so much of himself to everybody.

Tucker was like an older brother to me. He was so protective – I always felt that he'd be on my shoulder when I needed him. And he always made me feel that I could do something with the ball when I got it. He'd say, 'Here's your chance! Here's your chance!' He was a fantastic fellow and of all the players in that team who could have transitioned straight to the professional game, Tucker was number one. He was such an athlete.

People say to me, 'You only got seven caps.' I got more than twice as many as Colm Tucker – one of the most gifted players ever in Irish rugby.

Colm and Mossie are on either side of me in the photograph taken before the start of the All Blacks game. It's on the wall behind me in my office, above my desk. When I look at it I think, 'There but for the grace of God …'

Pat Whelan: Colm Tucker was one of the best footballers I've ever seen. He could do anything with a ball. He was a natural footballer, a thinker, a ball-carrier. And very strong. Incredibly strong.

Christy Cantillon: Colm got a virus that attacked his lungs. Then he was told he needed a transplant to stay alive.

Geraldine Tucker, Colm Tucker's widow: At first, we probably didn't realise how sick he was. It was a terrible illness, so unfair. Towards the end he was on oxygen 24/7, for the bones of a year. Four times he was called for a possible transplant, but every time it didn't work out. It was very, very difficult. You've got all that hope. An ambulance would take him to the Mater Hospital in Dublin, we'd wait around for hours and they'd come and say, 'No, sorry. It's not a match.'

So we'd have the journey home then. And you're trying to pick up the pieces, until the next time. Sometimes he'd say, 'I won't get one – look at the size of me. Where will they get a lung for my size?' But I always had hope.

Gerry McLoughlin: Colm kept himself to himself in the last years. We didn't have that much contact, even though we'd both go into Flannery's. Colm liked it there, because people left him in peace.

It was lovely to be in the same place as him. For two years we'd salute each other and that was it. I don't think we were very good at outward compassion. What's the word – empathy, isn't it? We'd sit at opposite ends of the bar, but just to salute him for those couple of years was lovely. We were both happy to do that. What could you say to somebody who was suffering, you know?

Geraldine Tucker: Colm loved his rugby career and he had great stories. He had that sharp wit, or a look. I still feel that look, here in the house. I'll think: *He's looking at me now.*

Everyone around him said he should have won more Irish caps. I was mad about it myself – his whole family was. He would never say anything about it, though. Not even between these walls – he just didn't want to hear about it. Whether he felt aggrieved or not, he took it. When he played so well on the Lions tour in 1980, he said, 'That's my answer. It doesn't matter how many Irish caps I have.'

Every single day during that Lions tour I wrote to him. Most days he wrote to me and all those letters are in a suitcase up in the attic. I kept a scrapbook too, cuttings from all the papers, waiting for him when he got home.

I had his Munster jersey framed in the house, the one from the All Blacks match. I had other things from his rugby days on the walls around the house, but we took them all down when he got sick. We were living in the same house, but it was different. The atmosphere had changed and our focus had to change.

We kept hoping, but he was getting sicker and sicker. He was moved to the transplant unit at the Mater, but he never got his transplant. We didn't really expect him to go as quickly as he did. But, you know, I think he'd had enough himself.

It's been more than seven years and, to be quite honest, I haven't even read the Mass cards. Every time I go to do it, I'm not able. I've never looked at those letters from the Lions tour either, but some day I might.

I have a note inside the suitcase, on the lid. I've left it for my children or my grandchildren, should they ever open it.

4. Kiernan

I'd light candles to Tommy. He pushed the boundaries. He was the difference.
Seamus Dennison, 2018

In July 2003, in the last of three long interviews for the original edition of this book, Tom Kiernan was asked a final question about his life in rugby: 'How would you like to be remembered?'

A more conceited man might have thought about it. Kiernan didn't. 'Just as somebody who was very keen and involved and who gave it a shot,' he replied quickly.

Fifteen years later, now in his eightieth year, he sits in an armchair at home, opposite the woman he married in the summer of 1966.

His memory isn't what it was. 'When did I go to Australia with Ireland, Maree – was it '68?'

'I haven't a clue, Tom,' she says. 'You came and you went and that was it.'

His days as a player and coach were only the start of the coming and going. Next he turned to rugby administration and held virtually every senior position open to an Irishman. In 2000, when he finally packed it in, Edmund van Esbeck wrote in the *Irish Times*: 'In every facet of the game he embraced, he made a profound impact. Kiernan's place at the pinnacle of Irish rugby will not depend on tradition, legend, hearsay or deceptive and exaggerated claims. The facts speak for themselves, for his has been a career without equal in the history of Irish rugby.'

'I gave up all of my leisure time to the sport,' he acknowledges. His years as an administrator were the most demanding of all, particularly after professionalism came. 'Every single day of the week I was up to my neck in it. It was just one bloody thing after another,' he recalls of the turbulent times when he fought to keep the European game from fracturing. He stuck to the task, as he did with every other challenge that came his way, because when you're in, you're in.

'I was just barely able to keep my show on the road,' he says. 'I don't have any regrets, but I don't know if Maree might have.'

Perhaps it helped that her own parents were steeped in the game too, Con people like his own. The way she tells it, matter-of-factly, things were never going to be any different in their marriage.

'I couldn't tell you much about this game or that game,' she says. 'We had six children, you see – and I only remember the departures. But it was what he wanted to do – and he was reared to it, by Uncle Neddy and the whole lot of them. We didn't sit down and talk about it. They were different days. He just did it because it was part of his growing up. Rugby was part of his life and that was it.'

It still is, but in a different way now. The rugby that interests him these days is also a reminder of his earliest – and perhaps happiest – sporting experiences.

You won't find him at the modern Thomond Park, but he never misses a Con home game at Temple Hill. Here he was once peerless under the high ball, on playing fields first levelled in 1953 under the supervision of his father, Michael Kiernan.

He has a grandson, Louis Bruce, who is fanatical about the game – full-back for Pres in the Munster Schools Senior Cup. He'd rather go and see the boy play than watch Munster on the big European stage, in a tournament he fought hard to bring about. When all's said and done, he is no different to the Munster players he once coached – loyal above all to the traditions that he grew up on.

There are few photographs or mementoes from his time in the game evident in the house and he rarely thinks about those times now. Of coaching Ireland to a famous Triple Crown in 1982, he says only: 'I coached them to a whitewash too, didn't I?' Munster's defeat of the All Blacks doesn't interest him much either. 'I don't think about it. I mean, Jesus, it's forty years ago.'

He leans forward, though, when Maree returns with an old cutting from the *Evening Echo*, which is dominated by a picture taken more than three-quarters of a century ago.

It captures the emerging talent of the day at Cork Constitution, lined up for a group photograph in the early 1940s. She points him out, the youngest of all, a tiny boy who still looks like he belongs.

'What photograph is that, Maree?' he asks. 'Is that the Conettes?'

Five minutes previously he had shaken his head when asked to recall his favourite memories as a player and coach. 'God, I have no favourite memory. I don't really dwell on anything.' Now, though, without even looking at the picture, he remembers the names of the older boys who are all around him.

There is Ray Hennessy, the star full-back who never got capped, because his thunder was stolen seventeen years later by a student who came from nowhere, his arrival confirmed in a *Cork Examiner* headline that read '*T. Kiernan is Ireland's Full Back For Match Against England*'.

There is Ted Crosbie, scion of the family that controlled the *Examiner* from 1856 until 2018.

There is Jim Kiernan, his older brother, who is standing next to Edmund van Esbeck, the future rugby scribe.

'I'm the smallest,' he says, 'not much bigger than the ball. The Conettes used to play up the Mardyke and my uncle coached them. That's my first sojourn now, what you see in that picture – I was three or four. They allowed me to kick the ball off – I remember I kicked it about two yards. That was the beginning of everything.'

5. Consequences

When anyone plays a game as tough as rugby football, they know there will be consequences. We knew it back when I played and none of us expected to walk away unscathed.
Moss Keane, 2005

Donal Spring: Shortly before Moss died, I went down to Portarlington on a Tuesday night to see him. He wasn't in great shape. Neither was I – I'd had two back operations in the space of fourteen days. I walked in the back door and I was bent over. He was sitting on a sofa, with pillows under his elbows. When he saw me, he put a finger to his mouth and said: 'Shhhh!'

At first, I wasn't sure what he meant. I hadn't said a word. Then he said: 'What you have is mechanical.'

What he was saying to me was, 'It's not going to kill you – so don't worry about it.'

Mossie motivates me every week. When he said things, there was always something in them – he was an incredibly deep and spiritual person. I've had three back operations – mainly rugby-related. But ever since that night, every time I get bad back pain I keep telling myself: 'It's only mechanical.'

I'll be sixty-two this year, but my mind is still playing rugby. I wake up some mornings and I feel like I could play again. Until I try to get out of bed.

Jimmy Bowen: Three years after the All Blacks game, I ruptured my knee playing for Lansdowne on the back pitch. Over the years I've had seven knee operations. I'll need to have the knee replaced, before long. I've been told my body will tell me when it needs to be done.

Gerry McLoughlin: I got a new knee in 2004. I had a bad limp and I needed to do something for my quality of life.

It was inevitable, really. I hurt the old one at sixteen and I played all my rugby without a cartilage in that knee. Bone against bone for twenty years.

Donal Canniffe: I got away fairly unscathed. Maybe I was cute.

Pat Whelan: I've dodgy knees. One of them I am going to have to get something done with. But that's about the size of it. I'm lucky.

Larry Moloney: I'll give my body to some museum, I think, when I'm finished with it. I broke every bone on one side – cheekbone, collarbone, dislocated shoulder, broken ribs, broken leg. I had serious hamstring problems, which stemmed from disc problems in my back. Eventually, at twenty-nine, I got a few discs taken out. I was still playing, but the medical advice was 'end of story'.

Since then, I've had two hips replaced. And now I've two knees giving me problems. I've got osteoporosis in both, but the right one is worse. Downstream, I'll have to get something done. To get up and walk is difficult, at times. But once I'm moving, I'm okay.

Back when we played, if you went down after a collision you'd be told, 'You're only winded – keep going.' If you had an injury, it was, 'Ah Jaysus, throw some ice on it. You'll be fine.'

Seamus Dennison: A bottle of water on the leg – and the water did the business. It was straight out of *The Art of Coarse Rugby*.

Donal Spring: I worry about the physicality in today's game. The collisions are mad and I don't think enough attention is being paid to the injury toll. It's shocking. The attrition is off the charts these days. When we played, the club sides hardly changed from week to week.

Jimmy Bowen: I don't know where the game is going, because it seems to be complete physicality now. I'm fairly broken up from rugby – and I think some of these guys today are going to be in a mess. Now, they're better trained and better advised about strength and conditioning, about diet and all that. But the hits that they are taking – it's phenomenal. You cringe sometimes.

Christy Cantillon: Their bodies are built up to take these collisions. We wouldn't have been in the same boat.

Seamus Dennison: I've had both of my hips replaced. I don't know if it was down to rugby. I'm sixty-eight now and I think it was just part of life – wear and tear. Just one of those things.

Olann Kelleher: I got a new knee eighteen months ago. It was an old injury, but I played through it. I was afraid of being dropped at the time. I had a back operation as well, five years ago. That had nothing to do with rugby, though. I just woke up with it.

Greg Barrett: Lower back pain, stiffness in my shoulder. Nothing serious, just wear and tear.

Moss Finn: Left knee a bit, lower back, shoulder, right wrist. I broke it playing against Garryowen on a day Wardy scored about a million points and it fucks up my golf. It didn't heal – they didn't have the pins that time. But nothing major.

Christy Cantillon: I've just got two new knees. They were banjaxed and impacting on normal life. Walking was becoming difficult and you can only tolerate so much pain.

I'd attribute that completely to rugby. When I was seventeen, a fellow drove through my left knee and opened it up. Then the cruciate in my right knee went when I was twenty-eight.

I've had slipped discs, a quadruple bypass five years ago and a tumour in my neck in the last year. Other than that, I'm fine.

Moss Keane (autobiography, 2005): I didn't really miss playing all that much. I did my best, but I was beginning to recognise my own mortality. My body was beginning to give in. My shoulders were shagged, my lower back was crocked; I also had a bit of knee trouble. I only had about 70 per cent rotation in my neck and it stiffened up if I had to reverse the car for more than a few metres. When you begin to worry about your physical well-being, it's time to give up. Up until then, the rougher and tougher the game, the more I liked it, but now I was just a different man, and the many stories of terrible rugby injuries troubled me. Time had moved on and so had I.

Sarah Keane: Later in life Dad had chronic pain in his right shoulder but he prided himself on never having joint replacements or surgery – unlike a lot of his team-mates. He put this down to a concoction of apple cider vinegar, blackstrap molasses, manuka honey and boiling water, which he mixed up in a mug every morning. He was a massive believer in the potency of the mix. He used to say that, only for it, he'd have needed an operation.

Geraldine Tucker: Towards the end of his career it was one injury after another with Colm. Every week he was ending up out at the Regional Hospital. I said, 'Colm, you have them baffled now – why don't you just give it up?' If he was still here I imagine he'd be having bits of him replaced. His right knee was giving him a lot of trouble. He always had a bad back. The players are looked after much better now, but I see the impacts and – oh my God – I worry.

Tony Ward: Sore knees, sore ankles – but they came from playing soccer. I got out of my rugby career virtually scot-free.

Seamus Dennison: Wardy never tackled anyone.

Brendan Foley: I'm okay, injury-wise.

Les White: I'm okay, I'm not suffering from anything. Not physically.

Gerry McLoughlin: As you go through life, the body can sometimes let you down, but I'd consider myself one of the lucky ones. On that 1978 team, not everyone was as lucky as me.

6. An Instant Bond

It was one of the wonderful days in my life. And it feels all the more amazing to me now.
Les White, 2018

Eleven minutes into the match, Joe McCarthy's Arriflex camera picked up more than just the passage of play that produced Munster's try. Twenty-one seconds elapsed between Pat Whelan's lineout throw and Christy Cantillon's grounding of the ball. From his distant vantage point well inside the Munster half, McCarthy's sixteen-millimetre lens held the action in mid-shot, tracking it all in one smooth sequence which is all the more compelling because the players on the field and the supporters massed around them on the terraces and the perimeter walls are captured together in every frame.

'The old-style camera had its own atmosphere,' McCarthy enthuses, pleased with a compliment for his work forty years on. Had he zoomed in as Jimmy Bowen surged ever closer to the All Blacks' line, the frenzied reaction behind the posts would never have been frozen in time, and the duffel coat thrown into the air a second after Cantillon dived over would not now be a prized exhibit in the Thomond Park museum.

The footage is still relied on by some to prove their presence in the ground that day, including Noel 'Buddha' Healy, who can be seen sitting on the high wall directly behind the goal line.

The 'I was there' stories are thick on the ground in Limerick still, and Buddha tells a good one. 'You'll often see Munster's try on TV and I'm there alongside my old pal Denis O'Lough-lin,' he says. A nineteen-year-old apprentice pipe fitter then, he secured his prime position after calling to his grand-mother's house in Ballynanty, which backed onto Thomond Park. 'We went in through the front door, out the back door, up on the ladder and we had the best seats in the house.'

A prop forward of the old school, you might say he was a slow starter: he spent seven seasons as understudy to Gerry McLoughlin at Shannon, unable to shift him from the front row until Locky upped and moved across the water.

The kid on the high wall who was getting into a few scrapes back in 1978 went on to become president of Shannon Rugby Club. Along the way he befriended Brendan Foley, playing alongside him in the lock forward's final season of senior rug-by, and then Brendan's son Anthony, who became his golf partner and best friend. 'We won our first Munster caps to-gether in 1995 – he was twenty-one, I was thirty-seven.'

Twenty-one years later, after his sudden death in Paris, a hearse carrying Anthony's remains slowed to a halt outside Thomond Park and his grieving friend Buddha Healy led hundreds of Shannon men, women and children in an emo-tional performance of the club's anthem, 'There is an Isle'.

The sentimental idea of the rugby community as an ex-tended family didn't seem out of place in the week Brendan Foley buried his forty-two-year-old son. 'The amount of help and support we got from everyone was unreal,' he says quietly, in his understated way.

Perhaps more than most teams from the same era, the Munster players of 1978 have collectively endured some difficult times. Even their moment of victory itself was interrupted by a jolt of pain from real life. Through it all they have been there for one another and that enduring team spirit is one of the reasons why their occasional get-togethers are always joyful experiences.

'I'm not usually one for reminiscing,' says Gerry McLoughlin, 'but last night I was looking at one of the letters I sent home from New Zealand, when I was on the Lions tour in 1983. It was in the middle of a pile of programmes I hadn't looked at in thirty years, maybe more. Reading the letter brought it home to me how lucky we were. I was telling Colette, my wife at the time, about all the activities we were up to.

'My God, life was a doddle for us back then. Playing rugby with your mates – what could be better? But then life moves on, doesn't it? And sometimes it's not a bed of roses.

'It really means something to meet the lads these days, because a lot of the stuff we've gone through has been pain. Between one thing and another, not many of us have had a smooth run, you know? So I just think that to be alive forty years on, to be able to appreciate each other, is a big thing.'

Tony Ward: People get asked, 'Would you change anything about your life?' The answer you often hear or read is 'No, I wouldn't – I'd do everything the same.' But behind closed doors there are issues or sadnesses in most houses. So, yes – there are a lot of things I'd do differently. I've made mistakes.

I got married much too young, the year after the All Blacks game. I've married twice and both times it didn't work out. Perhaps somewhere down the road I'll fall in love again. But I'm not looking for it, to be honest.

In my late fifties, I was diagnosed with prostate cancer, a pretty virulent form of it. For a few years it was very difficult, but I got through it. And I'm in a good place at the moment.

I don't think it's through selfishness, but I've got to know myself better. I didn't choose to be here, in my sixties, on my own – it's just the way it worked out. And I've got to like myself again, to enjoy where I am in life after all these years. I'm very aware that the ups and downs we go through are all relative. Brendan Foley has lost his son, other guys on the team have lost their wives.

People are nice. They stop me and tell me nice things about my rugby days. And that does matter, as you go on through life.

Jimmy Bowen: There's no point in looking back on things you can do nothing about. The way I look at it, I can learn from my mistakes and try to make life happy for myself and those around to me.

I enjoy life – it has been good to me. There's no massive bestseller in me, other than I was dragged out of Blackpool in Cork, which isn't exactly rugby territory. I've lost a few friends, lost a sister, but other than that it's been good. And I say thank you very much for that, because some people get a lot of hammerings.

Les White: In November 2011 I lost my wife, Moira. She'd had cancer for eight years. It started with the bowel and then went into the liver. In the end, the tumours came up where they couldn't touch.

It's life. You've got to live with it. People can lose their loved ones without any warning. I had eight years to prepare myself but nothing can prepare you, really. You've just got to get on with it.

I'd retired in 2009, but I went back to work for a couple of years because I didn't know what else to do with myself.

Over time, I met Jan. We live our separate lives, but we're very close, we're good for each other. She lost her husband the year after I lost my wife. So we were two lonely people, I guess. It was through rugby that we got together. So I'm very grateful for that.

Brendan Foley: You never expect to watch your son and your daughter play rugby for Ireland. When Anthony first started playing for Munster and then Ireland, we never expected we'd be there for so many fabulous occasions. We just took it as it came. We were spending the kids' inheritance along the way.

I remember the day he came home in 2006, after Munster won the Heineken Cup. We were all looking at his medal. Next thing, he went upstairs and he came back with two more – the ones from 2000 and 2002, when they were beaten in the final. He had thrown them in a drawer. 'Now they mean something,' he said.

In Paris, the day he died, I got a phone call from Niall O'Donovan [the Munster team manager and a fellow Shannon man]. I was walking with Joss Lowry, a friend of mine. We were out early, heading over to the game, going for a beer. Then I got the phone call. Shocking, you know? We got a taxi over to the team hotel, kind of hoping that it wasn't right.

The Munster lads were in bits when we got there. Everybody did as well as they could for us, in Paris and when we brought him home. As a family we're lucky in that we live around each other. You have to keep tipping. But, as the fella said, it doesn't get any easier.

Larry Moloney: Everything was fine for us up to about eighteen months ago. Not a worry in the world. Three kids.

Grandchildren. There was nothing on the horizon to tell me that anything was going to happen. I was reading the paper in the sitting room at home. Rose was on the phone to our daughter in America, Laura. The phone call finished and she just collapsed. All of a sudden, gone. Out like a light. Brain haemorrhage. I got the medics out as quickly as I could, but there was little they could do for her.

Other than that, I have no complaints about my life. Sometimes you ask yourself the question: why me? Why us? But no matter what cross you have in life, there's always somebody worse off.

Three of Rose's organs were successfully transferred – heart, lung and liver. They went to two men and a woman, so at least we have done our bit and there are other people enjoying life now. I won't say at our cost, because if you're not using it, give it. Give somebody else a second chance in life.

Geraldine Tucker: When Colm needed a transplant I'd listen to the news and sometimes I'd hear about a road accident – somebody dying at the scene. The first thing I'd think of would be, 'Could this be a donor?' For years, everything revolved around that waiting. For some people, it works out. They get another chance, more time with their families. Unfortunately, Colm wasn't one of them.

It's hard being without him, but it's important to remember all the good days as well. Jesus, we had a great old time. I always tell that to my own kids: we had a ball, on account of club rugby. I mean, we didn't come home until all hours after a match – it would be two in the morning. Different now, isn't it? It's all professional.

Colm would be looking for his gear on Monday morning.

'Where did I leave my gear bag, Ger?'

'I'd say it's still in Angela's, Colm.'

Two weeks ago, a package arrived here at the house. When I opened it, his Lions cap was inside, the most beautiful thing, with his number embroidered on the front – LION 568. It came with a letter from Tom Grace, the Lions chairman. Oh my God, it nearly broke my heart reading the letter, but it was so lovely to get it. For me – for all of us in the family – it was one of those emotional moments where time stopped.

Donal Spring: I've worked hard all my life, but I know I've been lucky too and I count my blessings. My dad passed something on to us, which we all have – it was that sport was sport, it wasn't your life. To me, playing on Saturday was what mattered. I only regretted that rugby didn't last more than eighty minutes. I just loved playing the game – all I wanted was the ball in my hands.

I look back at the All Blacks match and I know I didn't appreciate it at the time. I don't think Moss Finn or Jimmy Bowen were any different. When you're twenty-two years old, everything seems possible. I appreciate it now, though. And even back then I saw the significance of it in the faces of Moss Keane and Donal Canniffe and Seamus Dennison, guys who had played against them before and almost won. We hadn't gone through the same pain.

Seamus Dennison: Maybe the fact that we won has kept us together, but there was a bond between most of the fellas on the team before that. It didn't just happen on the big day.

Tony Ward: In 2008, Munster played the All Blacks again at Thomond Park. It was the thirtieth anniversary of our game and the first time they'd been back at Thomond since. It was the opening night of the new stadium and Pat Whelan organised a reunion of the 1978 team. I was on the opposite side of the ground, doing TV commentary. It was last place I wanted to be. I wanted to be with the lads.

Moss Finn: Munster were brilliant that night. They were winning with five minutes left. I was sitting next to Moss Keane in the stand. He turned to me and said, 'I hope to Christ they hold on, because we've had too much of this fucking thing for thirty years.'

Jimmy Bowen: Joe Rokocoko got the All Blacks out of jail right at the end. It was heartbreaking in one way, but another part of me was delighted that he scored. You could say that Dougie Howlett did us a big favour. When you're watching from the stand you can say what you like, but if I'd been on the wing that night I'd have gone out to meet your man, not let him come to me. So Rokocoko scored in the same part of the field where we got our try in '78.

Gerry McLoughlin: I didn't know how I felt. When Munster were ahead, I was shouting with the best of them: *'Come on Munster!'* But, to be honest with you, there was a part of me thinking that our achievement wasn't going to be out on its own any more, if they saw it out.

When the final whistle went, the first thought that came into my head was, 'Jesus, we're still the only team to have beaten them.' I felt sorry for the Munster lads – and for the supporters. It was a pity, in a lot of ways, that they didn't win that night. But then you have to win, haven't you?

Donal Canniffe: It was a great Munster performance – they tore into the All Blacks. Afterwards, a few people talked about me still being the only Irishman to captain a winning team against the All Blacks, but I had no interest in holding on to that. When Ireland eventually beat them in Chicago, a few years ago, it was such a big thing off their back. I watched that game on television. The youngest of my grandchildren was being christened, in Cork, and the family was all together. Ireland were always going to beat New Zealand one day – it should have happened before it did. I was delighted. The past is the past. There's only the future.

Gerry McLoughlin: I usually don't enjoy reunions, I'm not into them. They can be big occasions, with a lot of people in the room, and it can be hard to feel the connection with the fellas you played with in times past. But there was something different about the reunion at the Mansion House last year. We got presented with some kind of award, up on the stage. We weren't put on different tables – we sat down together and it was something special. I've never felt so close to the team. It's the closest I've felt to the team in fucking forty years.

Moss Keane's daughters were at the table. I could see what it meant to them, having that interaction with his old pals. And of course all the stories came out about Moss. The girls were mesmerised, listening to them.

I hope we can feel that again – and that everyone who's still around can come. I haven't seen Les White for a long time. I can't wait to sit down with Les again.

Les White: If there's a reunion for the fortieth anniversary, I'll be there. I feel very proud and honoured to have been part of the team. There was something special about being the only player based in England, especially when I think back to the seventies and how bad things were in Northern Ireland.

So, yes – for as long as I'm around, I'll always be available. I always was – I'd go anywhere for a game of rugby.

Tony Ward: I remember when we had our first reunion, in Abbeyfeale. Back then, we weren't thinking too far down the road. And when you're still young, you don't think these things are important. As the years go on, they become more important.

Seamus Dennison: We've had our ups and our downs. We've lost a few. But if you ask any of the lads, they'll all tell you it's nice that people still remember us. Because of what we did on a rugby field forty years ago.

Larry Moloney: Back in our time, club rugby was tribal warfare. There were fellas we hated playing against in Limerick, but when we came together with Munster, we'd fight for the guy. We were like a family. And I think those feelings for one another continue to this day.

Gerry McLoughlin: I think it took a long time to sink in – for me anyway – that we're not competing against each other any more. Meeting the lads now, it's more appreciation and love that I have for them.

When it comes to life, we're no different to twenty people who worked together in an office years ago and then went their separate ways. We just happened to play in a rugby match that, for whatever reason, people still want to hear about. Everyone I meet from that era has been at the match. Everyone. People still bring it up, constantly.

I never moved in the same circles as Pa Whelan, but we get on better now than we ever did before. That would be new to me – having conversations with Garryowen guys. But you mellow as you get older, don't you?

Mind you, I'm not sure if that applies to Pa.

Christy Cantillon: Any time we meet now, there's an instant bond. And when we get together next, for the fortieth anniversary, I think it'll feel like we're back in 1978 again. We'll enjoy reliving the small things that happened in the days before the match and after it.

Doing the fool on the boats out by Killaloe and drenching Tommy Kiernan.

Having a couple of pints the night before, to take our minds off what was coming.

Driving from the hotel to Thomond Park in our own cars and looking out at people walking to the ground – fellas who were probably thinking we were going to get hammered by thirty or forty points.

Jimmy Bowen: You can be sure there'll be plenty of slagging as well.

Seamus Dennison: Oh, definitely.

Donal Canniffe: What else is there to do now, except slag each other?

Brendan Foley: We wouldn't have it any other way.

Gerry McLoughlin: I'll probably get slagged again – for making out that I beat the All Blacks on my fucking own. But I'll laugh along with them – and anyway, I still maintain that prop forward is the position that matters most, because that's where you have the biggest confrontations.

It's like I said before – if you want to beat the All Blacks, you have to stand up to them.

APPENDIX I

Tom Kiernan is grateful that his Munster side got the breaks when they needed them, unlike teams from the past. Looking back at all the near misses, he says: 'Disappointment is a much stronger emotion than the feeling of winning. If you win, it's only a kind of relief.'

To a man, the players coached by him in 1978 speak of him with affection and huge respect.

'He was as straight as a die and fellas loved him,' says Moss Finn. 'There was no grey area. A fella went up to him once and said, "Why are you picking others ahead of me?" Tommy said, "Because you're not fucking good enough – is that all right?" He wasn't like the guys who said, "The other selectors dropped you." Tommy would tell you straight out. And you could identify with that.'

Kiernan went on to coach Ireland to their first Triple Crown in thirty-three years, in 1982. Under his leadership they also topped the Five Nations Championship table the following year. After coaching he turned to rugby administration and held a number of key roles in the Irish and international game. His final position as an administrator was director of the 1999 Rugby World Cup.

'He had tremendous vision,' says Pat Whelan, Munster's hooker in 1978. 'The European Cup was his idea. I got involved in the IRFU myself and I can remember him coming to meetings extremely well prepared, with all his notes under his arm, typed up. He had a determination to do things right and a huge, motivating personality. He's number one, as far I'm concerned, in terms of commitment to Irish rugby.'

In September 2015, Tom Kiernan was inducted into the World Rugby Hall of Fame. He still lives in Cork.

Gerry McLoughlin was capped for Ireland shortly after the All Blacks match, against France at Lansdowne Road. He won eighteen caps, the last of them against France in 1984. He was a member of the 1982 Triple Crown team coached by Kiernan. In the victory over England at Twickenham he scored arguably the most famous try in Irish rugby history and memorably claimed to have pulled the entire Irish pack over the line with him.

He lost his job as a teacher in Limerick when the Christian Brothers at Sexton Street punished him for going on Ireland's controversial tour to South Africa in 1981, and opened a pub, the Triple Crown. He was selected as a replacement on the Lions tour to New Zealand in 1983.

After winning the last of his five Munster Senior Cup medals with Shannon in 1987 he moved to Wales and stayed for fifteen years, running a pub in Gilfach Goch, Mid Glamorgan. He returned to Limerick in 2002 and resumed his teaching career. In 2004 he won a seat on Limerick City Council and he was proud to be elected mayor in 2012.

As mayor, he shunned the car that was a perk of the job, often preferring to cycle to the different functions. Now retired, he is regularly to be seen making his way around the city by bike.

Donal Canniffe retired from rugby in 1982 and became a coach and selector with Lansdowne. He took early retirement from his job with Aviva, the insurance company, which in 2010 bought the stadium naming rights to the home of Irish rugby formerly known as Lansdowne Road, for a reported €40 million.

Most of the Munster players attended the funeral of his father Dan two days after the All Blacks match. In 2014, on a trip to New Zealand, his wife Mary surprised him by arranging for some of the 1978 All Blacks to meet them at a hotel in Wellington, including his opposite number as captain. 'Mourie hadn't changed a bit. He was just like I remembered him. It was lovely to spend time with them after so many years.'

He still lives in Dublin.

Seamus Dennison retired from senior rugby three years after the match for which he will always be remembered, but then returned to play junior rugby for Roscrea for another four years. 'I didn't enjoy it as much as senior rugby. It was, "There's the fella that played for Munster against the All Blacks – kill him!"' He never added to the three caps he won between 1973 and 1975.

In 1999 his famous tackle on Stu Wilson was superbly dramatised in a stage play, *Alone It Stands*, by John Breen. In 2014 the play was added to Ireland's Junior Certificate cycle – alongside Oscar Wilde's *The Importance of Being Earnest* and George Bernard Shaw's *Pgymalion*. By then Dennison had retired as a teacher, but the school in Roscrea where he taught for forty years has asked him back every year since to tell pupils studying the play all about the day.

Brendan Foley went on to win eleven Ireland caps, the last of them in 1981. After quitting senior rugby at thirty-four, he was enticed back to the game by his childhood friend John Ryan and turned out for one final season of junior rugby for St Mary's, the club he played for as a boy.

His son Anthony, named after Brendan's late father, was a galvanising force in the Munster team for more than a decade, captaining them to their first Heineken Cup in 2006. In 2014, Anthony was appointed Munster's head coach. He was just forty-two when he died from a heart rhythm disorder in November 2016, just hours before Munster were due to play Racing 92 in Paris. His death shocked and saddened rugby people the world over.

Brendan's daughter Rosie, named after the mother who died when he was two, was also a distinguished international rugby player.

He continues to run a bus-hire company near his home in Killaloe, County Clare.

Tony Ward was voted European Player of the Year soon after the All Blacks match. Seven months later, he was sensationally dropped by Ireland on tour in Australia and replaced by Ollie Campbell. 'He couldn't believe it and he never got over it, definitely not,' says his former Garryowen and Munster team-mate Pat Whelan, who was also on the 1979 tour. His confidence broken, Ward would never be the same player again.

'My head was fried,' he says. 'The only two who looked after me down there were Mossie Keane and Pa Whelan. I'm bitter over the way it happened and the way it was handled. It was a profound blow to my sense of self-worth – all the doubts started creeping in. And there is a scar, still there, all these years later.'

Ward's supporters claimed he was targeted by the IRFU because they saw his glamorous image as a threat to amateurism. In the first of two autobiographies, he revealed the correspondence received from the union in the aftermath of his rise to fame. Four decades on, he says: 'They absolutely crucified me. It was just never-ending. I was getting letters giving out about everything and anything. And you had to toe the line back then – they ruled with an iron fist. You actually were in fear.

'Ned van Esbeck used to answer all those letters for me. I'd go over to his house and he'd pull out his old typewriter. But I was hurt by it.'

Twenty-four when he was dropped in Australia, he had won ten international caps. By the time he played his final match for Ireland, eight years later, the total stood at just nineteen. After the All Blacks match he opened sports shops in Limerick and Dublin but didn't enjoy the experience ('I felt like an animal in the zoo') and returned to teaching. He subsequently developed a career as a rugby broadcaster and journalist and has been director of rugby at St Gerard's School in Bray for many years.

Greg Barrett played for Ireland B and in a final Irish trial but never won a full international cap ('I'm told by Noisy Murphy that I lost one vote 3–2').

In 1981 his younger brother, Gus, broke his neck playing for UCC against UCD and became a quadriplegic, a tragedy that hastened the end of his own rugby career. 'My mother was losing her life over me playing. She couldn't cope with it,' he says. Gus died in 1989.

In 2002 he set up his own company, Greg Barrett Financial Services, which he still runs. He's heavily involved in rugby administration and was appointed chairman of the IRFU Rugby Committee in 2017.

He still lives in his native Cork.

Jimmy Bowen, the man who made the decisive break for Munster's try, became the subject of a joke told by Christy Cantillon, the try scorer. Bowen, it goes, is in the chair on *Mastermind* and Magnus Magnusson asks him: 'What did you do with the All Blacks' line at your mercy?'

'Pass.'

'Correct!'

He's convinced he did the right thing, 'but even my own son has said it to me – "Dad, could you not have gone in yourself?"'

He moved to Dublin from Cork in 1981, joining Lansdowne and later St Mary's, but his rugby career was blighted by injury.

'It's absolutely frightening that forty years have passed,' he says. 'Sometimes I wonder – how did we actually do it? They must have had 80 per cent possession. We never even gave them a shot at goal – and there were plenty of fellas well able to give away penalties.'

He lives in Dublin and runs his own finance company, Bowen Associates.

Christy Cantillon retired from rugby at twenty-eight, after suffering a second cruciate ligament injury while playing for Cork Constitution. He is considered unlucky never to have won a full international cap, but enjoyed considerable success as a coach. The highlight of his wide-ranging coaching career came when he led Constitution to the inaugural All Ireland League title after a memorable victory at Garryowen. He also coached UCC, Dolphin and Crosshaven – 'and I'm still involved with College'.

Previously an insurance broker, he has property interests in Cork and lives there still.

Moss Finn was picked for Ireland the following year and won fourteen caps, scoring four tries. He was a member of the 1982 Triple Crown team and played for Munster for fourteen seasons, sometimes at out-half. He runs Finn's Corner, the sports store in the heart of Cork city which his family has owned since 1878.

Like everyone else, he says the 1978 victory would not have happened without Kiernan, but believes Munster's out-half was equally crucial on the day. 'Wardy was at his imperious best. It was before all the trauma in his life. He was at the peak of his career and he was wonderful.'

Moss Keane, a late starter in rugby, was a permanent fixture in the Ireland lineout for a decade, playing his fifty-first and final international in 1984, five months short of his thirty-sixth birthday. Stories about him are legion and one of the most famous concerns Munster and the All Blacks. Late in the game, with the All Blacks a beaten team, Andy Haden is supposed to have wound up a big right hand, intended for the jaw of a Munster player. At this point, the story goes, Keane grabbed Haden by the arm and calmly asked him: 'Andy, do you want to lose the fight as well as the match?' Several eyewitnesses swear the story is true, but Haden describes it as 'bullshit' and, interviewed for this book, Keane also dismissed it as a myth. It lives on in folklore, however.

He died of cancer in 2010, aged sixty-two. At his funeral in St Michael's Church, Portarlington, his brother Brian recited the final words of Moss's 2005 autobiography, *Rucks, Mauls & Gaelic Football*: 'I'm not one that thinks of how I'd like to be remembered or shite like that ... I'd like to think that success never went to my head and that if someone, somewhere, was asked they might say, "Moss Keane? – Ah sure he did his best." He did his best. That would do me nicely.'

Larry Moloney played for Ireland against the All Blacks four days after Munster's victory, along with four other Munster players – Tony Ward, Moss Keane, Pat Whelan and Donal Spring. Drawing 6–6 late into the game, Ireland went down to a try two minutes from time. It was his final game in the green jersey and a total of four caps was a meagre return for his talent. He retired from rugby two years later, still in his twenties, after suffering one injury too many.

He spent his working life at AIB bank but took early retirement in 2007. 'It became very impersonal and I couldn't handle the technology. The machines didn't talk back to me, so I was banjaxed at that stage.'

He lives in Thurles and remains best friends with his old sidekick in the Garryowen and Munster backlines, Seamus Dennison.

Donal Spring won seven caps between 1978 and 1981, but then fell out of favour with the national selectors. 'At twenty-five I went to France for a couple of years and came back a 200 per cent better player – I never got another cap. I could give you a thousand reasons why – which aren't all to do with rugby. I used to harbour hopes, right up until the day I retired, that somehow I would get another call-up. But it's water under the bridge now. I'm long over it.'

Unhappy with the attitude of Munster selectors towards Dublin-based players, he subsequently declared for Leinster. 'You could say I didn't do an awful lot to make myself popular,' he says. 'I was always very quick to say what I thought was wrong with Irish rugby – what a bullshit system the selector system was, what an absolute farce. Tom Kiernan was a master at getting the team he wanted – but the very fact that he had to spend so much time and energy going through the process was ridiculous.

'Since the game turned professional, we are the most professional in the world. But when the game was amateur, we were the most amateur.'

He coached the senior teams at Old Belvedere, Lansdowne and – for one game, months before the arrival of professionalism – Leinster.

He heads up a prominent solicitors' practice in Dublin.

Colm Tucker, like his Shannon team-mate Gerry McLoughlin, was called up by Ireland for the international which followed the All Blacks' visit, but by the time he was through his career would represent one of the worst miscarriages of justice in the history of Irish rugby: two starts in Test matches for the Lions, two in the green of Ireland. In all played nine times on the Lions' 1980 tour to South Africa.

He later became a selector and manager of the Shannon team that were the dominant force in Irish club rugby after the All Ireland League was established in the early 1990s. He subsequently served as manager of the professional Munster team in its early days.

In 2001 he underwent a quadruple heart bypass operation, and while he recovered well he was later struck down with the lung disease that ended his life in 2011, aged fifty-nine.

Pat Whelan won nineteen caps for Ireland, the last in 1981, after years of contesting the hooking position for Ireland with Ken Kennedy, John Cantrell and – finally – Ciaran Fitzgerald. 'I went down to Australia in 1979 as first choice and got injured in my first match. Then I lost my place to Ciaran Fitzgerald. He was a good player, but if I'd been physically okay I might have resisted him.'

After hanging up his boots he coached Garryowen and Munster. He was coach of the province when the All Blacks next played Munster – and won 31–9 in Cork. Later, he turned to the administrative side of the game and rose up the ranks. He was elected chairman of the Six Nations Council in 2015, the first Irishman to hold the post since Tom Kiernan.

A builder and property developer, he ran into trouble in 2008 when the economy collapsed. 'I got caught in the recession – like nearly everybody else in the development world,' he says. 'It's been difficult because there are easy options and not so easy options. I took the one which was most difficult – which was not to go bankrupt.'

He lives in Limerick and turned sixty-eight in 2018, but is still working. 'I'll keep going for another couple of years.'

Les White, the oldest member of the team at thirty-four (he laughs off suggestions that he was older still), played for another season with Munster. He continued in the front row for London Irish until 1981 and played English county rugby until he was well into his forties. Next came a spell as coach of his native Hampshire.

He remains the only member of the team who doesn't live in Ireland, but his bond with the rest of the team remains extremely strong. He lives in Fareham and travels widely. 'Age doesn't really matter, it doesn't count,' he says. 'You've just got to keep body and mind fit.'

Jack Gleeson died of liver cancer in November 1979, aged fifty-two. The first indication that he was unwell had come less than three weeks after the Munster match, but the cancer was not diagnosed until after the All Blacks had returned to New Zealand. Hours after his death, an All Blacks team captained by Graham Mourie hammered Midland Division in Leicester, scoring five brilliant tries. 'That was for Jack,' Mourie said. Gleeson's sidekick on the 1978 tour, manager

Russ Thomas, died in 2000, aged seventy-three.

Graham Mourie is still considered one of the great All Blacks captains. He regards the Grand Slam tour as the highlight of an outstanding career that saw him wear the black jersey sixty-one times, fifty-eight of them as captain.

Always magnanimous in defeat, he says of Munster's victory: 'We had a strong team out – we weren't taking them lightly, not at all. You can use all the superlatives you want about how well they played – they were that good.'

While still captain he declared himself unavailable for New Zealand's tour to South Africa in 1981, because of his opposition to the apartheid regime. He played twenty-one Tests, the last a victory over Australia in 1982.

After accepting payment for writing a book he was suspended by the International Rugby Board for ten years, but was elected to the New Zealand Rugby Union board in 2002 and subsequently became chairman of the IRB Rugby Committee.

He coached Wellington and the Hurricanes and was inducted into the World Rugby Hall of Fame in 2014. Away from the game, he has had a lifelong involvement in dairy farming. He lives in Wellington.

Stu Wilson played for the All Blacks eighty-five times, including thirty-four Tests, two of them as captain. In his final international match he scored a hat-trick of tries against the British & Irish Lions at Eden Park in 1983, breaking his country's all-time try-scoring record in the process. Like Mourie, he was banned for accepting royalties for a book.

He became a real estate agent in Auckland, a weekend radio host and Sky TV rugby pundit. These days he works as an area manager for Pub Charities, an organisation that distributes funds raised from gaming machines to numerous community groups.

'The names of Ward and Cantillon will haunt me until the day I fall over, but every member of our touring party agreed we were stuffed by a well-coached team who had more passion and more grunt than we had on the day,' he wrote in a message which was read out at the launch of the first edition of this book. 'Rugby is about long-lasting memories and no matter how disappointed we were, we still felt that we had played our part in a history-making day.'

Corris Thomas, the match referee, handed in his whistle in 1982 but is still involved in rugby as a game analysis consultant, working with World Rugby and other bodies. He produces detailed reports on major tournaments, tracking in detail how the modern game is played. There is little meaningful comparison with the rugby of 1978, he says. His statistics show the breakdown is now vastly more influential in shaping the outcome of a game and there are far fewer line-outs and scrums.

He has fond memories of time spent with some of the Munster players late into the night of the game. 'The ones I remember were Moss Finn, Christy Cantillon and Jimmy Bowen. We went around a few bars and I found the atmosphere extraordinary. People weren't whooping it up – not at all. They had their pints in their hands and they were saying, "I can't believe it, I can't believe it." That it had actually happened still seemed unreal to them, long after I blew the final whistle.'

Johnny Cole and **Martin Walsh**, touch judges on the day, both continue to live in Limerick. 'The photograph of us with the Munster team will always be there,' Walsh says.

'People say to me, "Jaysus, there's one thing certain. You were definitely there."' He has enjoyed his association with the match and reckons he has had 'a good few free dinners off the back of it'. Four decades on, Cole is the official timekeeper at Thomond Park and a citing commissioner for World Rugby – both voluntary roles. 'The game is all about money now,' he says, echoing many of the interviewees for the updated edition of this book.

The Healy brothers remained inseparable until Sean's death in 1989, aged sixty-three. Stephen died in 2002, aged seventy-eight. They are fondly remembered by the saying that accompanied them throughout their lives: 'The two Healys are one.'

Bill O'Brien continued as secretary of the Munster branch for another five years, stepping down in 1983 after forty-two years. He died in 2002, aged eighty-nine. Lawson's menswear, for so long the home of the Munster branch, closed down in 1994, the year before rugby turned professional. The elegant gilt sign, protected by the local council, remains over the door where Billo and his father, Tommo, once ruled the roost. 'LAWSON & Co OUTFITTERS' it reads still.

Bill Walsh, the fish merchant who employed Donal Canniffe's late father Dan, says he often thinks of the man who was like a father to his staff. 'He was an exceptional person, a thorough gentleman.' For the past forty years, he has had a Mass said in Cork for Dan Canniffe on the anniversary of his death – 31 October.

The All Blacks next played Munster in 1989, once again arriving with a fearsome reputation. Not for the first time, the home team were given no chance by journalists previewing the match. 'There can hardly be anyone foolhardy enough to forecast anything but a clearcut New Zealand win,' wrote Sean Diffley in the *Irish Independent* on the day of the game. There wasn't – and this time the result went according to predictions: Munster 9, New Zealand 31.

Things were far closer in 2008, the only time the All Blacks have taken on Munster since. Before the game, the Munster team were presented with their jerseys by the men who wore the same numbers in 1978. Thirty years after the famous victory, the home team were leading 16–13 with four minutes left, but a late try gave the tourists an 18–16 win. Graham Mourie was one of several members of the 1978 All Blacks side who attended the game.

New Zealand have retained the aura that surrounded them in 1978 and before, producing many more great players and successfully exploiting their powerful 'brand' in the professional era. Two of the biggest names in the All Blacks' modern-day history, Christian Cullen and Doug Howlett, signed for Munster after ending their Test careers.

New Zealand won the inaugural World Cup in 1987. Subsequent failures resulted in huge national inquests, but they restored their reputation as the pre-eminent rugby nation by winning the tournament in 2011 and again in 2015.

Twenty-nine of the thirty-one players who saw action during the 1978 Grand Slam tour were still alive as the fortieth anniversary of that achievement approached. The exceptions, both forwards, were Gary Seear and Frank Oliver. The latter lined out in the second row at Thomond Park, up against Moss Keane, and some of the tributes to him following his death in 2014 echoed those paid to his fellow lock forward after his passing in 2010. 'He seemed indestructible,' said Andy Haden. 'He was a colossus.'

Munster, in the professional era, became the most passionately supported club team in the northern hemisphere, frequently taking thousands of supporters on their travels to France, England and Wales. Winning the Heineken Cup became an obsession and they were twice beaten in finals before eventually prevailing in 2006, against Biarritz in Cardiff.

One of the heroes in red that day, Paul O'Connell, has said that playing rugby for Munster 'is all about making a statement about where you come from', an echo of the words Donal Canniffe spoke to his players before they ran out at Thomond Park in 1978: 'Today, in this red jersey, we are representing the people of Munster.'

The Heineken Cup was claimed again in 2008, but Munster have failed to make a final in the years since, losing five semi-finals along the way.

They were unbeaten in European competition at Thomond Park for twelve years, from 1995 until 2007, a run that included thrilling victories which now have their own folklore status. In 2008 the capacity of Thomond Park doubled to 26,000 after a rebuilding project spearheaded by Pat Whelan, the Munster hooker in 1978.

The ancient divide between Cork and Limerick, which meant the Munster players were based at separate training bases sixty miles apart, was finally ended in 2016 when the squad moved into a multimillion-euro high-performance centre at the University of Limerick.

By long tradition, every big victory achieved by the modern Munster team is celebrated by the players in the dressing room after the game with a rousing rendition of their anthem, 'Stand Up and Fight'.

APPENDIX II

Record of the Eighth All Blacks Tour

18.10.78	Grange Road	Cambridge University 12
		All Blacks 32
21.10.78	Arms Park	Cardiff 7
		All Blacks 17
25.10.78	St Helen's	West Wales 7
		All Blacks 23
28.10.78	Twickenham	London Counties 12
		All Blacks 37
31.10.78	Thomond Park	Munster 12
		All Blacks 0
4.11.78	Lansdowne Road	Ireland 6
		New Zealand 10
7.11.78	Ravenhill	Ulster 3
		All Blacks 23
11.11.78	Arms Park	Wales 12
		New Zealand 13
15.11.78	Memorial Ground	South & South-West Counties 0
		All Blacks 20
18.11.78	Welford Road	Midland Counties 15
		All Blacks 20

21.11.78	Aldershot	Combined Services 6
		All Blacks 34
25.11.78	Twickenham	England 6
		New Zealand 16
29.11.78	Rodney Parade	Monmouthshire 9
		All Blacks 26
2.12.78	Birkenhead Park	North of England 6
		All Blacks 9
5.12.78	Linksfield Stadium	North & Midlands of Scotland 3
		All Blacks 31
9.12.78	Murrayfield	Scotland 9
		New Zealand 18
13.12.78	Brewery Field	Bridgend 6
		All Blacks 17
16.12.78	Arms Park	Barbarians 16
		All Blacks 18

APPENDIX III

Munster's Record against Overseas Teams, 1905–78

28.11.1905, Markets Field, Limerick: Munster 0 All Blacks 33
Munster: A. Quillinan (Garryowen), A. Newton (Cork County), B. McLear (Cork County), W. O. Stokes (Garryowen), R. M. McGrath (Cork Constitution), F. McQueen (Queen's College), Joe O'Connor (Garryowen), J. Wallace (Wanderers & Garryowen), T. S. Reeves (Monkstown & Garryowen), S. K. Hosford (Cork Constitution), W. Parker (Cork County), M. White (Queen's College), R. Welply (Queen's College), T. Acheson (Garryowen), T. Churchwarden (Cork County).
All Blacks: Booth, Smith, McGregor, Deans, Abbot, Mynott, Stead, Gillett, Newton, Tyler, Mackrell, Cunningham, Nicholson, McDonald, Glasgow.

8.12.47, Mardyke, Cork: Munster 5 Australians 6
Munster: J. Staunton (Garryowen), J. O'Sullivan (UCD), P. Reid (Garryowen), J. Mackessy (Cork Constitution), R. Dennehy (Dolphin), A. McElhinney (Dolphin), H. de Lacy (Harlequins & Garryowen), T. Clifford (Young Munster), J. C. Corcoran (London Irish & Sundays Well), B. Hayes (Cork Constitution), E. Keeffe (Sundays Well), P. Madden (Sundays

Well), C. Roche (Garryowen), T. Reid (Garryowen), J. McCarthy (Dolphin).

Australians: Windsor, McBride, Walker, Howell, Bourke, Broad, Cawsey, Davis, Dawson, McMaster, Shehadie, Hardcastle, Winning, Stenmark, Keller.

11.12.51, Thomond Park, Limerick: Munster 6 South Africans 11
Munster: P. J. Berkery (Lansdowne), M. Quaid (Garryowen), J. Horgan (UCG), G. C. Phipps (Rosslyn Park), M. F. Lane (UCC), J. Roche (Garryowen), J. O'Meara (UCC), T. Clifford (Young Munster), D. Crowley (Cork Constitution), D. Donnery (Dolphin), A. O'Leary (Cork Constitution), S. Healy (Garryowen), J. S. McCarthy (Dolphin), G. Reidy (Dolphin), D. Dineen (Bohemians).

South Africans: Keevy, Saunders, Lategan, Viviers, Johnstone, D. Fry, Du Toit, Bekker, Delport, Van der Ryst, Myburgh, Dannhauser, Barnard, Du Rand, S. Fry.

13.1.54, Mardyke, Cork: Munster 3 All Blacks 6
Munster: P. Berkery (Lansdowne), G. Kenny (Sundays Well), N. Coleman (Dolphin), R. Godfrey (UCD), B. Mullen (Cork Constitution), D. Daly (Sundays Well), J. O'Meara (Dolphin), G. Wood (Garryowen), D. Crowley (Cork Constitution), T. Clifford (Young Munster), T. Reid (Garryowen), M. Madden (Sundays Well), J. McCarthy (Dolphin), G. Reidy (Dolphin), B. Cussen (UCC).

All Blacks: Kelly, Tanner, Fitzgerald, Freebairn, Wilson, Haig, Bevan, Clarke, Woods, Skinner, Jones, Dalzell, Bagley, Oliver, Stuart.

21.1.58, Thomond Park, Limerick: Munster 3 Australians 3
Munster: R. Hennessy (Cork Constitution), S. Quinlan (Highfield), J. Walsh (UCC), F. Buckley (Highfield), D.

McCormack (Dolphin), M. English (Bohemians), M. Mullins (UCC), G. Wood (Garryowen), D. Geary (Bohemians), R. Dowley (Dolphin), T. Nesdale (Garryowen), M. Spillane (Old Crescent), M. O'Connell (Young Munster), T. McGrath (Garryowen), N. Murphy (Cork Constitution).
Australians: Curley, Morton, Potts, White, Fox, Harvey, Logan, Vaughan, Meadows, Davidson, Ryan, Shehadie, Yanz, Hughes, Gunther.

21.12.60, Musgrave Park, Cork: Munster 3 South Africans 9
Munster: R. Hennessy (Cork Constitution), P. McGrath (UCC), J. Walsh (UCC), T. J. Kiernan (UCC), F. Buckley (Highfield), M. English, T. Cleary (both Bohemians), G. Wood (Lansdowne), M. O'Callaghan (Sundays Well), L. Murphy (Highfield), T. Nesdale (Garryowen), M. Spillane (Old Crescent), L. Coughlan (Cork Constitution), T. McGrath (Garryowen), N. Murphy (Garryowen).
South Africans: Wilson, Antelme, Gainsford, Roux, Engelbrecht, Stewart, De Uys, Kuhn, Malan, Myburgh, Du Preez, Van der Merwe, Claasen, Van Zyl, Baard.

11.12.63, Thomond Park, Limerick: Munster 3 All Blacks 6
Munster: T. J. Kiernan (Cork Constitution), M. Lucey (UCC), J. Walsh (UCC), B. O'Brien (Shannon), P. McGrath (UCC), M. English (Lansdowne), N. Kavanagh (Dolphin), M. O'Callaghan (Sundays Well), P. Lane (Old Crescent), M. Carey (UCD), J. Murray (Cork Constitution), M. Spillane (Old Crescent), D. Kiely (Lansdowne), H. Wall (Dolphin), N. Murphy (Cork Constitution).
All Blacks: Herewini, Smith, MacRae, Davis, Watt, Kirton, Laidlaw, Lochore, Barry, Stewart, Horsley, Tremain, Clarke, Major, Le Lievre.

25.1.67, Musgrave Park, Cork: Munster 11 Australians 8
Munster: T. J. Kiernan (Cork Constitution), A. Horgan (Cork Constitution), J. Walsh (Sundays Well), B. Bresnihan (UCD), P. McGrath (UCC), J. Moroney (Garryowen & London Irish), L. Hall (UCC), P. O'Callaghan (Dolphin), K. Ging (Sundays Well), M. O'Callaghan (Young Munster), B. O'Dowd (Bohemians), J. Murray (Cork Constitution), M. Murphy (Cork Constitution), T. Moore (Highfield), L. Coughlan (Cork Constitution).
Australians: Ryan, Webb, Smith, Moore, Cardy, Brass, Catchpole, Thornett, Taylor, Prosser, Heming, Purcell, O'Callaghan, Taylor, Tulloch.

14.1.70, Thomond Park, Limerick: Munster 9 South Africans 25
Munster: A. Horgan (Cork Constitution), J. Tydings (Young Munster), G. O'Reilly (Highfield), B. Bresnihan (London Irish), J. Moroney (Garryowen & London Irish), B. J. McGann (Cork Constitution), L. Hall (Garryowen), P. O'Callaghan (Dolphin), T. Barry (Old Crescent), O. Waldron (London Irish), S. Waldron (Cork Constitution), E. Molloy (UCC), J. Buckley (Sundays Well), T. Moore (Highfield), W. O'Mahony (UCC).
South Africans: De Villiers, Grobler, Roux, Lawless, Nomis, Visagie, De Villiers, Myburgh, Barnard, Marais, De Wet, Carelse, Ellis, Jennings, Van de Venter.

16.1.73, Musgrave Park, Cork: Munster 3 All Blacks 3
Munster: T. J. Kiernan (Cork Constitution), J. Barry (Dolphin), S. Dennison (Garryowen), B. Bresnihan (London Irish), P. Parfrey (UCC), B. J. McGann (Cork Constitution), D. Canniffe (Cork Constitution), P. O'Callaghan (Dolphin), J. Leahy (Cork Constitution), K. Keyes (Sundays Well), J. Madigan (Bohemians), M. Keane (Lansdowne), C. Tucker

(Shannon), T. Moore (Highfield), S. Deering (Garryowen).
All Blacks: Morris, Williams, Hales, Skudder, Stevens, Parkinson, Colling, Lambert, Ulrich, McNichol, Holmes, Eliason, Haden, Wyllie, Sutherland.

9.11.74, Thomond Park, Limerick: Munster 4 All Blacks 14
Munster: R. Spring (Cork Constitution), P. Parfrey (UCC), L. Moloney (Garryowen), J. Coleman (Highfield), P. Lavery (London Irish), B. J. McGann (Cork Constitution), D. Canniffe (Lansdowne), O. Waldron (Clontarf), P. Whelan (Garryowen), P. O'Callaghan (Dolphin), J. Madigan (Bohemians), M. Keane (Lansdowne), C. Tucker (Shannon), T. Moore (Highfield), S. Deering (Garryowen).
All Blacks: Karam, Williams, Bruce Robertson, Morgan, Batty, Duncan Robertson, Going (Stevens), Tanner, Norton, Gardiner, MacDonald, Whiting, Kirkpatrick, Leslie, Stewart.

13.1.76, Musgrave Park, Cork: Munster 13 Australians 15
Munster: L. Moloney (Garryowen), P. Parfrey (UCC), P. Lavery (London Irish), S. Dennison (Garryowen), B. Smith (Cork Constitution), T. Ward (Garryowen), D. Canniffe (Lansdowne), G. McLoughlin (Shannon), P. Whelan (Garryowen), P. O'Callaghan (Dolphin), M. Keane (Lansdowne), E. Molloy (Garryowen), N. Elliot (Dolphin), B. Foley (Shannon), S. Deering (Garryowen).
Australians: McLean, Monaghan, Berne, Shaw, Ryan, Weatherstone, Hauser, Graham, Carberry, Meadows, Fay, Smith, Shaw, Loane, Cornelson.

31.10.78, Thomond Park, Limerick: Munster 12 All Blacks 0
Munster: L. Moloney (Garryowen), M. Finn (UCC), S. Dennison (Garryowen), G. Barrett (Cork Constitution), J. Bowen (Cork Constitution), T. Ward (St Mary's College),

D. Canniffe (Lansdowne), G. McLoughlin (Shannon), P. Whelan (Garryowen), L. White (London Irish), M. Keane (Lansdowne), B. Foley (Shannon), C. Cantillon (Cork Constitution), C Tucker (Shannon), D. Spring (Dublin University).
All Blacks: B. McKechnie, S. Wilson, B. Robertson (B. Osborne), L. Jaffray, B. Williams, E. Dunn, M. Donaldson, B. Johnstone, J. Black, G. Knight, A. Haden, F. Oliver, G. Mourie, W. Graham, A. McGregor.

Bibliography

General

Barrow, Graeme, *Up Front: The Story of the All Black Scrum*, Heinemann, 1985

Dixon, George, *1905: The Triumphant Tour of the New Zealand Footballers*, David Ling Publishing, 1999

Fallon, Ivan, *The Player: The Life of Tony O'Reilly*, Hodder & Stoughton, 1994

Haden, Andy, *Boots 'n All!*, Rugby Press, 1983

Howitt, Bob, *Beegee: The Bryan Williams Story*, Rugby Press, 1981

Howitt, Bob, *75 New Zealand Rugby Greats*, Hodder Moa Beckett, 2004

Jones, Lloyd, *The Book of Fame*, Penguin, 2000

Keane, Moss, *Rucks, Mauls & Gaelic Football*, Merlin, 2005

McCarthy, Winston, *Haka! The All Blacks Story*, Pelham Books, 1968

McConnell, Robin, *Inside the All Blacks*, CollinsWillow, 1998

McLean, Terry, *Mourie's All Blacks: The Team That Found Itself*, Hodder & Stoughton, 1979

McLean, Terry, *Willie Away: Wilson Whineray's All Blacks of 1963–64*, Reed, 1964

Mourie, Graham with Palenski, Ron, *Captain*, MOA Publications, 1982

Mulligan, Andrew, *All Blacks Tour 1963–64*, Whitcombe & Tombs, 1964

Mulqueen, Charlie, *The Story of Limerick Rugby*, 1978

Mulqueen, Charlie, *The Murphy's Story of Munster Rugby*, 1993

O'Flaherty, Michael, *The Home of the Spirit: A Celebration of Limerick Rugby*, 1999

Palenski, Ron, *The Jersey*, Hodder Moa Beckett, 2001

Quinn, Keith, *Grand Slam All Blacks*, Methuen, 1979

Reyburn, Wallace, *The Winter Men: The Seventh All Blacks Tour*, Hutchinson, 1973

Reyburn, Wallace, *Mourie's Men: The Eighth All Blacks Tour*, Cassell, 1979

Rothmans Rugby Union Yearbook, Headline, 1999

Scally, John, *The Good, the Bad and the Rugby: The Official Biography of Tony Ward*, Blackwater Press, 1993

Scally, John, *The Giants of Irish Rugby*, Mainstream Publishing, 1996

Smith, Sean, *The Union Game: A Rugby History*, BBC Worldwide, 1999

Thomas, Clem, *The History of the British Lions*, Mainstream Publishing, 1996

Verdon, Paul, *The Power Behind the All Blacks*, Penguin, 1999

Van Esbeck, Edmund, *Irish Rugby 1874–1999: A History*, Gill & Macmillan, 1999

Wilson, Stu and Fraser, Bernie with Veysey, Alex, *Ebony & Ivory*, MOA Publications, 1984

Club Histories

Cork Constitution, Garryowen, Shannon, St Mary's, Young Munster

Newspapers and Periodicals

Cork Examiner, Limerick Leader, Limerick Chronicle, Magill, Irish Times, Sunday Independent, The Times, Sunday Times, Daily Telegraph, Sunday Telegraph, Observer, New Zealand Herald, Old Limerick Journal, Rugby News (New Zealand), *Evening Echo* (Cork).

Acknowledgements

Note:
The Acknowledgements below are as they appeared in the first edition, apart from slight modifications. Naturally, I'm also grateful to all those who made contributions in different ways to this updated edition.

Convincing people to talk about Munster rugby was never going to be much of a hardship and writing this book has left me in the debt of many people. I interviewed the vast majority of the thirty-one players who appeared at Thomond Park that day in 1978, as well as replacements and match officials. Some, such as the main characters in the story, Tom Kiernan and Gerry McLoughlin, were exceptionally generous with their time and I could not have written it without them. Both are remarkable rugby men. But all of them have my gratitude, as do the many others I spoke to whose names crop up throughout the story. I will not list them again here, but they know who they are. Plenty invited me into their homes, others agreed to be interviewed in pubs; all in all, it proved a very agreeable assignment.

The day Munster beat the All Blacks is remembered for another reason, and I would like to thank the Canniffe family – Donal, the immortal captain, his wife Mary, brother Kieran and twin sister Deirdre O'Leary – for telling me the story of their late father, Dan. I also owe a great debt to Dan's former employer Bill Walsh, who recalled a painful day so movingly and who went out of his way to help me.

In Limerick, I paid several visits to the wonderfully hospitable Healy family to hear the story of two great Limerick rugby men, Stephen and Sean, and I would like to thank Stephen's widow Kitty, his son Gerry, and daughters Susan and Rose. Thanks also to the inimitable Mick Crowe, a great friend of the brothers, for taking me here, there and everywhere.

In addition, I would like to acknowledge the assistance of the following, though I am uncomfortably aware that it is by no means a comprehensive list: Willie Allen, Don Brennan, Tony Browne, Tommy Creamer, Len Dinneen, Noel Early, John English, Terry Fitzgerald, Ger Foley, Paddy Hayes, Noel Healy, Trudy Hopkins, Diarmuid Kelly, Sean Mac, Eddie, Paddy and Peggy McNamara, John Mason, Mike Murnane, Benny O'Dowd, Ken O'Dea, Michael O'Flaherty, Paul O'Halloran, Denis O'Shaughnessy, Pat Parfrey, Pa Rea, Paddy Reid, Frank Ryan, Gerry Ryan, Michael Noel Ryan, Jimmy Woulfe, Tom Wren.

I spent many productive hours at the excellent Limerick City library and the British Newspaper Library in London, and the library staff at the *Irish Examiner* also put up with me. In New Zealand I would like to thank Alistair Carlile at the Auckland War Memorial Museum for giving me access to the private papers of George Dixon. Bob Luxford, curator of the New Zealand Rugby Museum, was also most helpful. Journalists Ron Palenski, Keith Quinn and Bob Howitt, all of whom were at the match, provided assistance and encouragement, as did the venerable *Rugby News* publication. The great New Zealand rugby photographer Peter Bush revisited his files several times at my request. The Limerick photographer Michael Cowhey generously gave me access to many fine pictures he shot that day, and the photographic departments of the *Cork Examiner* and *Limerick Leader* were also supportive. I would also like to thank my colleague Andrew Mitchell for help in picture research. At RTE, the intrepid Sean MacAonghusa tracked down some long lost footage of the 1963 Munster–All Blacks match and provided me with what remains of the film shot in 1978.

For Yellow Jersey, Rachel Cugnoni commissioned the book based on not very much and when she moved on to bigger things Tristan Jones adopted it and saw it through with great care and skill, making several key structural suggestions along the way. Copy editing by Richard Collins was sensitive and shrewd. [*Thanks also to Tim Broughton at Yellow Jersey, who oversaw the updated* 2018 *edition.*]

I am fortunate to work for the *Sunday Times*, home to so many fine sportswriters, and I must thank my colleagues and friends David Walsh, Paul Kimmage and Stephen Jones for reading various parts of the manuscript and offering valuable feedback. David in particular has been a friend in good times and not so good and his enthusiasm was, as ever, infectious.

I cannot thank my brother Tom English enough. A terrific sportswriter himself, who covered Irish rugby with great distinction for eight eventful years, he encouraged me from beginning to end and read the entire manuscript, suggesting many improvements, all of which I incorporated.

My parents, Tom and Anne English, have backed me in everything I've ever done and this book was no exception. I hope they enjoy this story.

My greatest thanks go to my wife, Anne, and our children Aisling, Holly and Jack, who must have dreaded the all-too familiar words 'working on the book' during its long gestation period. They were, however, constantly supportive and I dedicate the book to them.

Finally, a note on the sources. Although I drew on some outstanding works of reference and on the rich tradition of All Blacks touring books, listed elsewhere, the vast majority of the material came from personal interviews. Even though many years have passed since the events written about here took place, dialogue employed in the book is true to the recollections of those I spoke to, or in some cases to accounts recorded at the time. Memory, as Hugh McIlvanney once wrote, is a tainted witness, and in a few instances, where recollections differed, I have made my own judgement on what seemed to me the most likely scenario, striving at all times to present a faithful account of a story that enthused me from start to finish.

The author and publishers would like to make grateful acknowledgement to the following for permission to reproduce photographs:

Michael Cowhey for the 1978 All Blacks line-up and the Munster Immortals; Empics for the All Blacks squad of 1905; the *Irish Examiner* for the 1963 Munster–All Blacks game, portraits of Seamus Dennison, Jimmy Bowen, Donal Canniffe, Christy Cantillon's try, Tom Kiernan on the touchline and 'Stand-off'; George Herringshaw for portraits of Tony Ward, Graham Mourie and Brian McKechnie; Peter Bush for portraits of Jack Gleeson and Graham Mourie, Christy Cantillon, the Munster and All Black packs colliding in scrum and lineout and 'Euphoria'; Mike Brett for portraits of Eddie Dunn and Stu Wilson; RTE for 'The Tackle'; the *Limerick Leader* for the portrait of Gerry McLoughlin and the All Blacks arriving at Shannon; and Billy McGill for the portrait of the 1978 Munster team, twenty years on.

Every effort has been made to trace or contact all copyright holders, and the publishers will be pleased to correct any omissions brought to their notice at the earliest opportunity.

Index

Abbeyfeale 9, 51–2, 136–7, 258, 282

All Blacks 2, 6, 13–14, 228–30, 296–7, 299–300
- 1905 tour 6, 16–19, 24–8, 29, 111–12, 125, 301
- 1924 tour 29, 125
- 1954 tour 45, 150, 252, 302
- 1963 tour 29–39, 119, 137–8, 150, 252, 254, 303
- 1972–3 tour 52–5, 112–15, 127, 135, 139, 149, 150, 231–2, 252, 304–5
- 1974 tour 56, 305
- 1978 tour 109–10, 112, 115–16, 120, 123, 124–5, 132–5, 140–1, 148–9, 158–60, 163, 167, 229–30, 231–9, 296–7, 299–300, 305–6
- 1978 team 5–6, 109–10, 124, 150–5, 169, 305–6
- 1989 tour 253, 296–7
- 2008 tour 252, 279–81, 297
- *see also* Munster–All Blacks matches

All Blacks–Australia 1978 Test series 109, 120

All Ireland League 244, 256, 289, 292

Alone It Stands (Breen) 286

Angel Hotel, Cardiff 114

Angela Conway's 30, 278

Argentina 129, 139, 150

Arms Park, Cardiff 69, 71, 132, 158, 233–8, 299, 300

Ashworth, John 233

Athanasius, Brother 46

Australia 44–5, 52, 108, 109, 120, 138, 140, 165–6, 202, 253, 254, 266, 287, 288, 292, 294, 301–3, 304, 305

Barbarians–All Blacks 1978 match 233–8

Barrett, Greg 9, 131, 185, 192, 196, 260, 271, 288

Barrett, Gus 288

Barrington, Charles Burton 21–2, 24

Barry, Johnny 88, 129

Bennett, Phil 234, 236, 237

Black, John 211
Bohemians Rugby Club 86–7
Bombing Field 23
Bowen, Jimmy 10, 94, 190, 191,
    192, 193, 215–16, 224–5,
    259, 269, 271, 273, 276,
    279, 280, 283, 289, 295
Bowen, Seamus 215–16
Breen, John 230, 286
Brennan, Johnny 241, 243–6,
    254–6
Brennan, Josie 243, 244–5
British Army 20, 23, 32, 100–1
Brosnahan, Frankie 68
Browne, Sam 255
Bruce, Doug 169, 209, 210, 222
Bruce, Louis 267
Bruree 8
Budd, Arthur 19
Bunratty Castle banquet 155,
    156, 167
Burgess, Bob 54
Bush, Billy 171
Busteed, Brian 141–3
Byrne, Ned 60

Cagney, Pat 30
Cambridge University Rugby
    Club 38, 132, 299
Campbell, Ollie 287
Canniffe, Dan 8, 88, 144–6,
    170–1, 204–5, 206, 212–13,
    219–21, 225–6, 286, 296
Canniffe, Donal 8, 96–7, 146, 158,
    219, 220, 225, 239, 246, 270,
    279, 280–1, 283, 296, 298

match, first half 176–7, 178,
    180, 188, 189–90, 196,
    197, 200
match, second half 205–6,
    211
career of after match 286
Canniffe, Kieran 4, 146, 213,
    225–6
Canniffe, Maisie 8, 145–6
Cantillon, Christy 2, 10, 57,
    192–3, 194, 205, 253, 261,
    263, 271–2, 273, 274,
    282–3, 289, 295
Cardiff–All Blacks 1978
    match 132–3, 158–60,
    163, 299
Cardiff Rugby Club 69–71,
    132–3, 158–60, 163, 299
Carroll, Tom 85
Casey, James 'Ter' 33, 170, 245
Casey, Paddy 'Whacker'
    22–3, 106
Catchpole, Ken 52
Charlie St George's 33, 256, 257
Cholley, Gerard 247
Christian Brothers 59, 61–4,
    72, 106, 248, 285
Clancy, Tom 255
Clarke, Don 33–4, 39, 167
Clarke, Peter 240–1
Clifford, Tom 1–2, 79
Clohessy, Peter 1–2, 244, 257
Clohessy, Tony 240
Clyde Road, Dublin 22
Cochrane, Paul 175–6, 205,
    207, 210, 216, 223–4

Cogley, Fred 40, 41, 158, 197, 212
Cole, Johnny 173–4, 178–9,
    193, 214, 215, 216–18,
    245, 253, 295–6
Collery, Tom 79, 80, 118
Condon, Hugh 129–31
Cork 7, 24, 43, 254, 281, 285,
    288, 289, 290, 296, 298
Cork Constitution Rugby Club
    7, 13, 35, 43, 44, 46, 50, 57,
    118, 161, 259, 268, 289
Cork Examiner, 6–7, 49, 58, 76
Costelloe, Morgan 171
Coughlan, Thady 108
Crescent College 167
Cronin, John 21
Cross, Mickey 255
Crowe, Mick 30–1, 34
Cullen, Christian 297

Daily Express 33
Daily Mirror 113
Daily Telegraph 212, 216
Dalcassian Bar 30–1
Dawson, Charles 20, 21
Deans, Bob 111
Deering, Shay 85, 165
Dennison, Danny 137
Dennison, Lally 134, 137
Dennison, Seamus 8, 9, 85,
    134–5, 136–9, 159–60, 217,
    232, 253, 258, 259, 265,
    270, 273, 279, 282, 283, 291
    match, first half 183, 184,
    185, 186, 195, 199, 201
    match, second half 205

    career of after match 271, 286
Desmond, David 43
Diffley, Sean 297
Dixon, George 18, 24–5, 26–8, 29
Dolphin Rugby Club 75–6
Donaldson, Mark 122, 200, 201–2
Duggan, Willie 72–3, 164
Dunn, Eddie 41, 169, 209–10,
    211, 222, 234, 235, 238

Edwards, Gareth 11, 69,
    233, 235
England–Ireland matches 50,
    61, 245, 268, 285
English, Mick 36, 38
Esbeck, Edmund van 266,
    268, 288
European Cup, creation of 252,
    285 see also Heineken Cup

Faldo, Nick 42
Feighery, Tom 60
Fermoy 83, 99–102, 134, 141
Finn, Moss 10, 57, 96, 185,
    186, 190, 217, 251, 253–4,
    262, 269, 271, 279, 280,
    284, 290, 295
Fitzgerald's Lane, Limerick
    20–1, 24
Fitzpatrick, Mick 4, 60
Fitzpatrick, Rose 49
Five Nations Championship
    284
Flannery, Kevin 72
Foley, Anthony, Sr 104–5,
    106, 108, 287

Foley, Anthony, Jr 103, 274–5, 277, 287
Foley, Brendan 10, 66, 102–3, 104–8, 143, 173, 178, 187–8, 189–90, 192, 253, 260, 262, 273, 274–5, 276, 277, 283, 286–7
Foley, Gerard 104, 105, 106
Foley, Rosaleen 104–5, 287
Foley, Rosie 287
France-Ireland matches 108, 234, 247, 285

Galwey, Mick 256, 257
Garryowen Rugby Club 7, 8, 23–4, 44, 60, 84–6, 87–8, 138, 160–1, 243, 247, 271, 282, 287, 289, 291, 292
Gibson, Michael (Mike) 38
Gilliland, Ray 52
Giltinane, Vince 89
Glasgow, Ossie 45
Gleeson, Jack 91–2, 109–12, 115, 119–20, 124, 129, 132, 133, 140, 148, 150–1, 153, 154, 156–7, 169, 171, 195, 199, 208, 209, 228–9, 230, 235, 293
Grace, Tom 55, 279
Graham, Wayne 210, 221–2
Grand Hotel, Fermoy 99, 102
Grand Slam 112, 125, 294, 297
Grange Road 132, 299
Grant, Peter 114
Gravell, Ray 133
Gray, Ken 111

Griffin, Minih 240

Haden, Andy 41, 122, 123, 148, 149, 152, 154, 189, 200, 201, 211, 290, 297
haka, the 40, 113, 137–8, 163, 179, 235, 236, 252
Hardcastle, John 45
Harris, Richard xiii, 230, 245
Hayes, Mick 107–8
Hayes, Peter 107
Healy, Dolly 31–2
Healy, Gerry 223, 226
Healy, Jack 32
Healy, Kitty 174
Healy, Noel ('Buddha') 274
Healy, Sean 31–3, 39, 169–70, 174, 223, 226, 296
Healy, Stephen 31–3, 39, 170, 174–5, 186, 191, 218–19, 223, 226, 296
Healy, Susan 174–5, 186, 191, 218–19
Heineken Cup 298
  2000 256, 277
  2002 277
  2006 252, 277, 287, 298
  2008 252, 298
Henderson, Noel 49–50, 274
Hennessy, Ray 49–50, 268
Herewini, Mac 36–7, 39, 170
Hopkins, John 110
Horgan, Sonny 48
Horsley, Ronald Hugh 37
Howlett, Doug 280, 297
Hurley, Gerry 93

Interprovincial champion-
ship 1978 253
Ireland 3–4, 49–51, 72–3, 96,
247–8, 249, 250, 251–2,
251n, 254, 260, 266, 267,
268, 277, 280–1, 284, 285,
286, 287, 288, 289, 290,
291, 292, 293, 299
Ireland–All Blacks 1963
match 33–4
Ireland–All Blacks 1973
match 54–6
Ireland–All Blacks 1978
match 232–3, 299
Ireland–England 1977 match 61
Ireland-France matches 108,
234, 247, 285
Ireland–Shannon practice
match 3–4
Irish Exiles–Munster 1978
match 96
Irish Exiles XV Rugby Club
94, 96
Irish Independent 317
Irish Rugby Football Union
27, 30
Munster branch 74, 76, 77,
80, 116–18, 296
Irish Times 22–4, 258–9, 266
Irvine, Andy 234, 237, 238
Island Field 23, 108

Jaffray, Lyn 5–6, 182–3
James, Carwyn 169
Johnson, Martin xiii
Johnstone, Brad 152

Karam, Joe 55, 152
Kavanagh, Pat 194
Keane, Anne Marie 258, 259,
262, 281
Keane, Moss 4, 10, 93, 168,
200, 201, 214, 216, 258–9,
262, 263, 272, 279, 280,
281, 287, 290, 291, 297
Keane, Sarah 258, 259, 260–2,
272, 281
Kelleher, Olann 88–9, 90, 211,
217, 271
Kelly, Michael 20–1
Kenihan, Jude 1
Kennedy, Joe 82, 155–6, 167
Kidney, Declan 72
Kiely, Cyril 246
Kiernan, Eileen (née Murphy)
43–4
Kiernan, Jim 46, 268
Kiernan, Maree 56, 57, 266,
267, 268
Kiernan, Michael 43–4, 47–8,
51–2, 228, 267
Kiernan, Tom
pre-match preparations 5,
11–15, 41–2, 81–2, 126,
157–62, 169, 176
training 6–7, 99–100,
101–2, 141, 167–8
on Limerick's love of rugby 19
1963 match 33, 35–6, 36,
37, 39, 138
views 1978 match video-
tape 40–2
scrapbook 42–3

Kiernan, Tom (*continued*)
   family background 43–4
   birth and early years 44
   introduction to rugby 44–7
   shooting 47–8
   first cap 50–1
   father's death 51–2
   and the Munster–Australia
      1967 match 52, 254
   1973 match 52–5, 139
   appointed Munster coach
      56–8
   and the Munster–Cardiff
      match 69
   and the London tour 78,
      80–1, 83, 89, 92, 93–5
   political ability 82
   1978 team 97, 116–18, 130,
      131, 257, 290
   and the first half 182, 189,
      195, 197, 198, 202–3
   and the second half 208,
      212, 213, 214
   match assessment 224–5
   victory celebrations 227–8
   and the Barbarians–All
      Blacks match 234
   career after 1978 match
      252, 265–8, 284–5, 293
Kirkpatrick, Ian 127, 152, 231
Kirton, Earle 38–9, 89, 91–2,
   148
Knight, Gary 3, 97–8, 152,
   171–2, 178, 179, 181–2,
   187, 197, 207, 222, 234
Knill, Mike 70

Lancaster Park 120
Lane, Mick 45
Lane, Paddy 37
Lansdowne Road 33, 54, 234,
   244, 255, 285, 286, 299
Leggoe, Dave 175
Leinster 3, 7, 234, 253, 291
Limerick
   and rugby 3, 7, 19,
      21–4, 27, 137, 170, 240–6,
      254–5, 256–7, 285, 298
   social conditions 18–21, 29,
      31–2, 249
Limerick Football Club 22
Limerick Leader 17, 25–6, 35,
   71, 90, 231, 243
Limerick Rugby Experience 255
Lions, British & Irish 12, 75,
   110, 234, 243, 265, 275,
   279, 285, 292, 294
London, 1978 tour 78–9, 80–1,
   83–4, 88–98, 118, 129
London Counties–All Blacks
   1978 match 134, 148, 299
London Irish Rugby Club 9,
   129, 293
Lough Derg 168–9
Lowry, Joss 277
Lynch, Jack 146
Lyons, Tony 231
Lysaght, Mogwah 255

McBride, John Willie 103
McCarthy, Jim 12, 45
McCarthy, Joe 193–4, 222–3,
   273–4

McConkey, Bob 86
McCourt, Frank 246
McGann, Barry 53, 55, 161
McGrath, Colum 33
McGrath, Pat 12, 37, 52
McGrath's pub, Carey's
    Road 241–3
McGregor, Ash 210
McKechnie, Brian 188, 189,
    191, 195–6, 237–8
McLaren, Bill 235, 236–7
McLean, Terry 37, 132–3, 152,
    153–4, 229
McLoughlin, Bridget 63–4
McLoughlin, Colette 275
McLoughlin, Gerry
  on the match 1–4
  match ball and 1, 245
  teaching career 59, 61–3,
    66–9, 72, 248, 285
  and rugby 59–61, 64–5
  education 63–4
  joins Shannon 65–6
  and the Munster–Cardiff
    match 69–71
  on the bench for Ireland 72–3
  and the London tour 83,
    88, 96
  rugby career 84–8, 248, 285
  and Gary Knight 97–8
  anti-Limerick bias 170
  comparison with Knight
    171–2
  and the first half 176, 177–8,
    179–80, 181, 181–2, 186–8,
    189, 192–3, 196–7

and the second half 206–7, 215
and the Barbarians–All
    Blacks match 233–4, 235–6
career after 1978 match
    247–51, 256–7, 285
and the Munster-Australia
    match 1981 253
Limerick rugby rivalry, on
    changing nature of 256–7
Colm Tucker death and 258
on Moss Keane 259
injuries 269–70
on bond between 1978
    Munster players 275,
    280, 281, 282, 283
and the Munster-All
    Blacks match 2008 280
McLoughlin, Mick, Snr 3,
    64, 247
McLoughlin, Mick 63–4, 88
McLoughlin, Pat 192–3
McLoughlin, Ray 85
McManus, J.P. 255
McNamara, Freddie 105
McNamara, Madgie 105–6
McPhail, Neil 30
MacRae, Ian 37
Malone, Andy 63
Mardyke, the 44, 45, 268
Markets Field 26
Mason, John 212, 216
match ball 1, 217–18, 241,
    245–6
Maxwell-Muller, Dinah
    141–3, 147, 158
Mays, Kevin 55–6

Meads, Colin 39, 56, 167
Middlesex–Munster 1978
    match 88–91, 118, 129,
    131, 149
Middlesex Rugby Club 7–8,
    88–91, 118, 149
Midland Counties Rugby
    Club 27, 299
Millennium Stadium, Cardiff
    252
Moloney, Larry 8–9, 101, 138,
    143, 157, 185, 259, 270,
    277–8, 282, 291
Moloney, Paddy 9
Moloney, Rose 278
Mordell, Bob 89
Morris, Trevor 53, 135
Morrison, Terry 89, 90
Mourie, Graham 109–10, 115,
    133–4, 150–2, 152, 169,
    230, 234, 236, 246, 286,
    293, 294, 297
  match, first half 186, 195,
    198
  match, second half 207–8,
    208–9, 212
Mulcahy, Frank ('Dollars') 255
Mulcahy, Ted 90
Mulconnery, Flash and
    Michael 65
Muldoon, Robert 153
Mulgan, John: *Report On
    Experience* xiii
Mulqueen, Charlie 71, 90
Mungret College, Limerick 137
Munster

1978 team 2, 4, 5, 6–15, 57,
    91–2, 96–7, 108, 116–18,
    128–31, 305–6
  bias against 3
  pre-match preparations
    5, 7, 12–15, 41–2, 81–2,
    157–62, 168–9
  training 6–7, 83, 92–4,
    99–100, 101–2, 134, 141,
    157–8, 167–8, 298
  motivation 14–15
  tradition 16, 24
1905 team 26, 301
1963 team 34–6, 170, 303
  jerseys 77–8
1978 London tour 78–9,
    80–1, 83–4, 88–98, 118,
    129
1973 team 135, 139, 304–5
  and the Barbarians–All
    Blacks match 233–8
  careers of players after 1978
    match 247–51, 284–97
  legend of 1978 achieve-
    ment grows in years
    after match 251–7
  Heineken Cup and 252,
    256–7, 277, 287, 298
  Interprovincial champion-
    ship 1978 253
  deaths of former players
    258–68
  reunions of 1978 team 258,
    259, 281–3
  injuries carried by 1978
    team players 269–73

320

bond between members of
1978 team 273–83
professional era and 298
Cork-Limerick divide
within ended 298
record against overseas
teams 1905–78 301–6
Munster–All Blacks 1905
match 17, 24–8, 301
Munster–All Blacks 1954
match 45, 150, 302
Munster–All Blacks 1963
match 3, 29–30, 33, 34–9,
137–8, 150, 152, 303
Munster–All Blacks 1973
match 52–5, 135, 139,
149, 150, 152, 304–5
Munster–All Blacks 1974
match 56, 305
Munster–All Blacks 1978
match
match ball 1, 217–18, 241,
245–6
McLoughlin on 1–4
spectators 1
lack of interest 4
videotape 40–2, 193–4,
222–3, 273–4
match scheduled 73
referee 126–8, 295
team line-ups 130, 153,
262, 305–6
tickets 143–4
first half 173–203
Munster scores first try
189–94

television coverage
193–4, 197, 212, 222–3,
230–1
Ward's drop goal 197–8
refereeing 198–200
half-time 201, 202–3,
205–6
the second half 204–16
Ward's second drop goal
212
final whistle 214–16
victory celebrations
216–26, 227–8
postmortem 228–30
Munster–All Blacks 1989
match 253, 296–7
Munster–All Blacks 2008
match 252, 279–81, 297
Munster–Argentina 1973
match 139
Munster–Australia 1947
match 44–5, 301–2
Munster–Australia 1958
match 302–3
Munster–Australia 1967
match 52, 138, 254, 304
Munster–Australia 1976 match
108, 165–6, 202, 305
Munster–Australia 1981
match 253, 266
Munster–Cardiff 1977 match
69–71
Munster Junior Challenge
Cup 108
Munster School Cup 61,
68–9, 71, 72

Munster Senior Challenge
    Cup 7, 24, 43, 44, 72, 78,
    84–6, 87–8, 108, 161
Munster–South Africa
    matches 45, 302, 303, 304
Murdoch, Keith 112–15, 124
Murphy, Colm 91
Murphy, Neddy 43, 44
Murphy, Noel, Snr 76
Murphy, Noel 43, 50, 53–4,
    73, 91, 131, 139, 177
Murphy, Ralph 82
Murray, Jerry 35–6, 37
Musgrave Park 53, 57, 71,
    128, 165

Nelmes, Barry 70
New Zealand Colts 119–20
Newport Rugby Club 38
Norton, Tane 151

O'Brien, Bill 74–82, 96,
    117–18, 143–4, 296
O'Brien, Brian 12, 85, 86,
    94–5, 256
O'Brien, Tom 74
O'Callaghan, Mick 3, 12, 37, 254
O'Callaghan, Phil 12, 53
O'Connell, Paul 254, 261, 298
O'Connor, Terry 132
O'Connor, Vincent 176–7
O'Donnell, Pat 87, 88, 215
O'Donovan, Niall 277
O'Gara, Ronan 254
O'Keefe, John 75, 77, 80
O'Leary, Anthony 130

O'Loughlin, Denis 274
Oliver, Frank 148, 152, 189, 297
O'Mahony, George and Betty 51
O'Mahony, Peter 254
O'Reilly, Tony 75–6
O'Sullivan, Micky 130, 250
Orr, Phil 60, 234
Osborne, Bill 159, 195

Palenski, Ron 152, 197–8
Presentation College 46,
    68–9, 72
Presentation Rugby Club 64, 66
Price, Eddie 87, 106

Quinnell, Derek 234

Ralston, Chris 89, 90
Reason, John 92–3
Rees, Elgan 234
Reyburn, Wallace 113
Rimutaka, SS 17–18, 111
Ripley, Andy 89–90
Rives, Jean-Pierre 235, 238
Robbie, John 132
Robertson, Bruce 149, 186,
    194–5, 208
Rokocoko, Joe 280
Rollitt, Dave 89
Royal Munster Fusiliers 32
RTE 4, 193–4, 231, 251, 311
Rugby Football Union 19
Rugby Special 158–60
Russell, Dermot 6–7
Ryan, Eamonn 64–5
Ryan, John 108, 287

Ryan, John Joe 64
Ryan, Noel 4

Sallon, Ralph 113
Scotland–All Blacks 1978
    match 232, 233
scrum, the 1–2, 179–80,
    181–2, 196–7
Scully, Fr Brendan 87
Seear, Gary 297
Sexton Street School 59, 61–3,
    66–9, 71, 72, 143, 285
Shannon Rugby Club 3–4, 7,
    10, 23–4, 59, 60–1, 65–6,
    72, 84–8, 108, 274, 292
Sheahan, Didi 255
Sheahan, Michael Danaher 245
Skrela, Jean-Claude 235, 236
Slemen, Mike 236
South Africa 45, 73, 155–6,
    187–8, 229, 248, 285, 292,
    294, 302, 303, 304
Sparling, Jimmy 218
Spillane, Brian 68
Spring, Donal 2, 10, 16, 188–9,
    201, 209, 213, 223, 258,
    262–3, 269, 270, 279, 291–2
Springboks see South Africa
St Mary's College, Dublin
    164–5
St Mary's Rugby Club 22, 23,
    106–8, 287, 289
St Munchin's College 167–8
Stanton, Ken 213, 219, 220
Starmer-Smith, Nigel 194
Stokes, William 21, 24

Sweeney, Hadah 107
Tanner, John 45
Tanyard Inn 240, 247
Thomas, Clem 6
Thomas, Corris 126–8, 184,
    189, 198–9, 214–15, 217,
    218, 238, 295
Thomas, Russ 112, 115–16,
    124, 153, 229–30, 232,
    235, 294
Thomond Park 29, 36, 39, 67,
    131, 137, 175, 243, 252,
    255, 256, 267, 274, 279–80,
    293, 296, 297, 298, 299
Times, The 140–1, 211
Todd, Eric 113, 114
Transfield Cup 24, 241
Triple Crown, the 42–3, 267,
    284, 285, 290
Tucker, Colm 2, 10, 41, 57,
    108, 157, 176–7, 178,
    180, 195–6, 211–12, 247,
    253, 258, 259, 263–5, 272,
    278–9, 292
Tucker, Geraldine 264–5, 272,
    278–9
Turnbull, Jim 81–2, 169, 208
Twickenham 148, 256, 285, 299
Tyler Cup 24

Wales–All Blacks 1905
    match 111
Wall, Henry 37, 138
Walsh, Bill 144, 204–5, 206,
    212–13, 219–21, 225
Walsh, Jerry 12, 138

Walsh, Martin 193, 199, 214, 217, 218, 295–6
Walsh, Paddy Steff 64
Wanderers Rugby Club 22
Ward, June 165
Ward, Tony 1, 10–11, 41, 87–8, 91–2, 96, 129, 160–2, 163–6, 253, 271, 273, 279–80, 282, 290, 291, 295
    match, first half 190–1, 193, 195, 196, 197–8, 202
    match, second half 212
    Kiernan's assessment of 224–5
    career of after match 273, 275–6, 287–8
West, Peter 211
West, Tim 76
West Wales–All Blacks 1978 match 133–4, 140–1, 299
Westmeath 43
Wheeler, Peter 234
Whelan, Pat 10, 11, 85, 90, 96–7, 177–8, 182, 187, 247, 260, 263, 270, 273, 279, 282, 285, 287, 291, 292–3, 298
Whineray, Wilson 30

White, Les 9, 93, 129–30, 169, 187, 200, 227, 273, 276–7, 281, 293
White, Moira 276
Williams, Bryan 133, 134, 149, 152, 160, 208, 210, 217, 222, 224, 234
Williams, Brynmor 69, 234
Williams, JPR 233
Wilson, Brian 54
Wilson, Stu 118–20, 121–5, 132, 134, 152, 159, 232, 234, 286, 294–5
    match, first half 175, 182–3, 183–4, 185–6, 190–1, 198, 199, 201, 202
    match, second half 209, 210, 216
Wolfhounds Rugby Club 89, 250
Wood, Gordon 1–2, 12
Wood, Keith 1–2
Workington–All Blacks 1972 match 231–2
World Cup, Rugby 251, 294, 297
Wyllie, Alex 54

Young Munster Rugby Club 24, 33, 82, 138, 241, 243, 244–5, 247, 254, 255, 256, 257